Not One of the Boys

Not One of the Boys

Sharon Carstairs

Macmillan Canada
Toronto

Canadian Cataloguing in Publication Data
Carstairs, Sharon
    Not one of the boys

Includes index.
ISBN 0-7715-9016-4

1. Carstairs, Sharon. 2. Manitoba – Politics and government – 1977–   .*
3. Liberal Party in Manitoba – Biography. 4. Politicians – Manitoba –
Biography. 5. Women in politics – Manitoba – Biography. I. Title.

FC3377.1.C37A3 1993   971.27'03'092   C93-094194-2
F1063.C37A3 1993

Macmillan Canada wishes to thank the Canada Council and the Ontario
Ministry of Culture and Communications for supporting its publishing
program.

Macmillan Canada
A Division of Canada Publishing Corporation
Toronto, Canada

1 2 3 4 5 97 96 95 94 93

Printed in Canada

To my husband, John, who has always supported me with his love, friendship and hard work, and to all the volunteers who have worked so tirelessly on my behalf.

Contents

Foreword

I knew even before I retired from public life that I wanted to write a book. Not only did I have a story I wanted to tell, it was, I felt, a story that needed to be told.

I hope that by discussing my abuse as a child, others—it will be worth it if it is only one—will be encouraged to face their abusers and begin the healing process.

I have no regrets about my political experiences. However, they will only be of true value if others can learn from them. There is now a woman prime minister, and the first woman premier has been elected in Prince Edward Island. It is my fondest wish that they will be able to reach out to other women and change political life as we know it in this country. They will only succeed if they dare to be different. Otherwise it will be politics as usual the Old Boys' way.

All of those who have been by my side for the last nine and a half years have helped me write my story. However, I would be remiss if I did not give two individuals particular credit for this book's final form. Leanne Matthes, my special assistant, has spent countless hours in the library, making changes on her computer and offering positive suggestions when passages were, to her, incomprehensible. Her help was invaluable. My editor, Kirsten Hanson, senior editor at Macmillan Canada, had, I think, some trepidation about taking me on. Just what she needed, another amateur author—particularly one who has been a politician and probably has the ego to go with it! Her comments, suggestions and clarity of thought were essential. I am deeply grateful to her.

Finally, to my readers, I want you to know that this has been the most cathartic experience I have ever had. I hope you enjoy reading this book as much as I enjoyed writing it!

Prologue

I woke on the morning of October 26, 1992, Referendum day in Canada, to beautiful fall sunshine. I was well rested. I frequently have difficulty sleeping because my mind is so busy cogitating I can't relax. However, this was not the case during the Referendum campaign—I slept the sleep of the just. Save for the counting of the votes, my heartfelt campaign for the No side and my long, emotionally taxing and exhilarating political career were over.

I packed an overnight bag because I was off to Toronto later in the morning to appear on CBC TV's live report of the results. Since I had such a busy schedule that day, I had voted at the advance poll the Friday before. Al Munroe picked me up at 8:30 and dropped me at the CJOB radio studio to appear on an hour-long program with Peter Warren, who hosts the most popular morning talk show in Manitoba. The morning format, Peter had explained, would have me as his guest from 9:00 to 10:00 for the "No" side and the Conservative premier Gary Filmon from 10:30 to 11:30 for the "Yes" side. To his surprise, the premier didn't arrive alone. He brought with him Liberal Lloyd Axworthy, New Democrat Gary Doer and the mayor, Bill Norrie. It didn't matter, because Manitobans weren't listening. They had already made up their minds. They were voting with the lone woman, not with "the boys"!

I arrived in Toronto, checked into the Four Seasons Hotel and went to visit my great friend Adrian Macdonald, who immediately took me off to have my hair cut! I had been trying to find the

1

time for the previous month but a speech always seemed to interfere. I had a quick visit with Adrian and her husband, former cabinet minister Donald Macdonald, after the haircut and returned to my hotel room to change. I felt a pervasive sense of calm.

When I arrived at the CBC's Jarvis Street studio all was hectic. This was a major production and things were at fever pitch. I watched with amusement because, as far as I was concerned, everything was finished. Peter Mansbridge asked me off air how I thought Manitoba was going to vote. I replied that, despite opinion polls to the contrary, it might be close. The polls had the "No" forces way out ahead, but I was unsure how the last-minute blitz advertising by the "Yes" side was going to affect the voters. Besides, it was still difficult for me to believe that the people were going to support my view over that of the establishment.

Newfoundland's results came in first. To no one's surprise they supported the view of Clyde Wells and voted "Yes." Prince Edward Island likewise supported their premier, Joe Ghiz, who like Wells had great popularity with his electorate. New Brunswick was different. There was a split beween the Acadian community, who overwhelmingly voted "Yes," and the anglophone community, who were very divided. However, the overall total showed passage in New Brunsick. Then came Nova Scotia, my native province and the place where I learned both my Liberalism and my value system. They voted "No." I was somewhat surprised, because all three political leaders in that province were on the "Yes" side. But I was not shocked. Quebec's results showed an overwhelming rejection. Thus, like most national election nights, things were decided before the results from the western provinces were even in. In the end, Manitoba did vote "No." Indeed, Canada gave a ringing "No" to the Charlottetown Accord. And I was finally at peace with myself.

It was all over—the Referendum campaign and my political life. I had been able to leave on a note that I hoped epitomized my life. My school motto had challenged me to Dare to be True. After the failure of the Meech Lake Accord, I took up that challenge to be true to myself. Now I had done so—and I had won!

one

The Legacy of Strong Women

My maternal grandmother's name was Sophie LeBlanc Martel. Born a few years before Confederation in Arichat, Nova Scotia, a small French fishing community close to Louisbourg, she always considered herself French. One of the treasures in my family home was a needlepoint picture of her local school flying the tricolour of France. As a child, it was clear to me that my French heritage was as important as my Irish one—and, because of this, the accusations over the years that I have been anti-French have hurt me a great deal.

In 1905, shortly after the birth of her seventeenth child, Sophie decided that there was no future for her twelve living children in this small community. She was determined that they move to Boston. My grandfather, Albert Martel, was not convinced this was the right decision, but she nevertheless packed the children on a boat and left. When they arrived in their new country she told them that English was now the language to be spoken. And that, more or less, was that.

My grandfather decided to join the family a year later, when it was clear his wife was not going to return to Arichat, and they had another child. She was my mother, Vivian Alma Martel. The only times she heard my grandmother speak French were when she said her prayers or attended church. My mother, as a result, spoke no French. However, one of the mementos that I now hang proudly in my home is a stained-glass window depicting a fleur-de-lis. Mum bought it at an auction to remind my father of her heritage, because, unlike his daughter Sharon, he was not in favour of official bilingualism as a policy for Canada.

There are many who feel that my personality and interests came from my father, Harold Connolly, who was an MLA, cabinet minister and, for a brief time, premier of Nova Scotia. He later served in the Canadian Senate for twenty-five years. He was certainly the one who gave me an interest in politics, but I think my personality to a very great degree came from Sophie LeBlanc Martel. Her stubbornness and conviction changed the future of her family. I would like to think those same convictions, and indeed stubbornness, helped to change the way Canadians voted in the Referendum of 1992.

My parents were married on New Year's Day in 1935. My sister Maureen was born the following year and in rapid succession came Dennis, David and me. I was born on April 26, 1942. My sister Patricia was born seven years later. But my mother also had the care of two other children immediately upon her marriage. My sister Catherine, born in 1930, was my father's child by his first wife, who died shortly after Catherine's birth. In addition there was my Uncle Dick, my father's youngest brother, who was still a teenager.

My father found himself, at the age of nineteen, the sole supporter of nine brothers and sisters. His father, Richard Connolly, was injured in the Halifax Explosion of 1917, and died a year later when gangrene developed. His mother died the next year. Dad told us she died from a broken heart. Mum always said she paused to think of all the responsibilities associated with raising ten children alone and died of shock. In any case, at the tender age of nineteen my father was overloaded with responsibilities. However, the expression "when the going gets tough, the tough get going" epitomizes my father. He went to work as a reporter with the *Halifax Chronicle*, and by the time he left to enter politics in 1936 he was the managing editor.

My mother was a nurse. As the youngest she was encouraged to fulfil my grandmother's dream: to have a child who practised a profession. My other uncles and aunts had been pushed by my grandmother to enter a number of different occupations; one was a secretary, one a furrier, one an electrician and one a mechanic. But my mother was to have a profession. Since she suffered from a severe hearing loss—a result of diphtheria as a child—nursing did not come easily to her. Mum told me of the difficulties she experienced in her training, particularly in the operating room. She had to be extremely quick, because otherwise she would not hear the doctor's instructions. At the end of her course they offered her post-grad training in surgery, not knowing what an incredible effort it took for her to be so quick. She could not take the training because of her handicap, but this did not slow her down. By the time she married Dad at age twenty-seven she was a supervisor of nurses.

I was born into this milieu, with two parents, neither afraid of hard work, both highly disciplined and both with over-developed senses of duty. My mother, in particular, thought life was hard work, and for her it was, both physically and mentally. There was great emphasis put on the need to be well educated. This meant that, other than wonderful Saturday night singsongs (particularly special for me because I loved music) and rainy-day games of Rummoli at our cottage at Grand Lake, there was not a great deal of family "fun." I don't think there was much fun in my parents' lives either. This is not to say that they were not happy. In their own way they were devoted to one another. If there were few signs of outward affection, it was probably a reflection of the era in which they lived, and also because of my mother's stoic personality.

My father, on the other hand, was more outgoing, as befitted a politician. But although he had great warmth of personality, it was not often shared with the family because his schedule gave him little time. He and my mother divided the duties. He looked after politics and she looked after the family. The arrangement worked well for both of them. In his unpublished memoirs, written at my request as therapy after his stroke left him paralyzed on his right side, my father wrote: "For we were in love, a love that lasted during our married life and between two such people these thoughts are privileged and sacred. I have honoured her always among all women and am so glad you have had such a wonderful mother."

I was a lonely child, a situation many people think strange in such a large family. My husband, who is an only child, found it inconceivable that you could be lonely with so many people around all of the time. My sister Catherine, who was twelve years older than me, looked after me for much of my babyhood. She was presented with me the day after her twelfth birthday—a belated birthday present—and because my mother was ill for a long time after my birth, Catherine became my substitute mother. I loved her dearly. She has all the warmth of my father, with a natural caring for people that makes her a very special human being. But when she married shortly after my seventh birthday I felt I had been deserted.

As if to epitomize my changed lifestyle, my mother decided that my hair, which was then my crowning glory, would be cut short. Before this disaster I would stand nightly between my sister's legs as she wrapped my long ringlets in rags. In the morning she would brush out my hair so that the curls hung, touching one another, at my shoulders. Mum simply did not have the time to give it the care Catherine had. It was because of that hair, I am sure, that I was chosen as an angel in grade two to lead the First Holy Communicants. And it was that hair that led to my presentation of flowers to the Princess Royal, Princess Alice, when I was four.

I was chunky as a child—I still have a weight problem—and I was convinced I had lost all of my beauty. Such are the concerns of childhood. (In fact, such, it seems, are the concerns of some of the electorate as well. My hair has come in for more criticism from them than even my voice.)

Little did I know that events of a much more serious nature were to befall me. I was soon to become the victim of the greatest betrayal of trust that can be perpetrated against a child.

two

From Adversity Comes Strength

When I was about nine years old I was sexually assaulted by someone who had both the trust of my parents and access to our home. The first time it occurred I had actually invited him into my house.

I came home one spring evening at about eight o'clock to discover that I was alone. With six children, two adults and normally a maid, my house was almost never empty. That night it was. I lived in a large, old home and that night, with dusk coming upon the city, it appeared to me both enormous and scary. Since I could find no one else I called this individual to tell him I was alone, and he immediately suggested he come to look after me. I trusted him, as did the rest of my family. When he took me to bed, undressed me and himself and began to rub himself against me I was filled with agony. Like all children I knew it was wrong, and, like almost all children, I didn't know what to do about it. I wondered if it was my fault. Had I done something bad? Was I wrong to have asked him for help? Others came home, but he had warned me not to tell anyone—it was our secret.

This person had always been a special part of our lives. He was there for birthdays and other family occasions. Like me, he loved music, and I trusted him. Perhaps this was why I was so confused when it happened. How could he betray me like this? I recognized that he had been drinking—that was a normal occurrence, and is perhaps the reason I am still so offended by people who drink too much. But that was no excuse for his foul behaviour.

There were several other incidents over the next two or three years when again he would find me alone in the house, but usually I was able to hide if I knew he was around. I learned to stay in my closet, hanging from the clothes rod so he couldn't see my feet should he open the door. I no longer wanted to be in my own home, and I spent as many hours at school as I possibly could. When I was required to be home I made sure that others would be there.

Why the attacks stopped I don't know. Perhaps he realized that if he kept assaulting me I would tell my parents. Certainly when I was in my early teens and my younger sister was getting to the age I had been when I was abused, I let him know that I would tell if he ever touched her. I am not sure where I got the courage finally to confront him. I do know that the "steely" tone of my voice often commented upon by my students was in my voice that day. He did not ever assault Patricia.

It was the only time I spoke to him about it, but he knew I detested him. In the presence of others he would make cutting remarks about me, but never when he felt I could make a retort. Like many children who have been assaulted, I felt ugly, and he would comment on my appearance, my weight, my hair. I remember the wonderful feeling of victory when he died. Family members were asked to make donations to his favourite charity. I remember my father was surprised that I sent four times what had been requested. I did it because it gave me such joy that he was dead.

Some readers are perhaps asking why I have never disclosed his name to anyone. I never will, for a very simple reason. It was only after his death that I began to feel comfortable—to a small degree —in speaking about my abuse. To disclose his name now would only create more innocent victims. He has children and grand-children, perhaps great-grandchildren. I deliberately have no contact with the family. If he abused any of them, they have already lived through their own particular hell. If he did not, then I have no desire to cause them pain. He alone should have been asked to pay the price, and I lacked the ability or courage to do that when it could have made a difference. My only regret is that, perhaps because of my lack of courage, others have suffered. I tell my story now in the hope that it will provide others with the courage I lacked.

It is hard to explain the long-term effects of such a betrayal on a young woman. At the age of fifty-one I still suffer from the occasional flashback. It usually occurs when my husband and I are making love, but with discipline I can force it aside. To this day I find it very difficult to be outwardly affectionate with any man other than my husband, John. Even the usual welcoming gestures of a kiss on the cheek are difficult for me, and I find it truly offensive when a man tries to kiss me on the mouth. I have always been somewhat relieved that I had daughters, because I always wondered if I would be able to express affection to a male child.

But these are just symptoms. What was of far greater importance was how it changed my outlook on the world, and my sexuality. I became even more self-contained and, therefore, more lonely. Since I had this great secret deep within me I couldn't get close to anyone—otherwise I might blurt it out, and I knew this was something I must not do. I shied away from deep friendships. As a teen I chose to date boys who would not put any pressure on me, since anything more than a very chaste goodnight kiss was impossible. It wasn't until my second year of university that I finally found a male friend whom I felt I could trust.

Reid Morden (now the under secretary of state for External Affairs) and I started to date soon after the school year began, but he was still a "safe date" since he had a girlfriend in Montreal. We decided to have a platonic relationship—particularly after he remarked that kissing me was like kissing a brick wall! (Perhaps I should have been insulted, but instead I was delighted since it meant he didn't even ask for a good-night kiss!)

Of course, Reid was not my father's idea of a partner for me. He was a Scots Presbyterian Tory who wanted to be a foreign service officer. My father's choice for me would have been an Irish Catholic Liberal lawyer. I couldn't convince my father that the relationship was platonic, and he made it awkward for our very close friendship to continue. At a certain point Reid broke up with the girl in Montreal and wanted a more romantic relationship with me. I simply could not do it, and we drifted apart. However, I have always been grateful to him for what he gave to me. Although I never told him about my abuse, he did teach me to trust at least one male member of the human race. Over the years we have kept in touch when events of importance occur to one another. Unfortunately our generation does not readily accept friendships between men and women without a sexual connotation, and we have not maintained the closeness we had achieved at university.

I think that, if there is any positive result whatsoever of my experience with abuse, it can be found in that aspect of my character that refuses to be bullied. Bullying is part of the political process, and there have been moments in my political life when members of both my own party and others have tried to use this tactic against me. It always fails! I am a sucker for the logical, thoughtful, compassionate argument, but threats of any kind simply make me defiant. Once you have stood up to the greatest bully of them all, the physical or sexual abuser of a child, you are not likely to be bullied by anyone else. In a display of just how well he knows me, Al Munroe, my executive assistant, organizer, driver and best political friend, once gave me a pair of red boxing gloves for Christmas! Although I never used them, it was clear that he, at least, had no doubt that I would and will fight politically with all weapons at my disposal when I think I am right.

One of the other positive aspects of my abuse was that it gave me an empathy with women that I have tried to carry with me throughout my political career. There has often been an unwillingness on the part of women politicians to admit they are feminists, and to take strong positions on women's issues. They are no doubt afraid they will be sidelined and treated as single-issue candidates and representatives. I am, however, beginning to see some progress.

I have tried hard to defend the rights of children and women who have been abused, sexually and otherwise. I have shocked members of the legislature by speaking openly about my abuse.

Those who operate shelters and treatment programs for women and children know they have a ready advocate in me. However, it is never enough. I live with the effects of my abuse daily, as do all women who have experienced it. I am still often filled with rage. I am one of the lucky ones since I have been able to direct my rage towards solutions; many direct their anger upon themselves. Despite my retirement it is my intention to continue to advocate, to raise money and to provide counselling for those I can help.

three

The Gift of Excellent Education

I began school at the age of five. Children in Halifax in this era went to either Catholic or Protestant schools. Both were funded with taxpayers' money and both came under the auspices of the Halifax Public School Commission. If you were Catholic you went to designated Catholic schools, and classes for you began at 8:40 a.m. so the first twenty minutes could be given over to catechism. If you were Protestant then school began at 9:00 a.m. As Catholics we were allowed to come late on certain Holy Days of Obligation because, of course, we had to go to Mass. This was particularly nice on All Saints' Day, November 1, because we could stay out later on Hallowe'en night. On my street it always seemed that we Catholics walked to and from school on the north side of the street and the Protestants on the south side. Since Cub Scout and Brownie groups were run in our respective churches we divided our extra-curricular activities along religious lines too. It extended even as far as the swimming and boating clubs.

I was raised in a strong Catholic household. It may be hard for kids today to realize the important role the Church played in our lives. It was not just our schools and our Sunday activities, it was the saying of the daily rosary, fasting at Lent and school visits to the church for confession. It was a very disciplined way of life. I lived in fear of committing a mortal sin and, like most children, I had to think hard about, even on occasion make up, sins to tell in confession. My father was very devout, frequently dropping in to visit a church during the day and was an extremely generous donor. My mother tended to be far more realistic about the Church, but she nonetheless insisted that her boys serve on the altar, her girls attend May Processions and all of us wear medals and scapulars. When my father died in May 1980, the Archbishop of Halifax, James Hayes, insisted on officiating at the funeral Mass, and my mother was quick to comment that it was being done for "politically correct reasons." When she died in December of the same year I sent a little prayer to her when the Archbishop appeared on the altar to say her Mass as well!

I went to this public Catholic school system for five years. I was always a good student, but when I finished grade five my father decided that my marks—consistently in the 90s, with no effort on my part—meant that I was not being challenged. Off I was sent to the Convent of the Sacred Heart, a girls' private school, as a day student. My father was a cabinet minister at this point and we were not affluent. However, my parents felt there was no sacrifice too great to be made towards the education of their children, and I was to get the best. There was no difference made in our family between sons and daughters in terms of what was expected of us. Each of us was to maximize his or her academic talent. My sister Maureen was already a student at the convent, having gone in grade ten. It was considered to be the toughest academic program in the city, and I loved every minute of it.

In grade eight I became a boarder at the school while my parents were on a holiday and, by choice, remained there for several months after they came back. It was the most secure environment I had ever experienced. Here, at least, I felt completely safe from assault. It was also the most disciplined. It was run by an order called the Congrégation du Sacré Coeur, or the Ladies of the Sacred Heart, sometimes called the female Jesuits. This was a semi-cloistered order of nuns whose personal education far exceeded the demands of the Department of Education. I was taught by nuns with Bachelor's and Master's degrees when one or two years of Normal or Teaching School was usual.

If I close my eyes today I can still see Mother Egan's notes on the French Revolution on the blackboards of Third Academic Class, grade eleven. And there were ceremonies, usually involving music, which filled me with joy. Memories of First Friday Benedictions and feast days like the Immaculate Conception are vivid. There was such beauty and pageantry.

But it had a downside, too. In hindsight, it truly was a paramilitary operation. We had a regular and a dress uniform. The former was a blue tunic with a pale-blue cotton blouse and blue-and-white polka-dot tie. It was really very ugly and flattered no one, perhaps on purpose, as vanity was unacceptable. It was worn with beige stockings and brown oxfords. Our dress uniform was a white sharkskin dress worn with white shoes and stockings. It was more attractive, but just barely! We wore this on special feast days like the Feast of Christ the King and the Feast of the Immaculate Conception, and, of course, for Prize Day.

To get the proper hem length for the dresses, we had to kneel while one of the nuns pinned the dress just where it touched the floor. It was not to drag on the ground, nor to ride up. We had white and black veils, the first for special occasions and the second for everyday visits to chapel (either of our own volition or because we'd been sent there by one of the nuns to reflect on our poor behaviour). The nuns did not raise their voices unless they were extremely agitated, so our instructions were given not by shouts but by clappers. These were made of two pieces of wood, each one hollowed out in the centre, and hinged together. They measured about one by two inches and were held in the hand somewhat like a castanet. When the nuns wanted our attention one clap was usually sufficient. Two meant we were in deep trouble. I am amazed at how obedient we were, and how completely cowed. We did not salute, but we did curtsey. I once reflected to an astonished group of friends that I probably curtsied about five thousand times in my six years at the school. There was no physical punishment. It was all mental, and extremely effective.

On Mondays at 3:00 p.m. we had Primes in the Assembly Hall. This was a ceremony in which all the students from grades seven to thirteen participated. The junior school held its Primes at 11:30 a.m. the same day. We would all stand as Reverend Mother, who was the head of the convent although not the school, entered along with the Mistress General and the Mistress of Studies. All of us would have on our regular uniforms, with the addition of white gloves as a gesture to the importance of the occasion. We sat arranged by height and not by grade so that the nuns could see each and every one of us. (The chairs were pressed oak, and I am sure they are worth a fortune today. I understand, though, that they have since been replaced by more modern chairs—typical of all modern education practice!)

Each class, beginning with grade seven and going up to Superior Class, grade thirteen, would parade up the centre aisle and form a semicircle in front of the assembled nuns. The Mistress General would then read that in Superior Class, or whatever the grade, all students had very good notes except for the following. It was then announced whether your notes were simply good, or indifferent, and the reasons for the inferior notes were given. As your name was read you were required to take a step backwards and to curtsey. After all the names were read students proceeded to get a card from Reverend Mother. Those with very good notes were given blue cards, pink were for those with good notes and yellow for those with indifferent notes. After you were given your notes, along with a quick comment if your card was pink or yellow, and after you had given the mandatory thank you (or apology) you took three step backwards, curtsied, turned towards the window, never the centre of the room, and returned to your chair. The worst situation of all was to be told your behaviour was so disgraceful that you received no notes. I can only remember this happening to students twice in the six years I went to the school. In this case you were so humiliated you immediately returned to your seat because you were in too much disgrace to appear before Reverend Mother.

For those of you who think this is all too bizarre to be believed, let me tell you that in six years, other than for absences (which warranted an automatic downgrading of your notes—sickness was no excuse for lack of attendance), I lost my notes only once, and that was in grade six when, on a dare, I threw my math books out of a second-storey window.

Only convent girls will know how truly effective this disciplinary technique was. But it didn't stop there. After all the cards were given out, medals were awarded in subject areas, to be worn by the recipient until the following Monday. These were not always given for academic achievement, they were also used by the nuns to encourage a hard-working student. In addition, politeness points were read. These were given for notable positive behaviour patterns. Four times a year ribbons were awarded: pink in the lower school, green in middle school and blue for the most senior students. These were worn daily as a sign of exemplary behaviour and were displayed with great pride by the recipients, as were the medals.

Among my caucus members, and before that my teaching colleagues, I had a reputation for being highly disciplined. After six years at the hands of these nuns I can assure you that I take no actions, or at least very few, without considering the consequences. Spontaneous I am not!

Another characteristic that is part and parcel of me and that I ascribe to the nuns is my compulsive neatness. (My daughters will be delighted I have admitted to being compulsive!) I am neat about almost everything, but particularly my office and my home. I cannot simply hand someone a piece of paper I have ripped out of a book, certainly not if there is a pair of scissors close by so that I can trim it. This kind of thing was simply unacceptable at the convent. I write many letters in longhand, and if I make a spelling mistake or the ink blots, I automatically rip the letter up and begin again. Old habits die hard, and I acquired these throughout my academic life, most particularly in my preparation of Feast Work.

Feast Work had to be prepared at least twice a year, once for Reverend Mother and again for the Mistress General. Math, chemistry or any subject chosen by your classroom teacher would be prepared as a perfect presentation piece for the reverend authority. And I do mean perfect. A lesson would be prepared in pen (not ballpoint!) on plain, white paper. Assignments were done over and over again until perfection was achieved. Spelling mistakes, sloppy penmanship, ink blots, poor underlining and inadequate drawings of experiments were all rejected. I remember recopying assignments at least four or five times. This attention to detail has stayed with me all of my life. When people wonder how I am able to get so much work done in a day I thank the nuns for the organizational skills, along with the penchant for detail, that was so much a part of my education.

Another valuable skill that I acquired from these role models is my ability to memorize very quickly. I am frequently asked how I can give a speech of twenty minutes or more without notes. The reality is I don't, but if I have read over a speech three or four times I can usually give it with little reference to the text. Memory-work was an integral part of my education. For example, we were required to memorize three or four verses of the New Testament each day and to recite when called upon first thing each morning. Of course we fudged a lot, but often it wasn't worth making excuses and we simply did it. Beginning on Ash Wednesday we were required to memorize the Passion in either St. Matthew, St. Mark or St. John. A certain number of verses were assigned each day, and on Holy Thursday we were given a test. A phrase was given and we were to write the text that followed, with perfect punctuation and spelling, until another phrase was given. There were usually three test passages. It was a great honour to have perfect marks, and someone usually did, although I must confess I wasn't one of them because my poor spelling always got in the way. After this kind of an exercise, getting a speech down pat is child's play.

I held the nuns in very high esteem. Like all children I had my likes and dislikes, but I was in awe of their dedication. Nevertheless, despite my eagerness to participate in all phases of school life, especially in musical activities, I never gave any serious thought to becoming a nun. I don't know if the nuns approached other students, but they certainly didn't ever press me. Perhaps they recognized in my young self what so many have commented on in my political life, my unwillingness to accept orders easily. I like giving them well enough, but I am not particularly happy in accepting direction if I think it is wrong or misguided. Certainly the vow of obedience, which requires a nun to obey even if she thinks the order is wrong, would have been unacceptable to me.

My difficulty with the vow of obedience was one reason that, although I remained a devout Catholic until long after I left the convent, I was already questioning the Church when I was still at school. Its regulation of male-female relationships was, even in my young mind, intrusive and wrong-headed. I knew how bright and dedicated these nuns were, and yet in the presence of a priest they often played second fiddle, when I knew the priest was both less articulate and probably less educated than they. I found it offensive that it was acceptable for the nuns to prepare students for religious occasions, decorate the altar and lead us in prayers and ceremonies as long as a priest was not available, but when a priest arrived it was expected that they fade into the background and obey the priest's instructions. Then, I found it insulting. Today I find it simply antediluvian.

However, my experiences at the convent did give me a strong belief in the value of single-sex education, particularly at the junior high school level, grades seven to nine, as well as a belief in the anonymity created by the wearing of uniforms. While female students in other schools were worried about their hair, make-up and clothes we concentrated on being involved in school activities. Make-up, even lipstick, was forbidden. (Friends watch with amazement and amusement when I put on lipstick without a mirror. It comes from desperation, and all my fellow students could do it. Mirrors were forbidden, as was lipstick, but there is only so much of it that will rub off if it has been heavily applied. Therefore, our application was heavy-handed. When the inevitable order came to remove it we were still left with enough on to make us look respectable.) Throughout my teaching career in mixed schools I watched with despair as girls sublimated their personalities and abilities in order to impress, or at least not offend, their fellow male students. I was often filled with rage while watching a very bright girl pretending to be a "dumb blonde" in order to get a boyfriend. It is one of the reasons my daughters, at least as long as they would let me make the decisions for them, went to single-sex schools.

four

New Horizons and New Challenges

By the time I was fifteen and in grade eleven I knew that it was time to move on. The convent was the only school in Nova Scotia, to my knowledge, that offered a grade thirteen. Because of its academic record, Dalhousie, considered the senior university in the province, would accept students from the convent who had completed Superior Class into third-year classes. My sister had gone to Dalhousie after Post Academic, grade twelve, and into second year. I decided that I wanted to start in first year, but I had a major problem. My father was not at all keen on his daughter leaving a religious education at the tender age of sixteen, which I would be in the fall of 1958. He was also not willing to send me to the Catholic universities of Mount Saint Vincent or Saint Francis Xavier, Brian Mulroney's alma mater, because he didn't consider them to be of sufficiently high academic standards, despite the fact that he sat on St. Francis's board of governors. So the challenge for me was to convince him that I had the maturity to go to Dalhousie at age sixteen.

Knowing how my father's mind worked helped. For the first time in my life I actually worked at school. I brought my average into the high 80s, which for the convent was considered excellent, and applied for a scholarship without his knowledge. After I received the announcement that I had been awarded an entrance scholarship, I presented it to him as a fait accompli. He was so proud he couldn't do anything except grant permission, and off I went to this secular university.

At this point my mother became involved in my academic program. I had wanted to be a nurse since the time I was a very little girl. Indeed, I am still intrigued by all things medical and devour everything I can on the subject. In the late 50s you could not become a Registered Nurse until you were twenty-one because of the regulation that forbade a youth from giving medications. I therefore decided to enrol in a Bachelor of Nursing program, which would take five years, the first two at Dalhousie and the remaining three at a nursing school. However, when I received notification of the faculty I was to enter, I found I had been accepted, not into nursing, but into premed! My mother had changed the application form without my knowledge. As she explained to me, no daughter of hers was going to spend five years to become a nurse when she could spend seven years to become a doctor! This was the first time she ever verbalized her conviction that I was to take a backseat to no one. It was at this moment that my feminist education began. I was somewhat shocked by her action, but it made me realize that she recognized a strength within me. I told my mother at her fortieth wedding anniversary celebration that she was a feminist. My father was horrified, but my mother just smiled as if to say what he doesn't know won't hurt him!

My first year at Dalhousie was a combination of great social success and academic failure. I barely passed my chemistry, biology and French courses and failed math and English. Since I had had a 99 percent average in math in grade eleven, I was stunned. But the reason was simple: I did everything that year except go to class and study. I became active in the Dalhousie Glee and Dramatic Societies, worked on the yearbook and student newspaper, joined FROS (Friendly Relations with Overseas Students, later to become the International Students Association), went to every home game, be it football, basketball or hockey (and I don't even like contact sports), attended every dance—and had a wonderful time. Rather typical behaviour, I think, for my age and the times. However, my parents were not amused, and if the truth be told, neither was I when the results came in. In the fall of 1959 I switched to Arts, much to my mother's chagrin. She made it clear, at every available opportunity, that she still wanted me to be a doctor. However, by the end of my second year my scholarship marks were reattained and I remained a scholarship student for the rest of my academic life. I also remained active in the many campus organizations that had so intrigued me in first year, but I now made better use of my time. I learned to maximize the limited study time available to me.

The organization that demanded most of my time was, of course, political: the National Federation of Canadian University Students, NFCUS. In 1961 I became the chairman at Dalhousie and Atlantic regional vice-president. It was student politics at its best. I am amazed at its dwindling popularity since that time. Without a single voice to speak on behalf of students in this nation, governments will continue to ignore students, to the peril of not only the students but our society as well. Politicians talk a good line about the value of education in our society, but if one looks at the funding to post-secondary institutions in the last few years, it is obvious that their actions belie their words.

One of the presentations I made in 1961 took me to Ottawa to address then Prime Minister John G. Diefenbaker. I was accompanied by Reid Morden, who was president of the Dalhousie Young Progressive Conservative (YPC) Club. Our thesis was that funding to universities should be based not on the provincial population, as was the practice, but on the number of students attending university in that province. Nova Scotia's universities, particularly Dalhousie, had always suffered from a lack of federal government funding because their enrolments represented a disproportionate number of students from across the country, but particularly from throughout the Atlantic region. Dalhousie was the only Atlantic province university in this era to have graduate programs in areas such as medicine and dentistry. I was able to persuade the other Atlantic universities to accept my proposal because we recommended that their grants be "grandfathered." This would result in no decrease in funding to them while the Nova Scotia universities caught up.

Our reception from the prime minister was cold to say the least. It probably was the result of an article—or perhaps I should say

non-article—written for the *Dalhousie Gazette* by student editors
Denis Stairs and Michael Kirby. (Denis is now a vice-president at
Dalhousie; Michael is a senator and a former staffer for Pierre
Trudeau.) The article opened: "The Rt. Hon. John G. Diefenbaker came to Dalhousie and addressed students in Room 24 of the
Arts Building. This is what he had to say." The editors then left a
completely blank column on the front page of the paper. The
prime minister was furious. Denis and Michael justified their
actions by saying that students would not be patronized. Those
of us who were fellow Liberals were delighted. Needless to say, the
YPCs were not amused—particularly Reid. I had to do some
cajoling to get him to join me in Ottawa for the presentation.

My involvement with NFCUS led to trips to other campuses
where I met students from across the country, many of whom
popped up in the Liberal Party later on. The university community was small in those days, and the contacts we made were
widespread and often significant in our later lives in whatever
field we chose. In my years at Dalhousie were future politicians or
public figures such as Clyde Wells, Michael Kirby, Russell
MacLellan, Paul Creaghan, Gerald Doucette, Rick Cashin, Ste-
wart McInnes, George Cooper, Reid Morden, Judith Maxwell
and Brian Mulroney. Joe Clark came the year after I left, and
Lowell Murray dated my sister's best friend at St. Francis Xavier.
It was truly a small world.

As the first female chair of NFCUS, I gained a reputation for
being different from the other women students. Certainly I was
the only female in most of my political science courses, and if I
didn't always have the best mark it was never below a third place.
I studied with some of the male students in my department, and
they treated me as a big sister rather than a "girl." In fact I was the
same age or younger than they, but I was dating "men" in the law
school, and my male classmates tended to use me as a sounding
board for their problems, particularly girl problems.

I didn't realize that other female students felt I was different
until I was interviewed by a reporter when I ran, unsuccessfully,
in Calgary Elbow in 1975. She explained, when I failed to recognize her as a fellow Dalhousian, that they had been intimidated

by me since I seemed to do things they wouldn't have considered doing. How strange, since I had assumed that my lack of closeness to people was just a habit of mine: a continuation of the pattern that I had begun as a child. It never occurred to me that I frightened or intimidated people. That same word, "intimidating," was used recently by Gary Doer, the leader of the New Democratic Party in Manitoba, as an explanation for why many of his female caucus members had failed to comment on my resignation as leader of the Liberal Party. His exact words were "You intimidate them." It gives me a deep sense of unease about our image of ourselves as women if it is true that strong women frighten or intimidate other women.

My father wanted me to go to law school after I completed my undergraduate degree, in part because he was never able to obtain a law degree. My mother was still determined I would go into medicine. I was twenty and had never lived away from home, and my first desire was to go someplace new. It was a bit of a problem, since my parents really didn't have the money to send me away to graduate school, and I knew that if I took either medicine or law it would have to be at Dalhousie. Student loans were unheard of in 1962, and female students could not earn enough money in the summer to pay for the cost of room and board in addition to tuition, books and spending money.

Early in my final year I saw some applications on a bulletin board for a program called a Master of Arts in Teaching at both Harvard University and Smith College. I had, like many women of my era, considered the so-called feminine serving professions, and teaching was one of them, but teaching small children didn't really interest me, and in those days one seemed to have to teach one's way to the top, from elementary to senior high. This degree was specifically geared to the high school teacher, and since they were offering fellowships I applied. To my amazement I was accepted by both, though only Smith College offered me a fellowship. However, I had at last achieved partial approval from my mother who, having been raised in Boston, was delighted that her daughter had been accepted by such "prestigious" universities. To this day I regret not having gone to Harvard, and when my daughter Cathi was accepted as an undergraduate I urged (begged) her to go, even though she wasn't convinced at the time of the value of the opportunity. She is now, fortunately; she graduated in 1990, during the Meech Lake crisis.

Despite my regrets over not going to Harvard, my experience at Smith College was first-rate. The assumption was made that, since we all had undergraduate degrees worthy of entrance to Smith, our education courses should be meaningful and at a graduate level, despite our lack of undergraduate prerequisites.

Half of our course work was in the area we were to teach—in my case history—and the remaining work was in education. Our education courses were directly related to our subject areas. It was a wonderful year of training, and one that should be emulated at our universities. I was dismayed to discover, upon returning to Canada, that full courses in audiovisual aids were offered in the education faculties of many universities. It seemed so unnecessary when there were so many other things essential to know before one entered a classroom. The audiovisual course at Smith consisted of one lab, in which we were introduced to every piece of equipment on the market and told to learn how to use it. We did, but on our own time. I am so very tired of students in education telling me what a boring course it is and how useless it all is when they find themselves in a classroom. My Smith year was both practical and stimulating.

To my astonishment I discovered that I loved teaching. From the moment I entered the classroom I found it challenging, rewarding and entertaining. When I proposed to reporters on announcing my retirement the notion of my return to the classroom they pooh-poohed it. Needless to say they have never seen me in a classroom, and they don't know what a real turn-on it is for me. My staff knows because some of them have accompanied me to classes I've been invited to teach, and they all know that I never turn down an invitation to have students in my office.

During the summer following my second year at Dalhousie, I had started dating an American naval lieutenant, Shirley Holt. He was stationed on the USS *Essex*, an aircraft carrier that docked in Halifax for a week that summer. Shirley, whom I quickly nicknamed Lee, and I began an arm's-length romance that lasted until 1964—"arm's length" because we rarely saw one another! Yet another example of my refusal to get too close to anyone. Obviously since we rarely saw one another I didn't have to worry about my sexuality. He hoped to have a posting in Massachusetts or Maryland in the fall of 1963, and I decided to remain in the United States when I graduated from Smith in order to give the relationship a chance. I took a teaching job at Dana Hall School for Girls in Wellesley, Massachusetts.

In the *Official Preppy Handbook* Dana Hall is listed as the number-one preppy girls school in the United States—and that it was. The students were bright and wealthy. As teachers, it was our job to get them into first-class universities, beginning with Radcliffe and the other "Seven Sisters" if possible. Dana Hall was where I truly recognized the depth of talent in women. Not only were the students very bright, but many were excellent athletes, artists and potential public figures. Yet most of them still thought a white knight would come along, pull them up onto his horse and ride away into the sunset. We did not, as a staff, do our best by them, even though some of us tried to get them to face reality, and also value themselves more highly.

It was here that I also learned of the enormous pressures faced by teenagers. Several months after I began teaching I was visited by a ninth-grader. A bright, bouncy young woman, she was extremely homesick. Elaine told me she was considering committing suicide. I spent three hours talking with her and sent her back to her residence to get ready for dinner, convinced that I had comforted her and that she was back on an even keel. But that night she took an overdose of sleeping pills. Fortunately, she was found and, after her stomach was pumped, her parents took her home to the Midwest. I felt both guilty and furious with myself for presuming to have a capacity and ability I did not have. I never saw her again, but I did learn two valuable lessons that stayed with me throughout my teaching career. First, you don't ever undervalue a threat to commit suicide, and second, you do not offer a service for which you are not qualified. Classroom teachers today are asked to be counsellors, nurses and even doctors. Not only is it not fair, it is dangerous. When I am in the classroom I am a trained teacher and that is all. I am not a health-care professional or a social worker, and when those roles are expected of teachers, their attention is distracted from their true work and focused on areas in which they lack both training and effectiveness. It is one of many problems in the school systems throughout this land.

Eventually my romance with Lee ended, and by that time my longing for this very special country was palpable. I left my position at the end of my second year, despite efforts by the administration to get me to change my mind, and came home. I remember driving from Boston to the Maine/New Brunswick border with mounting excitement. Crossing over I was filled with the joy of homecoming. I had always been home for holidays during my three years away, but now I was home for good. I didn't have a job, and I certainly didn't know what to do with the rest of my life, but this was home and I never wanted to leave it again. To this day I don't even cross-border shop!

I was home for no more than a week when both parents started encouraging me to go back to school. It was not enough that I was their first child to have a Master's degree, they were determined that I would go to professional school. My Dad was still enthusiastic about the law degree he had not been able to obtain. My mother still wanted me to be a doctor. I was only twenty-three and they knew a lifetime lay ahead of me. It was difficult to convince them that I really did love my teaching, since they both considered it a profession inferior to law and medicine. Having lived on my own for three years I knew that I could not return to live in the family home through three or four more years of education. I wanted to continue to evolve as a person able to manage her life on her own.

What has always intrigued me about my parents was that they never put pressure on me to get married. Perhaps it was because my mother did not marry until she was twenty-seven. Certainly most of my friends seemed to be pressured to get on with their lives in this way. The pressure I felt was to make something of my life, and marriage was considered to be merely a part of this.

Oddly enough, the next step I took in my career led me, indirectly, to John Carstairs.

I discounted the idea of medicine, but I was still curious about law, so I again made inquiries at the Dalhousie Law School. (I had applied during my last year of Arts but had withdrawn the application when I accepted the fellowship at Smith.) But that summer I received a call from Jack Earle, then an administrator with the Calgary Separate School Board. He had met my sister Maureen, who had just moved there, and learned that I was unemployed. He offered me a job in Calgary. I took it and began my life in western Canada. I have not looked back.

My first teaching experience in Calgary was in complete contrast to my years at Dana Hall, and like a step back into the Dark Ages. The school I taught at was St. Mary's Girls Senior High School. The principal was a member of the order of the Faithful Companions of Jesus. Their habits were almost identical to those worn by the nuns who had taught me at the convent. But all comparisons ended there.

These nuns were as narrow-minded as mine had been progressive. On my second day of teaching I was called into the office and told by the secretary that I couldn't wear sleeveless dresses without a sweater on top. She had been asked to broach this subject with me by the principal. I was flabbergasted. After all, this was 1965. When I inquired as to the reason for such a directive, I was informed that the students had a dress code forbidding any garment without sleeves, because "such clothes might inflame the passions of the other girls." I was dumbstruck, but not for long. I told her to tell the principal that I considered my clothes both reasonable and fashionable, and I would make no changes. Instead, they changed the students' dress code! But what a hollow victory that was. I soon learned that Sister Geraldine, the librarian, diligently blacked out all words in library books that she considered inappropriate for young minds. Unfortunately, I was able to do nothing about this far greater impediment to the girls' academic development.

There were some amusing moments. One of the school rules decreed that the boys' school was to be let out fifteen minutes ahead of the girls'. They were supposed to go immediately about their business so the girls could go home without any interference. This, of course, was nonsense, as the girls simply met the boys at cafés or other teenage hangouts. One day I looked out my second-storey window and saw two girls sitting on a low fence speaking with a couple of boys. Within seconds Sister Geraldine pounced on them. The girls were dragged up the stairs, and as they passed my room on their way to the office I heard one of the girls bleat, "But Sister, we don't go to this school!" It turned out they were students at Western Canada, the public high school some blocks away. I doubt they ever sat on the fence outside of St. Mary's again.

Although my teaching experience was not all that I wanted, it was during my first year in Calgary that I met John Esdale Carstairs, who within a matter of months was to become my husband.

I was chosen early in 1966 to be part of a Young Liberals team competing on a television program called "Challenge." The team was comprised of three young men and a token female. The woman I was to replace, who was coincidentally John Carstairs's girlfriend at the time, had gone home to England, and Gary Holland suggested me to fill in. This was my first meeting with John, who was one of the team, but it was not an auspicious one. The Young Liberals had been Grand Champions the previous year. This was the first match of the new season and we went down to crushing defeat against the Okotoks Toastmasters Club. The questions were primarily on nursery rhymes. The Toastmasters, for the most part young family men, knew the answers. I did not. John didn't think he had to since these were obviously answers to be found in a female's repertoire. I did not make a favourable impression.

We met again about two months later at a debate between the YPCs and the Young Liberals which, fortunately, we won. We went out for a drink afterwards, and he asked me out to dinner the following night, St. Patrick's Day. Six weeks later, on April 30, he asked me to marry him. The best decision I have ever made was an instant "yes," and we were married in August.

Our entire life, at least until my retirement, has been closely tied to our overwhelming interest in politics. Indeed, he told me once that he married me because I was the first woman he had ever met who shared his passion for politics! His constant encouragement and support gave me the impetus to continue to challenge the society in which I lived.

It was during our brief courtship that I told him of my abuse, although I had never discussed it with anyone else. His reaction was to hold me and to allow me to cry. When I looked at him he too had tears in his eyes. For the first time in my life I felt free to welcome my sexuality. What a joy it was to feel like a whole woman!

My faith in Catholicism began seriously to waver while I was teaching in Calgary. Like so many of my problems with the Church, my concern at this time dealt with a women's issue, which I felt all the more intensely because of my newfound sense of myself and of being a woman with John. One of the teachers in the division, whom I had met during orientation meetings, came to see me. I didn't know her well, but she must have decided I would have a sympathetic ear. Perhaps it was simply that I was the same age and was more prepared than most to tilt at windmills. She told me that she was pregnant and wanted to have an abortion. Like all Catholics of this period I believed abortion to be murder. Yet here was a young woman, beginning her career, with no opportunity for marriage. I became incensed when I learned that the man involved was a professor, and had been her teacher and counsellor at the University of Calgary. He had used that relationship to have an affair with her and was now unwilling to do anything to help.

I was caught in a dilemma: did I obey my Church or help this needy young woman? We talked of alternatives, but there appeared to be none. Her mother, she believed, would consider her a slut if she knew of her pregnancy. I didn't have the financial resources to help, and although I could turn to my parents for most things, this was not one of them. I decided to take on the professor. For the first and only time in my life, I used blackmail, and it worked. I told him that either he paid for the abortion or I went to the president of the University of Calgary. He paid. In hindsight, I realize I should have also gone to the president in order to protect other students, but obviously someone did, because he was dismissed a year later. From this experience I learned two things: men could be held accountable for their actions; and the Church was far too absolute in its rules and regulations.

I began to have serious doubts about the Church because of other things, too. The priests from the boys' school would some-times come to teach our catechism classes. Other priests were brought in for two or three days to conduct retreats in which the students would be subjected to hour after hour of lectures on morality. More and more often I found myself in real conflict with their teachings. They were so unrealistic about the lifestyles of young people that I felt compelled to openly disagree with them. One priest in particular, Father Moran, seemed to target my class. When he walked in I would walk out. When he questioned me about my behaviour I told him he had a choice. Either I left or he could argue with me in front of the students when he began his lectures about sexuality. In my opinion, he knew nothing about the experiences these girls had or were going to have shortly, and he was giving them no help in the decisions they would be asked to make. After that he didn't question me. His visits to my class became infrequent. (When I gave birth to my first daughter, Cathi, he was visiting pastor at Foothills Hospital, but when he came into my room and saw who it was he turned on his heel, acknowledging with finality that we had nothing to say to one another, and walked out!)

I left St. Mary's after two years and moved to St. Francis Senior High, which was co-ed and run by non-religious faculty, although it was part of the Separate School Board. I had made the decision that I could not, in all conscience, teach religion, but I did offer to teach an optional course on dating and marriage to grade twelve girls. I was so happily married that I felt I had something to offer in urging them to take the time to make the right choice. John and I were thirty-three and twenty-four respec-tively when we married; these girls were seventeen and eighteen.

I also knew that my views on issues like birth control and abortion had radically changed as I entered my twenties. I had readily accepted Church dogma in my teens, as they did, and I wanted them to have the luxury of time to think through decisions that would affect their lives forever. They were starved for information, and my classes were always oversubscribed. This was the first example of any form of family life education in the Separate School system, and I am proud to say it grew from there.

I was told by the head of Religious Curriculum for the division that I could not raise the issues of abortion or birth control. Implicit was the instruction that if they came up in class I could not deviate from the Church's official position. I made it clear to the students from day one that there were certain topics I could not bring up myself, but that I would answer all their questions to the best of my ability. It usually took them about two weeks to discover that all they needed to do was ask questions! Looking back now on what we discussed, I realize it was really very limited, but it did give them the opportunity to learn where they could get more information if they wanted it. I marked my success not by tests and examinations but by the number of engagements I broke in any given year. Far too many of these young women were planning to get married immediately after high school. I persuaded many to continue their education and to put off marriage for the future.

My philosophical outlook was constantly evolving during that period. I learned an enormous amount from my school and from the politically radical environment of the 1960s. St. Francis was a school with a diverse ethnic mix. We had especially large numbers of first-generation immigrants from Poland, Italy and Hungary. Most of the fathers were labourers and the mothers housewives or minimum-wage earners. It was difficult to persuade them of the need for their children to obtain a post-secondary education, particularly their daughters.

I remember one very poignant case. Mary was brilliant, with not a mark under 95 in grade twelve. Her brother was in university, but her father was determined his Mary would take a secretarial course. The staff was determined she would go to university. We all spoke to her father and asked her brother, a former student, to intervene on her behalf. All to no avail. But on Prize Night, Mary not only walked off with most of the academic prizes, she was awarded the prize as the student making the most outstanding contribution to school life. Her father came up to me, tears streaming down his face, to say we had won, Mary could go to university. "I hope I have not lost my daughter," he said. "She is a good girl." It wasn't until then that I understood the magnitude of the decision he had to make. For me it was a simple decision of maximizing Mary's talents, for him it was a moral decision, about her soul. I was not so smug after that and tried, as much as possible, to get a better understanding, not only of the young people I taught but of their homes and families.

It was while I was at St. Francis that Cathi was born. At that time I was deeply influenced by Betty Friedan's *The Feminine Mystique*, which John, who had already read it, had urged me to read. I was not going to be like the mothers before me. I was going to have it all—the career, the marriage, the children, the perfectly decorated home and more. Unfortunately none of the authors of such advice told us how we were to fit all of these activities into twenty-four-hour days, nor did they teach us how to live with the guilt!

I had chosen to have my first child. John was quite indifferent about whether or not we had children. He recognized that the majority of responsibility would be mine and so therefore it should be my choice. I love children and wanted five! Unfortunately, blood pressure problems were identified early in my pregnancy, requiring bed rest for the last month and hospitalization for a week before delivery. During my second pregnancy I spent almost six months resting for at least half a day in bed and five weeks in the hospital. We decided shortly after Jennie was born that she would be the last. John tells me he made that decision much earlier, when the doctor told him both the child and I were at risk. I was actually offered a medical abortion after my second pregnancy was identified and my blood pressure was already on the rise. I told the doctor to go to hell. My mind would allow me to give the choice to other women, but my Catholic roots would still not enable me to do it myself. Besides, I wanted the baby very much, and as I wrote to Jennie on the day she graduated from high school, she, like her sister, has never given me anything but joy.

When I am asked what is my greatest accomplishment, and the question is not directly related to my political career, it is easy for me to reply that I have the greatest pride in Cathi and Jennie. Yet they are not my accomplishment, they are their own. I watch, with complete amazement, these two young women, now twenty-four and twenty-one, who have strengths and capacities well beyond mine at the same age. Cathi has her father's gift for intellectual pursuit; Jennie, a natural athlete, is gifted with creativity. I cannot tell what kind of mother I have been; that judgment is theirs alone to make. I do know that they have sometimes felt left out of the closeness John and I share, and they consider me to have been a harsh taskmaster. I hope they also know that the greatest gift I could give them was teaching them to fly on their own. This is harder on the parents than on the children, for it is much more comforting to keep them tied to your apron strings. I have pushed them out. I am sure they often misunderstood my actions as a sign that I didn't love them. To the contrary, I was trying to show them how much I loved them by giving them the opportunity to be their own people. If I could only get them to share my passion for neatness, then life would be perfect!

All of the feminist "superwoman" theory was particularly difficult for an A-type personality like me. I returned to the classroom when Cathi was six months old, and for the next eighteen months I ran myself ragged trying to do everything perfectly. If I stayed longer at school to help a student, I felt guilty about Cathi. On the other hand, if I went home I would feel guilty about the student. The worst part for me was going home and finding that Cathi was fast becoming more attached to Theresa, our live-in housekeeper, than she was to me. There is nothing worse than arriving home, giving your young daughter a kiss and a hug and having her say she is going downstairs to visit Theresa (who lived in a basement suite in our house with her husband and two sons). In retrospect it was probably more fun for her, since Theresa's boys doted on her and played with her constantly. But it devastated me.

In the fall of 1971 I was suffering from a bleeding ulcer and decided to end my teaching career. If I had been given the option of teaching part time I would have accepted it, but, unfortunately, this was not part of the mentality of the early 1970s. I am of the opinion that job sharing and part-time work in the classroom result in higher productivity, because two teachers under less stress and with a more enthusiastic outlook are better teachers than many I have watched, burnt out at the end of a day or week. I also know that when I returned to part-time teaching in 1978 after my youngest daughter, Jennie, entered grade one, the schools received much more from me than my 50 percent paycheque warranted. This is the way of the future for both men and women who want to take a more active role in child-raising. Everyone benefits—the workplace and the home. Unfortunately too many employers are stuck in the ways of the past. Without new ways of thinking Canada will never be able to maximize its potential in the twenty-first century.

Although I was now formally out of work—in other words I didn't get paid for all the work I did—I began to devote more and more of my time to what was to become my life's work—politics.

five

Is There Life Without Politics?

I remember my very first political experience, although my mother maintained I was a political animal from the first time my father kissed me on the day of my birth!

I was in grade two at Oxford Street School in Halifax. It was June 9, 1949, an election day. My father was running, as usual, in the constituency of Halifax North. His Conservative opponent was Richard Donahoe, who later became attorney general in the province and replaced my father in the Senate. He is the father of Terence Donahoe, the former Nova Scotia Minister of Education, and Kathleen, who was in my class. We were friends, frequently walking to and from school together. At the end of the day our teacher, a member of the Sisters of Charity, announced to the class that our fathers were running against each other in the election, that she wished them both well and hoped the best man won. As we formed our line to exit the room, as was the practice of the day, Sister called me back. She told me to remind my father that all of the nuns were Liberals. So much for separation of Church and State!

That evening my father was the first Liberal to be declared elected. I was at election headquarters, and we all loaded ourselves into trucks and cars to make our way to the premier's headquarters in Halifax South. As we went by St. Theresa's Convent, where the nuns lived, on the corner of Oxford and North Streets, my father ordered the horns to be blown, and the convent, which had been in darkness, lit up like a Christmas tree. It was his special thanks to the Liberal nuns!

The following school year Kathleen and I were both slated to be skipped to grade four. Kathleen's parents agreed; mine did not, believing me to be too young. Whether it was because we were no longer in the same grade or because of our fathers' rivalry, we were never friends again, simply nodding acquaintances.

My next political experience was not nearly so pleasant. In April of 1954 the premier of Nova Scotia, Angus L. MacDonald, died. The suddenness of his passing led the Liberal caucus to ask my father to form a cabinet, and he was sworn in as premier. The decision was unanimous. Although precedent in politics to this date does not require a leadership convention on the death of a leader, my father called one for September of that year. It took place at the Halifax Forum.

During the months between April and September an interesting phenomenon developed. A number of candidates stepped forward; all of them were Protestant. It was apparently thought that it was not fair for a Catholic to replace a Catholic. (Although he had made no secret of his religion, many Nova Scotians didn't realize that Angus L. MacDonald was a Catholic until his funeral Mass took place at St. Mary's Roman Catholic Basilica!) There was no question that a Connolly would be Catholic, since the Halifax Irish were almost all Catholic, and the Scots Presbyterians in Nova Scotia weren't having any of it. I remember well sitting in the Forum watching the results on election day. At the age of twelve I learned my first tough political lesson.

The myth of the "Protestants' turn" was precisely that—a myth. In the history of Nova Scotia there had been only three Catholic premiers—Sir John D. Thompson, Angus L. Mac-Donald and my father—but revisionist history spread like wildfire on the convention floor. Perhaps part of the explanation is the strange custom of the city of Halifax, which, in the election of mayors, did alternate every two years between a Catholic and a Protestant, a custom that died out when Haligonians elected a Jewish mayor.

On the first ballot that awful 1954 day, my father received 224 votes, not enough to win outright. His closest opponent had 83, and Henry Hicks, the ultimate winner, had 81. On the sixth ballot Hicks won. There was no victory parade. Instead, party officials hustled the new leader away because fights broke out, people were in tears and the police were called. My father was mobbed on the platform by weeping people. I watched from the stands and couldn't understand how, if he was so well loved, he had lost.

Within the week Dad had received a call from Robert Winters, the federal cabinet minister from Nova Scotia, asking if he would accept an appointment to the Senate—an appointment made in July of 1955. The federal Liberals were very concerned about the negative fallout in the Liberal Party from the convention. In the next provincial election of 1956, the Liberals were badly trounced by Robert Stanfield and the Progressive Conservative Party. All those who ran against my father were defeated either in this election or the one to follow. It is not true to say my father gloated then, but he didn't shed any tears!

This was my first direct experience with prejudice in any form, and one that was difficult, at age twelve, to understand. Prejudice in the Liberal Party was also given, by L. Ian MacDonald in his book *Mulroney, The Making of the Prime Minister* as one of the reasons why Brian Mulroney, a good Catholic boy, chose to become a Conservative, despite his family loyalty to the Liberal Party.

The political lesson I learned on Christmas Day of 1954, following my father's defeat, made an even greater impression on me than the convention. Like most Catholic parents, mine went to midnight Mass on Christmas Eve. As we became teenagers we joined them, but in our younger years we went to early Mass on Christmas morning. My brothers would usually get to the presents at about four o'clock in the morning. I would be roused at five o'clock and taken to see my gifts and stocking. We would dress and trudge off through the snow to six or seven o'clock Mass. I am sure we didn't always have a white Christmas in my childhood, but with the convenience of selective memory I can't recall any other kind. After Mass and breakfast we would move to the living room to watch my parents open their gifts. There seemed to me always to be thousands of presents, and it took forever. First were the gifts from family members, including the stockings which were, by family tradition, filled in alternating order by one child each year as a gift from that child to my parents. Then it was on to the political presents—boxes of chocolates, cigars, bottles of liquor, the occasional fruit basket, the tinned fruit cake. But Christmas 1954 was so different. All the non-family presents disappeared, with the exception of those from close personal friends. Interestingly, they all returned in 1955 after my father had been appointed to the Senate. Even to a child it was a telling lesson about the fleeting fame of politicians— an important thing to learn for anyone choosing to enter this crazy game. Having had those early lessons, I was one politician who entered the game with my eyes wide open. That is not to say that I didn't have my share of disappointments, I simply expected them and was, therefore, better prepared than most, who had to learn on the job.

When I was in grade six, at the age of ten, I decided the time had come to get to know my father. In families with large numbers of children you don't get a great deal of individual attention. My father, as a busy politician, had less time than most for the affairs of children. I was at the convent, which was located halfway between our home and the Nova Scotia legislature. On days that the legislature sat, instead of using my return bus ticket to go home, I would go from school to my father's office in the Provincial Building. If he wasn't there I would cross the street to the Assembly.

The Nova Scotia legislature is a small, granite, Georgian building and its only office is that of the premier; it is not large enough to house any other offices. I soon got to know the pages and the ushers and they would escort me to the ladies' gallery. The Speaker of the day, John Smith McIvor, would usually notice me (I was often the only one in the galleries other than the reporters) and would doff his tall silk hat in acknowledgement—very impressive to a ten-year-old. My Dad always sat next to the premier. Although he was just over five-foot five, his height was all in his upper body, so, seated, he appeared to be much taller than he actually was. Perhaps like all children I thought my father was very handsome. Certainly he was very dapper and often won awards as one of the best-dressed men in Nova Scotia. I was very proud of him. Dad would wave, the signal that he would drive me home when the session adjourned, or earlier if he could get away.

I spent many hours watching, struck by the majesty of the spoken word and the drama of the events, most of which I didn't understand. I could, however, identify the strong speakers from the weaker ones, and I still have a great love of good oratory.

My siblings soon labelled me Dad's favourite, but I am not sure they understood how hard I worked to get that attention. On our drives home he would discuss his day and the political events that had transpired. My father always spoke to me as an adult, which perhaps led him to the conclusion that I was fully mature at age twelve. Of course I was not in most parts of my life, but perhaps I was by that time in terms of comprehending adult conversation.

My father assumed, as did everyone else, that I had an undying interest in politics. In fact I had an undying curiosity about my father! My visits to the legislature soon paid off in terms of outings with my father elsewhere. Mother Agnes Lahey, the Mistress General of the convent, would get phone calls saying I was to be picked up at such and such a time, and off I'd go with Dad to Antigonish, Sydney or Yarmouth, where he'd be attending political meetings. The one I remember best was Allan J. MacEachen's federal nomination meeting, at which there was a bomb scare. With the advantage of youth I didn't even have enough sense to be frightened, but my father was concerned for my safety. (Perhaps someone already knew what all of us were soon to learn, that Allan J., once elected, would become something of an enfant terrible in terms of the power he would wield in Nova Scotian politics, and wanted to stop him before it began!)

By the time I was in high school I was truly a political animal. At Dalhousie I became active in the Young Liberals and participated in model parliaments along with Young Progressive Conservatives like Judith Maxwell (then Judy McMahon), who would later become head of the Economic Council of Canada (ECC), and Reid Morden. I remember with some amusement the stories in *Maclean's* in the 1980s when Reid was appointed to the Canadian Security and Intelligence Service (CSIS) and Judy to chair the ECC. The thrust of the articles was that the people who were given these posts were political eunuchs. But some of us have very long memories and know that Brian Mulroney, who very carefully tried to hide his year-long attendance at Dalhousie, was active in the YPCs at the same time as Judy and Reid. Both were very well qualified for the jobs they were given, but they also had important political connections.

I took my political interests with me when I moved to the United States in 1962. Shortly after I arrived at Smith, Edward Kennedy, who was running for the United States Senate, was in a plane crash in the town of Springfield a few miles from the college. It was announced that he would be unable to campaign personally, and the call went out for additional volunteers. I signed up and quickly learned the very distinct differences between Canadian and American elections. The door-to-door canvass, so much a part of the Nova Scotian scene, with a poll captain in each poll and a worker for almost every block, was not employed to the same degree in the United States because, even in a state like Massachusetts where citizens had a high level of education, many were ineligible to vote because they were not registered. It seemed appalling to me that you were required to register—I had always believed that was the enumerators' job. This, of course, is the reason why a 50 percent turnout is average in the United States whereas a 70 percent turnout is considered poor in Canada. Americans tend to wear their belief in democracy on their sleeves, but when the chips are down, they fail to exercise it!

This was my first introduction to direct-mail campaigning and phone canvasses. Since you wasted too much time going door to door speaking to unregistered voters, you worked directly from the registered voters lists and wrote to them or phoned. Ted Kennedy's election campaign was interesting and I was glad I participated, but there was not the same excitement—or I suppose commitment as there is working for a candidate running in your own province or country.

It was with some amusement that my fellow students in residence watched me, with my ear attuned to a poor-quality radio signal from Montreal, listening to the returns in the federal election on April 8, 1963. They had certainly never heard of Lester B. "Mike" Pearson and couldn't understand why this crazy Canuck was jumping up and down because Diefenbaker, whom some had at least heard of, had been defeated. It was particularly baffling because I had given a speech on campus justifying Mr. Diefenbaker's decision to prevent American Bomarc missiles from being stationed in Canada unless they were under Canadian control. Since Mr. Pearson had taken the position that the Americans could do as they pleased, they had reason to believe I wouldn't support him. In trying to explain that Liberal blood was thicker than water, I am afraid I lost them. It was not the first time, nor would it be the last, that the Liberal Party and I were not in agreement.

It had become a matter of national pride to me that Americans should not just assume that, as their friends, we would be willing to sacrifice a small piece of our sovereignty to them, and that is what I thought they were asking of us in the missile issue. I had become particularly vocal since I had been refused permission to practise-teach in the public high school because I wouldn't swear allegiance to the American flag. When I explained that, in good conscience, I couldn't do it because I was a Canadian citizen, they told me I simply could not be trusted to teach American history to vulnerable young people! So I did my practise-teaching in a private school.

That academic year also brought the world a major event in the Cold War, the Cuban Missile Crisis. It was a disturbing time to be living in the United States, and because of where I was located, I was personally touched by the events.

In 1961, Lee Holt, my U.S. naval lieutenant, left the navy to fly helicopters in Thailand, I now assume for the CIA. When he returned many thousands of dollars richer and tried to enrol in law school, he was issued a demand order to return to the navy because of his specialty. He was on leave visiting me in Boston when he was recalled suddenly to a base in Puerto Rico. This was my first intimation that something big was coming down.

Several days later my residence was in complete upheaval. Four of the graduate students were from Turkey and they couldn't get in touch with their families. All indications were that if the United States attacked Cuba the USSR would retaliate against American bases in Turkey. It was a scary time for all of us, and I, for one, was not helped by a letter from Lee telling me he would be perfectly prepared to head a suicide mission to assassinate Castro. I suddenly realized that we did not think in the same ways, and I was quite frankly horrified by the thought of such a personally violent act performed by someone I thought I loved!

It is hard to describe the daily tension faced by everyone. Security was extremely tight. None of the "foreign students" was allowed to visit a fellow student living on a nearby air force base because the base was on full alert, and we were not to be trusted. We were told to carry our green "alien" cards with us at all times. Everyone attended classes, but certainly no one seemed to be paying much attention. Most of us truly believed that World War III was about to begin.

I found that at home in Canada during this time there was certainly an atmosphere of tension, but not to the same degree as those of us living in the United States experienced. For me, it was a time when I was acutely aware of not being an American, and I felt a fierce devotion to everything I have come to believe is the essence of what we are as citizens of Canada. It is strange indeed to have discovered that the fiercest Canadian nationalists are often found among those of us who have lived, for at least part of our lives, outside of this country. Certainly it gave me a strong desire to not be an American, the opposite desire being something of a disease that many Canadians suffer from, including, I think, Brian Mulroney. I can admire what they are but have no desire to be one of them. Perhaps living outside Canada for part of one's life should be a requirement for anyone who aspires to be prime minister.

The next event that shaped me as a political animal was the assassination of President John F. Kennedy. Like all of my generation I know where I was when I first learned of this disaster; however, my experience had a peculiar twist. I was coming out of a hair salon in Wellesley, Massachusetts, and ran into a grade nine student of mine who was hysterical. She blurted out that the president had been shot and so had my father. One part of me was filled with dread, the other a sense of unreality. As the story unfolded it appeared that she, who knew that my name was Connolly and that my father was a politician, had leapt to the conclusion that Governor John Connolly, shot at the same time as the president, was my father! I walked her back to her residence, where house-mothers and teachers were making the rounds in an effort to be supportive to the youngsters, and began a process, which would last for days, of working with students one on one and in groups helping them to understand the incomprehensible. It was particularly difficult for me to explain since, on the one hand, my knowledge of American history taught me that assassinations and attempted assassinations of American presidents was a relatively common phenomenon, but on the other hand, one that was relatively obscure in Canadian history and experience.

The students, like most Americans, were devastated. This was the first president to represent youth. He was the Camelot president, with all the magic that represented. I remember standing in the chapel that Friday night as students assembled on a voluntary basis. As we began to sing "America the Beautiful," the tears streamed down my face, as they did on the faces of all assembled, and I was struck anew by the differences between our two nations —one willing to settle differences by the use of guns and violence, the other rejecting violence but prepared to exhaust itself with talk as a means of settling its often felt incompatibility.

There was another, perhaps more philosophical influence on my political views at this time. My father had represented the constituency of Halifax North throughout his political career. This was the part of the city in which he grew up, and where the Halifax Explosion of 1917 had made its greatest impact. It was the poor part of town. We were not raised there. I grew up in the west end and moved to the south end, the affluent part of Halifax, shortly after my father was appointed to the Senate. But it was to the north end that Dad always returned, even when handicapped by his stroke. When we asked where he would like to go on his drives following the stroke, he would give directions to proceed up Gottingen or Barrington Street to the north end. He would want to drive past his old home, still standing and now the offices of a housing co-op, and past St. Patrick's Church. He had a story for every block. He loved this part of the city, and he had compassion for those who lived their lives in poverty.

I was not very old when he took me for the first time to visit Africville. Africville was a black squatters' community near the Halifax dump. He told me of the unfairness suffered by those born into poverty, who, through no fault of their own, couldn't break the cycle. He felt particular compassion for the women he knew, for the most part, to be hard-working yet mired in prejudice in their own city. It was on this outing that he told me that more was expected of me because I had been born with so much. In my father's eyes we had every advantage, and I suppose from his perspective, as he had been forced to leave school and to give up his dream of becoming a lawyer because of his family responsibilities, it must have looked as if his children had the world by the tail. But we were not to be complacent, and the need to give of ourselves to our community was a recurrent theme.

It is therefore hardly surprising that my brother Dennis has served as an alderman in the City of Halifax, and has run, unfortunately unsuccessfully, for mayor, and that my sister Patricia is a school trustee. Service from the Connolly children was expected. It is why I become angered with citizens who don't participate and, in some cases, don't even vote. They are convinced in their own minds that politicians are only in the game for self-aggrandizement. Perhaps some are, but the vast majority of those in public life that I have met are motivated by a deep sense of responsibility to their fellow human beings. That is not to say I have liked them all. I have not. But I rarely question their reasons for becoming politicians.

It was with this legacy that I watched with interest the career of the Reverend Martin Luther King, Jr. Here was a black leader in the United States preaching active involvement in society and non-violence at the same time. I heard him speak in Boston and I was deeply touched by his commitment to his people. Finally, I thought, blacks have someone to lead them to a better life. I thought of Clara Adams, a Ph.D. student in chemistry at Smith who had become my friend. She told me of growing up in the then segregated city of Baltimore and being forced to sit at the back of the bus. I learned of her being spat upon, of being forced to sit in the undesirable parts of the movie theatre and of going to segregated schools. I could only imagine how very bright she must have been in order to have accomplished so much. Yet when she came to Smith her assigned roommate had refused to live with her because she was black. Our friendship began when I offered her a bite of my Nova Scotia McIntosh apple. I was unaware that you didn't share food with a black person. That summer when she found that apartments were magically filled every time she went in person to rent one, I rented one and sublet it to her. Now she and her people had a leader who would help them gain the respect they deserved.

At the same time it forced me, in my Canadian smugness, to re-examine how we treated our black Canadians and Aboriginals. What I saw was a history of racism and bigotry that made me ashamed. Martin Luther King taught me to look beyond that shame and look towards actively changing these patterns of behaviour. It was the reason I went to Washington, D.C., on August 28, 1963, and listened in front of the Lincoln Memorial when he gave his famous "I have a dream" address. That is why, when I announced my retirement, the comments of two Manitobans were so highly treasured. Wayne "Kojo" Williams, a leader of the black community, said:

She will be remembered for opening up the doors of the Liberal Party so that it now reflects the society in which it operates. Blacks and other minorities in particular, and Manitobans and Canadians in general, will sadly miss this great woman politician, who remained human throughout her career trademarked with the words conviction and heart.[1]

Oscar Lathlin, who is now an NDP MLA but when I first met him was the chief of The Pas Indian band, said:

> The Leader of the Liberal Party, in my mind, has contributed immensely, not only to her party but without a doubt I think she has contributed tremendously to this Legislature and to the people of Manitoba. I think the Leader of the Liberal Party is a very principled person and for that I admire her. May the Creator be kind to her, give her peace of mind, contentment, good health, happiness and a good family life.[2]

They made me feel that the lessons I learned from Martin Luther King had somehow been put into practice.

In the summer of 1965, on my return to Canada, I was asked to attend another Liberal leadership convention at the Halifax Forum. Gerry Regan was running against Bob Matheson, and once again it appeared that a Haligonian would be rejected as the leader of the party. For some reason, one can only assume fear of the big city, Nova Scotia Liberals had never elected a leader from the capital city of Halifax. My father thought Matheson, a Haligonian, to be the superior candidate, and he was particularly incensed when the Regan camp began to tell delegates it was a Catholic's turn. My father wanted that kind of prejudice on both sides eliminated from the political process, and he wrote an open letter to the delegates to that effect. When I was passing out the letters, one elderly gentleman became quite agitated and insisted that Harold Connolly couldn't possibly have written such a letter. When I insisted that he had, I was ridiculed. When I pointed out that I was his daughter he became silent. My father stood tall for the principles by which he lived, and that has been part of his legacy to me. It certainly didn't affect the result, though, as Regan, known in his radio days as "Gabby," won and went on to be the premier.

Finally in 1992, the Nova Scotia Liberal Party elected a leader from the urban area of Halifax-Dartmouth (Dr. John Savage is now the premier, and in his caucus is Wayne Adams, the first black MLA in Nova Scotia). It probably helped that he was the mayor of Dartmouth! Politics is like every aspect of life: the old ways are hard to change.

In Calgary, I maintained my political ways. I had been there for less than a month when the 1965 federal election was called. By now I was like an old workhorse politically. An announcement would be made and I would show up at election headquarters prepared to go to work. Harry Hays, the Minister of Agriculture, was the candidate in Calgary South, where I lived, and I volunteered to take a poll. When I finished that I went back to take another one. Gary Holland, the campaign chair, was absolutely amazed when I offered to take the second one. In those days it must have been unusual to have young women on the campaign in Calgary, because I certainly came in for my share of good-natured teasing. Perhaps it was just that I was working for Hays who, despite being one of Calgary's more popular mayors, turned out to be a one-election wonder when it came to federal Liberal politics. Not surprising in Tory Alberta.

Nick Taylor, who eventually became the leader of the Alberta Liberal Party, showed up at my classroom door one day to meet me. He explained that he couldn't believe his ears when his daughter Patrice, his eldest of nine and a student in my class, informed him she had a Liberal for a teacher. This he had to see for himself. I was certainly beginning to get a reputation.

six

Liberals Are an Endangered Species

M y husband John's introduction to politics was somewhat different from my own. John was born in Montreal in July of 1933, and although his mother was a Canadian, his father was a British citizen. The family returned to Great Britain shortly after John's birth, and John and his mother didn't return to Canada until July 14, 1940, his seventh birthday. The Blitz had begun in Britain. His father had enlisted in the Royal Air Force and would have little contact with the family for the duration of the war. John's parents decided that he and his mother should accept the Canadian government's offer to ship Canadians home for one pound each. John's father remained overseas in the RAF.

John's experiences in private schools, particularly Ashbury Collegiate in Ottawa, gave him no insights into Canadian politics, despite the fact that future politicos like Donald "Thumper" Macdonald and John Turner were there with him. His real political education began in 1950 at the University of New Brunswick. He was sixteen. His landlord was a Liberal organizer, and he asked John if he would like to make twenty dollars on election day. John, who has always been keen to make a dollar, leapt at the opportunity. His job was simple—he would drive voters to the polls. After they had voted "correctly" he would give the men a mickey of scotch or rum and the ladies a box of chocolates.

How did you guarantee they voted correctly? It was really a

simple scam. The first Liberal voter of the day didn't cast his or her ballot. After receiving the ballot from the returning officer the voter left the polling station instead of casting his vote and delivered the unmarked ballot to the organizer. It would be marked with a Liberal X. The next person taken to the poll would be given this marked ballot and, in order to receive his or her gift, would be required to deliver an unmarked ballot to the organizer. On and on it would go throughout the polling hours. Effective, no doubt, but absolutely illegal. Amazingly, it made him a Liberal. It has always been a source of some amusement in our family that the upright corporate lawyer not only earned his political stripes in this way but also has always been more to the left of the party than me! I am sure it was always assumed by the business community that it was John who kept me from being "a left-wing fanatic." In fact, he would have had my policies go much further to the left. I am the small-c conservative in the family.

It is truly difficult to describe my political career without talking about my marriage. When I realize that fellow women politicians like Sheila Copps and Kim Campbell have sacrificed relationships because of their political goals, I know what a truly charmed life I have led. John has been my number-one supporter throughout. He was perhaps better known on the doorsteps in River Heights, my constituency, than I was since he was there more often, persuading the voters to cast their vote for "beauty wonder" (his favourite expression for me) while I was off travelling the province. Throughout three provincial elections he was the corporate fund-raiser, in all cases raising more money than we spent! Perhaps he can best be described through our daughters' rueful admissons that it will be tough for them to find husbands who live up to their father's example of a truly liberated man. He is much more than liberated. He has an inner confidence that leaves him with only joy in the promotion of others. For me he has always been the wind under my wings, encouraging me to soar higher and higher, all the time letting me know that I flew with the security of his love to cushion any falls.

My image as a politician is one of a tough competitor. The public rarely sees me as a wife and a mother, and yet these are the roles in which I take the greatest pride, and I believe if you fail to understand these roles, you do not have a true picture of me. My devotion to John is total and complete. Had he ever asked me to retire at any time in my political life I would have done so, knowing he would not have asked if there was not a good reason.

We came very close to this in 1985, only one year after I was elected leader of the Liberal Party in Manitoba. It was clear, even in early 1984, that the corporate offices of Inter City Gas, the company John worked for, would be moved from Winnipeg to Toronto. Prior to my running for the leadership, John spoke with Bob Graham, the company president, about the possibility of such a move affecting the legal department of which John was the head. We were told not to worry. Exactly one year to the week of my election, John came home from work on a Thursday night looking somewhat down. He told me he had good and bad news. "Which do you want first?" he asked. The good news was a large raise. The bad news was that the company wanted him to spend it in Toronto.

The next day was the opening of our Annual General Meeting of the party. Did I tell the delegates of the possibility of such a move? Did I say nothing and get through the weekend hoping that the company could be persuaded to change its mind? At no time did we consider the solution of breaking up the family with my living in Winnipeg and John living in Toronto and commuting back and forth. This was simply not an option. I had watched my mother and father live this way with my father in the Senate in Ottawa, and I watched them develop separate lives. That is not what either of us wanted from our lives together. And since John's salary was almost three times my own, his quitting was not a viable option either.

We went to visit Otto and Adrian (now Macdonald) Lang, political friends. They recommended that I say nothing to the membership of the party until I had a definitive answer from the company. But Adrian knew how vulnerable I was and stuck close by me throughout the meeting. After I had given my accountability session to the delegates, I left the stage to find her waiting, which was just what I needed. I immediately asked her how I had done, and she said, "You were terrific. Why?" Adrian knew I didn't fish for compliments. I said, "Because I don't remember a single thing I said up there. All I could think about while I was speaking to them was that this might be the last time." After that, she didn't let me out of her sight! All politicians need friends like her.

We didn't tell Cathi and Jennie and decided to take them to Mexico for a week while the company was sorting out what it intended to do. Several days before we left on our trip a reporter showed up at my office. His wife had a friend at Inter City Gas and the news had spread that senior corporate moves were in the offing. Doing his job, he processed that information and sought me out for some answers. I asked for five minutes to call my husband. It was decided that we would pick the girls up from school and tell them about the possibility before the early news, since it looked as though this reporter had a scoop. I then gave the interview and went home. The girls were told. Cathi, who was in grade eleven, immediately announced that she wasn't moving anywhere, at least not if they didn't have an International Baccalaureate program, a rarity in Canada. Jennie was just confused.

The next day it was the big story and interviews were conducted nation-wide. The reactions covered all the bases from Elizabeth Gray of the CBC's "As It Happens," who simply couldn't understand why we wouldn't live apart, after all others did it, to, "Isn't that just like a woman anyway," to genuine sympathy. The decision ultimately made by the company was that all the senior corporate officers would move to Toronto with the exception of the legal department. We knew this, in essence, would mean a certain degree of red-lining for John. If you are not where the decisions are being made your corporate influence is lessened. However, we decided that my political career was important to both of us and decided to take the gamble. Many didn't understand exactly what had happened. John actually became a bit of a folk hero for some women because they thought he had sacrificed his job for his wife!

It was John who encouraged me to run for the first time in the Calgary constituency of Elbow, now held by Ralph Klein, the recently elected leader of the Progressive Conservatives and premier of Alberta. John and I remember when Ralph was a Liberal; indeed, we reluctantly admit to writing his very first pamphlet when he sought political office at the municipal level. In the 1960s and '70s that was one of the things we did in our volunteer work. Pamphlet writing is a skill, and we practised it with many. Unfortunately most of our candidates were not victorious since they ran for the Liberal Party—not a great favourite in Alberta. Or perhaps it was the pamphlets!

The party did some really stupid things. One of the worst, in our opinion, was the defeat of Bill Dickie, then a provincial MLA, by Pat Mahoney at the federal nomination meeting in 1968 in Calgary South. Bill was the only Liberal left in the provincial legislature and he had paid his dues. Because of asinine membership rules—rules that unfortunately still exist in the Liberal Party—the Mahoney team was able to stack the meeting with teenagers. Because one need only be fourteen years old to vote at a nomination meting, it was possible to "persuade" teenagers with hamburgers and beer. Pat won and went on to be a cabinet minister. Bill Dickie crossed the floor and joined the Lougheed team in the provincial legislature. There are many in the party who still think this is smart politics. On the contrary, it is stupid politics and leaves such a bad taste in the mouths of so many that the long-term pain outlasts the short-term gain.

This was also the year Alan Sulatycky won the riding of Rocky Mountain. Like so many candidates, Alan entered the race wanting to raise his profile in the Liberal Party while recognizing that his chances to win were minimal. However, the Conservative Party split in two at the nomination meeting, and the defeated incumbent ran as an Independent Conservative. As a result Alan was able to win the riding with only 38 percent of the vote. Within days he began to believe he had won the riding all on his own merits, a failing common to almost all politicians I have met and one that leads to disaster for most of them. Pat and Alan were defeated in the next election in 1972. Both received their Liberal rewards, serving on the courts of this land.

In 1974 Nick Taylor was chosen as the leader of the Alberta Liberal Party. An election was called the following year, and he asked me if I would run in the Calgary riding of Elbow, where both he and I lived. He had decided to run in Glenmore because that was the most recently held Liberal seat. I agreed, with John's help, to do it, but we determined that no workers or money would be drained from Nick's campaign. As a result the entire campaign was run from our kitchen. We even used our home phone number as the campaign number. Through my father's financial assistance and a campaign visit by my brother, Dennis, who brought with him "Where You Vote" cards when he arrived from Halifax, we distributed four pieces of campaign literature and our expenditures were less than $2,500.

A typical campaign day would find me off to the printer to deliver a new pamphlet while John went to work at his corporate law office. Then I'd go to a coffee party given by a neighbourhood friend. I spent the afternoon walking Jennie around the riding. She was two, and Cathi was in school. John and I would both head out at 5:00 and would remain on the streets until 9:00 or 9:30 p.m. We had knocked on every door in the constituency by election day. We would then come home to write the next pamphlet, usually in bed! The pamphlets were fun, and we had nothing to lose. Liberals had always run fourth in this riding, so we were prepared to try anything. One of the pamphlets was actually called "Fathers Don't Always Know Best, Why Not Try A Mother For A Change!" Whether it was our energy or our craziness, I am not sure, but we came second—albeit a very distant second—and Peter Lougheed was quoted as saying he wouldn't mind having me on his team!

In the midst of all of this activity, an extraordinary thing happened that once again challenged my own assumptions. My housekeeper, Theresa Fagan, a Cree from northern Alberta, was afflicted with Bell's palsy. The whole left side of her face collapsed. The prognosis was poor and she was told by local doctors that rest was the only hope. After a few days she told me she wanted to visit the reserve she had grown up on. It was cold and I was concerned for her health, but she was determined to visit the medicine man. You can imagine my reaction to such an announcement. At that time in my life medicine men were ranked along with witches and goblins in my mind. However, we cared deeply about Theresa, who had provided both wonderful care and a unique value system to our daughters since our eldest, Cathi, was six months old, so we helped her on her way. Imagine our shock when she returned home several days later with her face fully restored. Would it have happened anyway? Was it faith? Who knows? But I have had great respect for alternative health care since that time. Once again the values I held dear were questioned. I was forced to broaden my narrow way of thinking and reach out to new experiences.

Throughout our years in Alberta both John and I had served the party in a number of ways. John had been a member of the federal campaign committees in 1963, 1968 and 1972. I had chosen the executive route and in 1976 was elected president of the Liberal Party in Alberta, another first for a woman.

The party at this time was joint, so I was president of both the federal and provincial wings. I remember well my first executive meeting in Ottawa. Women were rarities in those days in positions other than female vice-president, a position as token as its name would imply. For the most part I was dismissed as we greeted one another until Jim Coutts came up to me immediately before the meeting and gave me a big hug and a kiss.

Jim and John had been friends for years. John had co-chaired Jim's bid to be the president of the Young Liberals of Canada at the 1962 convention in Banff. That led to Jim being given the job as appointments secretary to Lester B. Pearson. In 1966, on his way to Harvard to take his MBA, Jim stopped in Halifax to be the best man at our wedding. Now that he had publicly supported me, I was supposedly someone to be reckoned with, since Jim was the principal secretary to Pierre Trudeau.

During the national executive meeting we sat in a rectangle with Trudeau at the head. I sat two to his left. Beginning on his right, we went round the room so that provincial presidents and other members of the executive could give him information from their regions regarding the state of the nation. I couldn't believe my ears. Most of the statements were the most mealy-mouthed hyperbole I had ever heard. To listen to this bunch you could only believe that there were no problems in Canada, that everything was perfect. I can only assume they were all protecting their potential patronage appointments!

When it was my turn I burst. You could see the cringing as I raised issues such as the unacceptably high unemployment rate, the unpopularity of the National Energy Program and our failure to sell bilingualism. I made it perfectly clear that I was in favour of our language policy but that I needed some hard facts. The average Albertan was of the opinion that everyone was to be forced to be bilingual, that there would be no jobs in the federal civil service unless you were French-speaking and therefore, in their minds, from Quebec. Albertans were also under the impression that all RCMP officers as well as all members of the armed forces had to be French-speaking. I wanted facts to contradict this ignorance. Because there were no elected Liberals in the Alberta legislature or in Parliament at this time, the role of president was perhaps more public than in most provinces, and I wanted support. In addition I explained that I thought there were many Liberals who still did not understand the language policy, and it was up to us as an executive to make it clear to them. Mr. Trudeau was not absolutely sure of my position but appeared to accept it— and me—at face value.

The next question was posed in French by the French-speaking female vice-president. Mr. Trudeau replied, as he should have, in French. There was frantic waving from the other side of the table. The president of P.E.I. whined that he couldn't understand why, since all of us could speak English, we didn't! Trudeau gripped the edge of the table, his knuckles turning white, and translated both the question and the answer into English. He then turned to me and said he now had a better understanding of what I had been trying to say. He and I have never been offside in our vision of this country; he taught me well. Though I have never considered anyone other than my husband John to be my hero, if I were asked which living Canadian public figure I hold in the highest respect, I would not hesitate to pronounce Pierre Elliott Trudeau as my choice.

Less than a year later John and I and the girls moved to Manitoba, and our political adventures in a new province began.

Tony's grandfather, Douglas Campbell (the former Premier of Manitoba) to this day -- at age 90+ -- holds Trudeau in absolute contempt. He said he'd to bring the Constitution home allowed this country to fall into financial ruin because of his inattention during this period.

seven

Manitoba Sets a
New Direction

We arrived in Winnipeg in July of 1977. John had been employed for about five years by Canadian Hydrocarbons, recently purchased by Winnipeg-based Inter City Gas, as corporate secretary and head of the legal department. In 1976 the company decided they wanted all senior officers to be located in Winnipeg, and John and I had a choice to make. Either he would return to his corporate law practice in Calgary, or we would move to Winnipeg. We both decided Manitoba was a good place to live.

A provincial election in Manitoba was called for October 11, 1977, and, because of our recent arrival, John and I were ineligible to vote. However, this didn't prevent us from becoming involved. Soon after we arrived I contacted Lloyd Axworthy, who was the Liberal MLA for Fort Rouge, our constituency. It was not the first time I had met Lloyd, although I suspect he forgets that we first met in our house in Calgary.

John and I had owned a spacious home in Calgary. Since there was never any money in the Alberta Liberal Party, when a political celebrity arrived in town we were often asked to host the reception. We absorbed the costs as our contribution to the party. My mother had ensured upon my marriage that I had all the things necessary to entertain in large numbers. I suspect she knew one of us would choose a career with a public profile. In any case, I can entertain fifty for dinner and one hundred for a reception with ease. At one such reception the visiting members attending a Western Liberal Policy Conference were the invited guests and Lloyd, recognized as an up-and-coming young western politician, was among them.

First impressions are important to me, perhaps too important since they can sometimes be false. In any case, I am afraid Lloyd scored a goose egg. I found him conceited and arrogant. Unfortunately, my initial impression has been reinforced over the years, and he was my nemesis throughout my leadership. Could we have worked together? I don't know. We didn't, and, unfortunately, that was not in the best interests of either one of us. Liberals throughout the province were aware of our conflicts and were often forced, they thought, to choose sides.

When Lloyd appeared at our Winnipeg home in the summer of 1977 I told him that I was in a difficult situation. Having just stepped down from the presidency in Alberta, I felt somewhat awkward to find myself starting at the bottom again, but I was also sensitive to the feelings of others and I did not want to step on toes. Lloyd asked if I would come to work for him as a volunteer and, after discussing our earlier work as pamphlet writers, asked if I would chair his publicity committee. It was the last time I heard from him during the campaign. When the election writ was issued we phoned to volunteer again and were told we could take a poll. We of course agreed because John and I have always believed that everyone in the campaign should do a poll, if only to get a sense of what the voters are saying at the door. But when I asked what else I could do I was told that was all. Although we shared the work, John was the poll captain of record since by this time I was mildly annoyed. My only overt act in this campaign was putting a sign on our lawn.

Wellington Crescent, where we lived, is a beautiful tree-lined street leading to Assiniboine Park. It is frequently described as a street of stately mansions. Our house was magnificent, and only in Winnipeg could such a home be purchased for so little. Built of brick and trimmed with tyndall stone (often called Manitoba Marble), it was filled with oak and mahogany panelling and the French doors were paned with bevelled glass. Our den, a wonderful 400-square-foot room finished in oak with leaded-glass doors on the bookshelves, made living in cold Manitoba winters quite bearable as we all snuggled up with books in front of the fireplace. In the debate about our possible move to Toronto in 1985 realtors decided that to find a similar home in Toronto we would have to look in Rosedale, and the company would be required to give us four-and-one-half times the value of our house in an interest-free loan in order for us to live in equivalent accommodations. This beautiful housing is one of the great secrets of Winnipeg that some of the younger generation are now beginning to discover.

There were few admitted Liberals living on this street. Shortly after the writ was issued, signs for the Progressive Conservatives went up on either side of us. Sidney and Senator Mira Spivak lived across the street, and since he was running for the PCs in a constituency that began with the next street to the west, they put up a large sign, too. John and I had thought we'd wait and see what use they made of signs in our new city before we made our move, but this was too much for me. I phoned Lloyd's headquarters and told them to bring the largest lawn sign they could find. The woman on the end of the phone said, "We don't get many requests for Wellington Crescent." I replied, "You do now!" Izzy Asper, president of the Global Television Network, former leader of the Liberal Party in Manitoba and also a resident on the Crescent, drove up several days later. He acknowledged that he was very curious about these new Liberals on the street since he had, until this time, considered himself to be an endangered species.

In 1980 the Liberals were in opposition in Ottawa, having been defeated in the 1979 election. Joe Clark and his government had a minority and, as with all minority governments, the threat of defeat hung over their heads at all times. Lloyd, who had moved to the federal scene in the 1979 campaign, asked John to lunch. He wanted John to become his constituency fund-raiser. John was reluctant. Despite all the fund-raising efforts John has made on behalf of the party, he hates the job and has to steel himself mentally to make the calls. He also felt he was too recently moved to the community, and although he had a relatively big job in Winnipeg terms, he wouldn't be able to call on old friendships and associations as a means of raising funds. But Lloyd was desperate, and John took on the job, raising more than enough money to fight and win the election in Winnipeg Fort Garry.

We tried for six months following the election to have Lloyd hold a cocktail party for the donors. Once again we were prepared to pay the cost. John knew that if Lloyd was to be successful in fund-raising in the future, donors would have to be encouraged to have contact with him. His staff finally found a date, because Lloyd was now a busy cabinet minister and didn't have time for unnecessary socializing! We tried the next year to hold a similar event but the minister couldn't fit it in!

Sometime in 1982 John received a phone call from Leo Cholakis telling him that he was now Lloyd's new fund-raiser, and John was to turn over the lists. We heard not a single word from Lloyd. This callous abuse of people was to become a recurring theme in our relationship.

I do not usually hold personal grudges against those who hurt me in politics, but no one is allowed to hurt one of mine! John was terribly hurt by Lloyd's actions, and while I have been able to explain away many other things that happened to me in our relationship over the years, this unnecessary hurt directed to John has always infuriated me. It could have been avoided so simply. A call to John, thanking him for his efforts and telling him that he had been able to find someone with more profile in the community would have done the trick.

A provincial election was called for November 1981. As with the 1973 and 1977 campaigns, the Liberals once again were unable to run a full slate of candidates. The campaign, under the new Liberal leader Doug Lauchlan, a former senior staff person and protégé of Lloyd's, was a disaster. I became the office manager for Beverly McCaffrey, who was running in the Tuxedo constituency. I recognized that the Liberal campaign in general was in very bad straits. There were neither campaign manuals nor policy manuals. Candidates like Beverly were left on their own to sink or swim. Like the rest of them, Bev sank! In addition, there was no money. It is not surprising that our popular vote was 6.68 percent. The only sitting Liberal member, June Westbury, who had replaced Lloyd in a by-election in Fort Rouge in 1979, wound up third in her constituency despite noble efforts during her two years in the House. After that election there was no Liberal member in the Manitoba Assembly. Lauchlan resigned shortly into the new year, and the Manitoba party was leaderless throughout most of 1982 and all of 1983.

In mid-December 1983, the executive of the Liberal Party in Manitoba decided to announce a leadership convention. The debt, which had been enormous after the 1981 campaign, was now down to manageable levels. They had recently begun to actually pay for the services of one of the "Gang of Eight," a group of eight women who ran the office on a rotating basis as volunteers for about eighteen months, and Doreen Froese became a full-time office manager. I had worked with her during my chair of the Fund-Raising Dinner in the fall of 1983 and I called her to ask if there were any potential names being dropped as leadership contenders.

She told me that, as far as she knew, the only one interested was Bill Ridgeway, a close friend of the president of the party, Diana Ryback. It became clear that the timing of the convention in March and the late call in December was designed to propel Bill into the leadership. I was dismayed. I didn't know Bill well but I honestly didn't think he had the ability to lead the party. For one thing, he was a farmer from rural Manitoba, and while this would not result in instant disqualification, it was clear that the Liberal base of support was in urban Winnipeg, and there would be little acceptance in the city of someone without urban roots. I had also worked with him in a limited way on the Fund-Raising Dinner and questioned whether he had the contacts to raise the money and the desire to do the hard slogging necessary to rebuild the party.

I did what so many women have done for generations. I went out in search of a male candidate. I made contact, or asked others to make contact, with men like John Shanski, Leo Cholakis and Ed Coutu. The latter two have been real enemies of mine in the party, the former has always been a supporter. None of them showed any interest. After diligently searching for several weeks to no avail I decided, at my husband's suggestion, to run for the job myself.

John and I sat down and made a list of my strengths and weaknesses. On the negative side was my lack of knowledge about Manitoba. I had lived in the province for only seven years and there were many parts of the province, such as the north, that I had never visited. My knowledge of agricultural and mining issues was very limited, and to a great degree these are the lifeblood of the province. I thought my profession was a weakness. Political leaders in the past had tended to be lawyers or so-called sophisticated business people. I was neither of those things. I also recognized that I had a weight problem and that television would not be kind to me. On the other hand, I understood organizational politics from the ground up, loved the Liberal Party and knew I could and would work very hard. And I was no pushover. In the back of my mind I was still willing to back out and support the perfect candidate, but I had the confidence I could do more for the party than Bill Ridgeway. The other two candidates that announced, Stephen Zaretski and Al Dejardin, were not really in the race. It would be a heavy load for a few months because I continued to teach school every morning and had no intention of giving that up just to campaign! But balancing competing pressures was something I was getting used to.

In January of 1984 I announced my candidacy. As Lloyd was the only sitting member, provincially or federally, I went to see him out of courtesy prior to my announcement. I saw no sign of interference on his part during the leadership campaign. My sense was that he preferred Bill, but it became very clear that the majority of the Liberals in Lloyd's constituency were supporting me and it was best for him not to become involved. Certainly when he phoned on the afternoon of March 4, shortly after I was declared the leader (a call necessitated by the fact that he had returned to Ottawa the night before and had not remained at the convention to cast his vote), he was obviously shocked at my victory, particularly as I had won it on the first ballot with 307 votes, compared to 238 for Bill.

I was never more proud to be a Liberal than during this leadership campaign. Manitobans had been deeply divided by the decision of the Howard Pawley NDP government to extend

French-language services. The Roger Bilodeau case was to soon go to the Supreme Court of Canada. He was appealing a parking ticket because the summons had been printed in English only. The government was fearful that the ruling would be similar to that of the Forest case in 1980, which implied that Manitoba statutes were invalid because Section 23 of the Manitoba Act of 1870 had stated that laws must be available in both English and French. The decision raised the serious issue that all statutes passed in the province of Manitoba since 1890 might be considered unconstitutional. All statutes would, in this case, require translation. Since many of the laws were obsolete and the costs of translating all of them extremely high, a decision was made by the NDP provincial government to compromise by offering an extension of French-language services.

The offer of an extension of new services acted like a lightning rod to all the bigots of the province. The Progressive Conservatives, under their new leader, Gary Filmon, knew no shame. Grant Russell, an active member of the Tory party, began a movement called Grassroots (at its worst fomenting bigotry, and responsible for much misinformation), which literally worked out of the PC caucus room, although the Filmon Tories denied any direct affiliation. The federal Tories, to their credit, dissociated themselves from the group. There were huge marches on the legislature. Frances Russell, a columnist for *The Winnipeg Free Press* who supported the government in her columns, was subjected to death threats. Eventually the government backed off and agreed to the translation of all statutes since 1890, even those no longer in effect, if necessary, and withdrew the idea of new services. The government sent a reference to the Supreme Court of Canada for further instructions as to what they must do. It was a backward step but one for which the government could not be faulted. They had tried their best.

In the midst of all of this our political leadership race was held. My campaign committee urged me to soft-pedal the issue but I could not. I had fought the battles for bilingualism in Alberta and had the flat nose—from doors slamming in my face—to prove it. These were legitimate constitutional rights and they could not be denied. It has always fascinated me that it has been anglo-phones, most of whom have been found in the Liberal Party, who have been the quickest to defend the minority rights of franco-phones outside the province of Quebec. Francophones inside Quebec have rarely come to the defence of those living elsewhere. As an example, one need only point to the position taken by the government of the province of Quebec in opposition to the extension of education rights for the francophone community of Saskatchewan. Quebec politicians were always fearful that if francophone rights were extended outside of Quebec, then ang-lophone rights would require respect and further protection within Quebec!

That is of course my position: that rights must be protected for people no matter where they live, despite the wishes of the major-ity or the so-called collectivity. My campaign committee pointed out the difficulties inherent in my position. However, I explained to them that I didn't want to be the leader of a political party unwilling to accept the notion that as others are granted rights out of respect for their individual needs, one's own rights, far from being denied, are enhanced. As I travelled throughout Manitoba only one Liberal raised any objections to my position, and that was Bob Lundale from Lundar. But he chose to run with me on a Liberal slate in the 1986 election. This was my party—idealistic, caring and prepared to stand up and be counted.

It is important, I think, to understand that Liberals on the Prairies are a very special group. It was always so much easier provincially to be NDP, PC or even Social Credit. If you joined a political party for some reward, then there was not much future for you in the Liberal Party. Those who remained dedicated to the party did so on principle and, in my opinion, worked harder than in any other place in Canada because there were so few of us. I often became angry in national strategy meetings when officials from Quebec and Ontario would tell us we just didn't campaign properly. Little did they know about the shortage of bodies, the antipathy to the federal leadership, the anti-bilingual, anti-metric and other negative feelings directed towards Liberals. And yet campaign after campaign these dedicated troops would pull themselves together and hit the streets on behalf of their Liberal candidates.

It was difficult enough in federal campaigns. Provincial campaigns were even more tough because the lawyers, engineers, architects and accountants whose only reason for being Liberals was the hope of a patronage reward saw no advantage to working provincially and chose to become active at that level in other parties. So it was these dedicated provincial Liberals who supported my message on the rights of francophones. Bill Ridgeway, who had taken a much softer position on the issue at the beginning of his campaign, was won over to my position by the delegates at the time of the convention.

I also learned a very important lesson in this campaign. Not only had I looked for a male candidate, but I had chosen a male chair to head my personal campaign for leadership. It was to be the last time. In my races for a seat in the Manitoba Legislature I always had a woman co-chair or, in the last two campaigns, chair the committee. Women have been the true heroines of my nine years of leadership. They gave me their devotion, loyalty and effort. It is because of them that I avoided becoming "one of the boys"! Why is it that women have been so reluctant to recognize the abilities of their own gender? For me, I think it was my lack of self-confidence expressing itself in the need to surround myself with people I perceived to have greater ability than me, while at the same time not having the confidence that one of those could be a woman. What foolishness. It is not that there aren't lots of capable men who can run campaigns. But more to the point, there are lots of fabulous women who also can do the job, and if we as women fail to make use of their talent, why should we expect others to do so? This lack of willingness on the part of women to recognize our own strengths and talents must be overcome. I tried as the years went on, but in the first few years I was as guilty as anyone in failing to recognize the talents of 52 percent of the Canadian adult population.

I was dismayed by the comments of Catherine Callbeck, the new premier of Prince Edward Island, to the media the day after her election as the Liberal leader of that province. She went to great lengths to dissociate herself from the women's liberation movement. Does she not realize that, were it not for the hard work of "libbers" who, through the years, have demanded that women be given equal opportunities, she might not have achieved such stature? However, the media plays a role in suppressing the wide-ranging knowledge and accomplishments of women as well. Since the media is, for the most part, still dominated by men, they are quick to stereotype. For example, I found they would quickly come to talk to me about children's issues, rapes or murders of women, but they were not so sure I was knowledgeable about the economy.

I travelled throughout the province during that campaign, much more than my principal opponent did. In the past, Liberal leadership races had often degenerated into a rural versus urban battlefront. In 1980, for example, Hugh Moran, a realtor from Portage la Prairie, received most of the rural votes but very few delegates from Winnipeg. Doug Lauchlan won that race on the strength of the delegates from Winnipeg, where 60 percent of Manitobans live and where approximately that percentage of delegates can be chosen. I knew that if the party was to be truly rebuilt my support should come from all over.

I went to The Pas and Thompson in search of northern delegates and received the majority of the delegate support from this area. I travelled to southern farm areas and, while I didn't get the majority of the delegates, I had the support of enough that the delegates were divided between Bill and me. By my campaign committee's estimate, seventy of the delegates were Young Liberals, and we always believed that sixty-nine of them supported me. The Young Liberals have always been among my most dedicated workers. My teaching experience and my love of young people was invaluable here. Jeff McLaren is the one Young Liberal we knew who supported Bill. Jeff came to work for the provincial Liberal caucus as an intern shortly after the 1988 campaign, and I kept him on as a researcher. It was only after he attained his goal of being accepted by the federal government as a foreign service officer that I told him I knew he had been the odd person out!

There was only one moment during this campaign when I lost my cool and gave notice that I was not going to be put upon. Susan Anderson, a fellow teacher, drove me to one of the delegate selection meetings in Winnipeg. Since we were late she dropped me at the front door and left to park the car. When she later walked into the room she was approached by Myroslaw Tracz, one of Bill Ridgeway's workers, who asked her who she was going to support. Susan decided to fish for a little information and said she was considering supporting Carstairs but had not yet made up her mind. He told her she really couldn't consider an aggressive, loud-mouthed bitch for the leadership. Susan, who is as proud to be a feminist as I am, replied that yes, she could.

I decided that there was only one way to approach this kind of smear campaign—deal with it directly. At the next meeting as I was giving my speech I said, "It has come to my attention that some of the opposition workers are saying that you shouldn't support an aggressive, loud-mouthed bitch. However, it seems to me that what this party needs is someone with some aggression to get this party moving again, and a loud mouth to be heard in the process." There was dead silence in the room, then loud applause. Those words were never used again. Myroslaw later apologized and told me he admired my style. We have worked closely together since that time.

The balloting at the convention was on Sunday morning. There were fewer than six hundred delegates but we had to wait and wait for the results. Because I had won on the first ballot, the co-chair of the convention, Tom Robson, deliberately held off announcing the results in order to build excitement! The tension became more and more unbearable. Rumours spread throughout the room. Some said there was a tie, others that there were too many spoiled ballots. Finally the results were announced. The tension was released and the room filled with excitement. The Young Liberals started chanting "Sharon! Sharon!" If the photos are to be believed, my whole family was ecstatic.

There were not many rifts following my election. More money was raised on my behalf than was spent (as I have been able to do in every campaign I ran) and I offered the remainder to Bill's campaign chair, Keith Ryan, in order to pay off his debt. The offer was refused; I suspect they thought I was lording it over them. In reality, I considered it Liberal money to be used for Liberals, and Bill was certainly one of those. Instead, we put the balance into an account known as "the Leader's Fund." This fund, which provided my travel expenses, was secured for the next four years at the bank by a $10,000 Canada Savings Bond of my own.

Of all the photos taken by the media during that convention weekend the one I treasure the most is a picture of John on a very high ladder hanging a "Carstairs Ready to Go the Distance" sign. I treasure it because I alone know how terrified John is of heights, and it was one more example of the love that has enwrapped me for twenty-seven years. It also reminds me of his organizational skills. When he realized how high the ceiling was in the room, he rented every single high ladder in the city, paying in advance, even though most were not only not used but were not even picked up. He cornered the market! Our campaign was the only one with signs at the top of the room.

Victory had been achieved. Now the work began in earnest.

Immediately following the announcement of my victory I was swarmed by the media. For the first time, stories about my voice were written. When John and I had made an inventory of my strengths and weaknesses neither of us had thought to list my voice. No one had ever commented about it before. I had done some script-writing and presentations for Calgary and Region Education Television in the 1960s and no one had critiqued my voice then. Now it seemed to be the whole focus of attention. That, and my red suit. Of the four outfits I wore that weekend only one was red, but I was immediately dubbed "the Lady in Red." Even the day I retired comments were made about the red jacket I wore. Of course they failed to mention that my skirt and blouse were black! My voice also came in for its share of comments after my resignation. *The Ottawa Sun* said I had "a machine gun delivery that raised [my] voice to a Minnie Mouse pitch," and *The Edmonton Journal* said, "She sounds like she has been inhaling helium."

Were the comments on my voice and the colour of my clothes sexist? Certainly there were comments about the plaid jackets of Frank Miller of Ontario and John Turner's errs, but they have never been quite so persistent. It was all so irrelevant, and it had a way of belittling and trivializing whatever I had to say. One such story, which appeared in *The Winnipeg Free Press*, written by Fred Cleverley (whose columns were usually an apology for the federal and provincial Conservatives), refers to "the Lady in Red" who, on the particular day about which he was writing, was wearing a navy-blue silk skirt, yellow jacket and white blouse!

The comments on my voice, however, led to several positive things. In the 1984 by-election in Fort Garry I used it as my slogan —"A Voice With A Difference." When Paul Walsh, the co-chair of my River Heights campaign of 1986, made the comment at a roast shortly afterwards that Sharon Carstairs was living proof that Donald and Daisy had offspring, I adopted the line. By making fun of myself and my voice the voters could empathize, and the sniping eventually lessened. I suppose I could have stopped wearing red, but I like it!

During one of the interviews at the convention, Linden Soles, the television news anchor for CKND, one of Izzy Asper's Global stations and the only one giving live coverage throughout the convention, asked what I would do if the provincial party was not in agreement with ideas of the federal party, which was the government of the day. I replied we would have to agree to disagree. The provincial party, I went on to say, would be required, on occasion, to take positions different from the federal party since our areas of responsibility would be different, and so be it. The day after my leadership win I received a phone call from John Conlin, head of Lloyd Axworthy's ministerial office in Winnipeg, who told me that such a statement was unacceptable. Such reprimands to my "errant behaviour" were to become commonplace. It was not an auspicious beginning to my newly formalized relationship with the federal minister!

On Monday morning, having asked for the day off from my part-time teaching job, I arrived at Campbell House, the party offices (named for the last Liberal premier of Manitoba, now a member of the Reform Party, Douglas L. Campbell). I was told that the party president had moved out of her office on the second floor for me, and I was escorted in. My first impression was not positive. I could not imagine giving media interviews there; it was truly shabby. When I went to straighten a poster of Pierre Trudeau on the wall I discovered it was hung on an angle to cover a hole! I called John, always my first line of attack, and explained the situation. He told me to have it painted at his expense. John and I had been supporting the Liberal Party for so many years out of our own pockets, we could do it one more time. The painters arrived within a day or so. That weekend we went out and purchased a series of prints by a local Manitoba artist, A. Paquette, and the office began to look professional. Meanwhile, I was divesting myself of a teaching position.

At the time I was teaching junior high at St. Norbert Collegiate. St. Norbert is a community in Winnipeg, but the school was located in a rural division. Also teaching at the school was Brian Dixon, the chair of the largest school division in the province, Winnipeg School Division Number 1. The principal, Ed Laboissiere, despite being a Liberal, couldn't imagine having two active politicians on staff, so he made my resignation easy. Within the week a replacement had been found. The students gave me a farewell party, and it was hard to say goodbye because I always became very attached to my students. But I hoped that by acting as their advocate for a more effective education system I could continue to serve them. One week after the convention I was ready to be a full-time leader in a freshened-up office.

The following week we held an executive meeting. It was clear that many of the executive, including the president, had not supported my leadership bid. It was also clear that recognizing the authority of the leader was not instinctual for these people. When the party had announced the convention the previous December they had also announced that the financial picture was brighter, and that the position would pay $36,000 a year, since it was clear the leader would not be in the legislature and drawing a salary as an MLA, at least not for some time. At this first executive meeting the treasurer, Jim Smith, who was also

Lloyd's official agent, announced that he wasn't sure if they could afford to pay me, and that the newspaper story had misrepresented the facts. The decision to pay me was deferred until the next meeting. When I went home that night, John, always unflappable, announced he had never expected me to be paid, so not to worry.

I have never known what prompted the statement from Jim Smith. I have believed it was a first attempt to control me with money as they had the previous leader, Doug Lauchlan, and I suspect that when the ploy failed—I never asked a single question about the money—they decided it wouldn't work. Meanwhile, they were going to look very foolish to the membership.

At the following executive meeting a salary of $35,000 was announced. At my request this was to be reduced to $15,000 when I was elected to the Legislature, that being the amount paid to the leader of a third party in the House, but for which I was ineligible because we did not have the four seats requisite for party status. This was eliminated, again at my request, when I was elected leader of the opposition in 1988. At the same time I was told there was no money for staff, and the party secretary was not to be used by or for me unless she had extra time. Doug Lauchlan had had a staff of four but I was to make do with none! Fortunately, Doreen Froese made a joke of it. She would come into my office at noon and again at four-thirty to announce that she was "off" and what could she do for me? Without her support my leadership would have been in tatters before it even began.

Three days prior to the opening of the provincial leadership convention, Pierre Trudeau resigned. Manitoba Liberals were too busy in the initial days with our own leadership convention to be overly concerned, but the talk soon turned to choosing the next federal leader. It appeared that John Turner would be the first choice of the majority of Liberals throughout the land. He had not been in the public limelight for some years and absence made the heart grow fonder. It was his to lose, and he nearly did!

eight

The Federal Liberals Choose a New Leader

I knew John Turner was the one candidate I would not support. My father had the terrible habit of one-lining people and, unfortunately, those one-liners tended to stick. His line on John Turner was that he had once danced with Princess Margaret and never got over it.

John Turner had left the cabinet in 1975 abruptly and, to some degree, rudely, because his opportunity to become leader in the short term had disappeared. However, to my mind his far greater sin was to write negatively about the government after he left. Loyalty to the party has always been high in my books, and he committed a cardinal sin. To top it off, he had insulted my husband. I remember during the 1968 leadership convention that John Turner, when at a meeting in Calgary, had leapt over a table on his way to greet John, recalling their days at Ashbury Collegiate. When we met him once in Winnipeg, after he had left politics, he didn't have the time of day for John. I admit I'm a bit of a mother hen about my family. Either you respect them or you do not; using them for your own purposes and then ignoring them is not the way to influence me!

Jean Chrétien called me within days of my selection as leader. I told him that if Jim Coutts was going to run he had my support and I explained why. Jean told me that he thought that even if Jim ran the final ballot would be between himself and John Turner, and asked me what I would do then. I had known Jean since the late 1960s when I was asked to take him to events in Calgary as part of the 1968 election campaign, and I liked and admired him. I told him there was some value in the alternation policy that had been used in the Liberal Party for some years, as we moved back and forth from a French-Canadian leader to an English-Canadian leader. He chided me about this. I responded finally that if it was between John and Jean, then Jean would have my vote. In the early days he was the only one to call. John Turner never did contact me, under the belief, I assume, that Lloyd was taking care of me.

That night when John came home I was in the kitchen making an inordinate amount of noise. When I am upset I tend to bang pots and pans while cooking, and Jean's challenge of my acceptance of alternation was preying on my mind. John asked what I was angry about. I told him of my conversation with Chrétien. It was John who reminded me about my father's experience, and it was he that first put the idea in my head that perhaps it was time for the Liberal Party to remove this anachronism from its history. It weighed more and more on my mind as the leadership race continued and the whisper campaign began to do its work, spreading the word that Liberals could not vote for Jean Chrétien because he was a French Canadian and it was an anglophone's turn.

Ten days after my election I was asked by John Conlin to meet with the minister, Lloyd Axworthy. I suggested Campbell House, but I was told the minister's time was limited and I would be required to attend at his ministerial office in Osborne Village, just a block away from Campbell House.

I arrived early, as I always do, at about 11:20 a.m. for an 11:30 meeting. (Another one of my legacies from the nuns and from my father is the penchant to always be early. Dad had me ready to go up the aisle at my wedding fifteen minutes before the scheduled time!) By noon the meeting had not yet started, and at 12:15 p.m. I was very annoyed, making up my mind to leave if it didn't begin soon. Lloyd is as habitually late as I am early. Finally I was ushered in, with no apologies. To me it was clear that I was being put in my place; however, when I later learned everyone was treated this way I tried to take it less personally. I try my best to keep no one waiting, and if I do I try to make amends.

Lloyd told me that he was considering running for the leadership. I told him of my commitment to Jim Coutts, which he appeared to understand.

I don't think Lloyd perceived Jim to be a real threat. I explained to him that if Jim did not run and he did, he would have my support as a favourite son from Manitoba. He then said that if he did not run he would support John Turner, for whom he had worked during the 1968 leadership and whom he had served as an executive assistant in his younger days. I told him that under no circumstances would I support John Turner, and why. However, I also told him that if neither he nor Jim ran I would probably remain out of the fray.

Circumstances were to change my stance, and he seemed to feel I had betrayed him because I did get very involved for Jean Chrétien. However, as events unfolded I considered the betrayal to be all on his side.

My support for Jim Coutts goes back a long way. He has been a very strong supporter of mine throughout my career, raising money for me in Toronto and actually working on polls in my constituency in each campaign. John and I wanted to show our friendship when the subject of Jim's running for the national leadership was raised. There is no question that I would have supported him over any other candidate. But it was not to be.

A meeting to discuss Jim's candidacy took place in Toronto shortly after my meeting with Lloyd. Senator Keith Davey, Marty Goldfarb, Dan Casey, Tom Axworthy and others, all Trudeau loyalists, were present. It remains for John one of the saddest days in politics. The group not only told Jim not to run, but they also, to our shock, said that they were prepared to desert him if he chose, despite their good advice, to do so. Friendships in politics are only as solid as your ability to win. There is more than a little irony in the fact that most supported Turner only to desert him over his constitutional position because it was the antithesis of the Trudeau position, a problem they would not have encountered in supporting Jim.

The process of my alienation from the Manitoba federal Liberals began in earnest on March 19, 1984. I was at a meeting of farmers in MacGregor when a call was put through to me from *The Winnipeg Free Press*. Turner had announced his decision to run for the leadership and he was immediately asked about his stance on the French-language crisis in Manitoba. His response was that the problem must be settled in Manitoba. By this time, the Manitoba government had referred the matter to the Supreme Court because it was tearing Manitobans apart. What did I think, the reporter wanted to know. I told him that it was naive on Turner's part to think it could be settled in Manitoba and it had gone to the Supreme Court out of necessity. John Turner had been out of the public arena for some time, so it was understandable that his knowledge of some issues would not be up to snuff. This turned out to be the case throughout the campaign, and it almost cost him the leadership. I suppose I should have used a softer tone, knowing as I did that he would probably be the leader and I would have to work with him. However, I was outspoken throughout my career, so I have no regrets about saying what I did.

The next day the headline in the *Free Press* read "Turner Naive on Language Issue." That afternoon, John Conlin called to demand I hold a press conference and retract my statement. I refused. He then informed me that I was no friend of Lloyd's. When I pointed out that the comment had nothing to do with Lloyd and, indeed, Lloyd had not yet declared in favour of Turner, I was told that he soon would and I was now considered offside with the minister. (Lloyd's own bid wasn't very serious; he knew there was no support-base for his candidacy.) With that the conversation was terminated. The relationship deteriorated rapidly. I was cut off from the ministerial office and rumours floated that I would quickly be replaced as leader, as soon as the federal leadership race was over. As usual, the bullying didn't have any impact on me, other than causing me to dig my heels in.

Meanwhile, my friends Richard and Hillaine Kroft had phoned to tell me they were heading the Chrétien campaign in Manitoba and were delighted to know that I would support him over John

Turner. I told them, as I had told Lloyd, that I would probably not get involved. However, as the antagonisms grew I became more defiant. Finally, in order to clear the air, I invited Richard Good, the federal affairs chair, for a drink at our home. I had known Richard for a number of years and liked and trusted him. He had not played a role in my own leadership race because of his position, but I felt he had been supportive; certainly his former wife, Andrea, had been. I explained to him all that had transpired over the previous few weeks and proceeded to make a threat of my own: essentially, if relations did not improve within the week I would openly support Jean Chrétien. He looked at me with complete astonishment and said, "You wouldn't dare." I said, "Just watch me." I assume he told the powers that be in Lloyd's office, and perhaps Lloyd himself. Nothing changed, and on April 11, 1984, before a crowd of nine hundred enthusiastic supporters at the Westin Hotel in downtown Winnipeg, I announced my support for Jean Chrétien by saying he was "everything good and noble about the Liberal Party." I believe that as much today as I believed it then.

The Turner committee was out for my head. Throughout the campaign stories circulated about how they planned to do me in once the leadership race was over in June. Izzy Asper, the chair of the Turner campaign, did his best to keep the lid on things. For example, he phoned to apologize when I was physically barred from attending a Turner lunch on April 26, 1984. That day two leadership candidates were in Winnipeg. I told the Turner campaign that I would come to the reception prior to the lunch but that I could not stay to lunch since I felt I had to drop in at the lunch for Donald Johnston. When I arrived the workers at the desk demanded a luncheon ticket. When I explained I was not staying for the lunch they refused to let me in the room. Izzy told me that feelings were running high, but that he personally would try to keep them from going overboard. Izzy, as a former Manitoba leader, knew the problems I was facing and has always given me his support both personally and financially. I think he also had a grudging admiration for me playing David and taking on Turner's Goliath. He, too, broke with Turner on the Constitution and worked with me on both my Meech Lake and Referendum campaigns.

That summer I hired Sean Saraq as my executive assistant. The money came from a combination of funds I had personally raised and a STEP (Student Temporary Employment Program) grant from the provincial government. Sean, along with Prabet Jha, now a physician, a Ph.D. in epidemiology and a Rhodes Scholar, had actually been hired earlier in the year to work as researchers for Lloyd Axworthy during that summer. In reality they were set to work on the Turner campaign and, therefore, were dismissed when they decided they would support Chrétien over Turner. They were fired before the work began, but they were determined to stand on principle. I was sorry for both of them. I can be as hard-nosed a politician as most, but my one exception is young people. I try to encourage their idealism as much as possible. Prab was able to find a job in a lab and I hired Sean on minimum wage.

One of our more amusing experiences that summer was running out of gas on a stretch of Highway 1 just outside of MacGregor on our way back to Winnipeg. It was pouring rain. Sean was driving the car and so I didn't think to look at the gas gauge. Sean is a brilliant young man, but he does not focus well on practical, everyday living skills. The car stopped dead. Sean valiantly tried to wave down a passing car or truck, but they all swished past leaving Sean soaking wet. He finally climbed back into the car, announcing that, if this was an indication of the votes we were to get in the next election, our campaign was not going well! Finally an RCMP officer arrived. Sean explained the situation. The officer couldn't believe there was a Liberal leader in our car. "What leader?" he asked, looking straight at me. It was decided Sean would go to get gas with the officer and I would remain in the car and listen to music. I was tired, having just given a speech in Brandon. I locked the doors and was quite happy to remain where I was.

But the officer had second thoughts and decided it was not wise to leave "what's her name in the car by herself." Sean came back to tell me the Mountie insisted I go with them. I got out of the car and, of course, locked the door. Sean, looking at me in abject horror, rain pouring down, wailed that the keys were in the ignition because I had wanted to listen to the music. There we were standing in the pouring rain getting drenched. The car not only didn't have any gas, it was locked. I thought it was funny but Sean was not amused. The RCMP officer was convinced this crazy woman was hopeless, and I am sure he determined on the spot never to vote Liberal. We arrived at the gas station and picked up gas. The young officer drove us back to the car and, with the help of a coat hanger, unlocked the door. Sean and I continued on our way.

This episode led to another Christmas present from Al Munroe, who soon became my organizer. This time it was a red plastic container for gas.

I finally got mine back with Al at the Brandon Winter Fair in 1989—sort of. Lois Fjeldsted, an active Liberal in Brandon and a provincial candidate in 1988, and Sandi McNabb, a farmer and someone I hope will become a Liberal candidate federally or provincially when her children are a little older, were at the fair with Al and me. After I had completed the usual tour, including a visit to the animals (which I'm totally allergic to), we went back to the car to discover the engine running and the doors locked. Lois, who knew how much teasing I had taken about the gas incident, started to laugh, and so did I. Through our gales we explained to Sandi that maybe Al was not quite perfect after all. As it turned out he almost was. He nonchalantly opened his wallet and extracted an extra key and unlocked the doors. That is why he has been my organizer throughout my career. He has been prepared for all emergencies and I have had absolute confidence I would never be let down.

They say that timing is everything in politics. Following John Turner's election as leader, he decided to call a federal election almost immediately. If he had waited and built an image of his own perhaps the results would have been different. I remain convinced we still would have lost, Canadians being tired of Liberal administration, but perhaps we would not have lost so many seats. On the other hand the timing was perfect for me.

The Liberals who had determined they were going to get rid of me were now too busy running the federal election. I, on the other hand, took advantage of the campaign to travel the province. As the polls kept getting worse and worse for the Liberals across the country, many senior cabinet ministers, who could usually be counted on to travel to other constituencies to give them a boost, remained at home trying to eke out the last remaining votes they could.

Richard Good had announced, early in the campaign, that Adrian Lang Macdonald would be the co-chair of the federal campaign. Adrian and I were friends then, and as the years have passed we have become closer still. We did not meet until we were adults and both active in politics, she as the wife of Otto Lang, senior federal cabinet minister, and I as the president of the Liberal Party in Alberta. In a quintessential Canadian way we learned through chatting that we were born in the same hospital in Halifax, four days apart, and had been delivered by the same doctor. Our husbands always wondered how the hospital survived, convinced that the two of us were probably already trying to organize the world our way!

Richard and Adrian were desperate to get people into constituencies to give upbeat speeches. Since there were no federal troops ready to do battle they turned to me. This gave me the opportunity—at federal campaign expense—to meet Liberals throughout the province and to win their support. I visited thirteen of the fourteen federal ridings. Only the candidate from Churchill, Jack Kennedy, said he didn't want me because he didn't think I was well enough known and I had not supported Turner.

As with all elections there are stories to be told. My visit to the nomination meeting in Portage-Interlake where we nominated a farmer, Abe Suderman, led to a showdown with the federal campaign chairs. The meeting was to be held in Minnedosa, about two and a half hours by car west of Winnipeg. The Liberals in Portage la Prairie decided to rent a bus and drive the one and a half hours from that community. The campaign committee asked me to drive to Portage and take the bus from there, and do the reverse on the return to jolly up the troops. I agreed. I was later to

learn that Lloyd was to be flown to the meeting by private plane—
a trip of about thirty-five minutes. To add insult to injury, he
didn't acknowledge my presence on the platform. I told Richard
and Adrian that if it happened again I was out and they could do
their own cheerleading. I was at least acknowledged, if not gra-
ciously, from there on in.

Al Munroe, who at this point was working for federal affairs,
became my partner in travel. Together he and I sold a party
membership to Peter Rampton in his cow barn in Dauphin,
Manitoba, competing with about five hundred flies. If only Liberals had wanted to be as close to the leader! Peter ran and lost the
federal nomination but was to go on to run, unfortunately unsuccessfully, as the provincial Liberal candidate in 1986, 1988 and
1990, and to serve as president of the party from 1989 to 1991. It
was at the federal nomination meeting in Dauphin-Swan River
that I first met Jean LaPierre, who eventually left the party over
Jean Chrétien's election as leader of the Liberal Party of Canada
and his position on the Meech Lake Accord. LaPierre was convinced of a Liberal victory, he said, but to be safe he was hurrying
home to his Quebec constituency! He and I were to cross paths
again, unhappily, at John Turner's leadership review in 1986.

I was the guest speaker at many of the nomination meetings,
but it is safe to say I was not the main attraction. Those in
attendance were only interested in listening to me until such time
as something better came along such as the results of the balloting. Al and I developed hand signals. I would speak while the
ballots were being counted and for as long as the count took.
When I saw Al waving his hands at the back of the room it was
time for me to wind down my speech and for the results to be
announced. We worked well as a team.

No one in the Brandon-Souris campaign will forget the Turtle
Derby in Boissevain. Politicians are asked to do many things;
racing turtles is perhaps among the more novel. The Turtle Derby
is this community's summer fair. David Campbell, the Liberal
candidate, was using the opportunity to do some campaigning. I
was sent down to campaign with him. When I arrived, David had
apparently decided that, because it was Sunday, he really didn't

want to do the rounds and shake hands. He also didn't want to race turtles. We spent the day jollying up David, finally getting him to do some mainstreeting. His rueful comment on the turtle races, which we lost (True Grit, our turtle, never even came across the starting line), was that our only mistake was not to name the turtle after Bryce Mackasey, since he would be sure to run straight for the money! This was the headline in *The Brandon Sun* the following day. Bryce Mackasey had been a cabinet minister in the Trudeau government and had a penchant for getting into difficulties. He had just been appointed ambassador to Portugal in one of a raft of patronage appointments for which Turner would give the infamous explanation, in the leaders' debate, that he had had no choice.

In the dying days of the federal campaign everyone was getting depressed. It looked as though we would be lucky to hold on to the incumbent seats of Fort Garry and St. Boniface. Workers were pulled from campaigns and sent to work in Fort Garry, Axworthy's riding. St. Boniface was believed to be more secure, and besides, Axworthy, as a cabinet minister, was more important. In the opinion of many, Bob Bockstael, the member of Parliament for St. Boniface, should also have been in the cabinet. Many in St. Boniface thought, however, that Axworthy had prevented it. Certainly Bob had not made a secret of his support for Chrétien, so if the campaign committee was trying to impress the new federal leader, Turner, then the support had to be given to Axworthy.

On federal election night, September 4, 1984, the results showed a victory for Lloyd Axworthy but a defeat for Bob Bockstael in St. Boniface. The Liberals had won only forty seats across the country. The party had been devastated, and everyone was exhausted.

nine

A Provincial Liberal Party Is Rebuilt

Bud Sherman, the PC candidate in the federal constituency of Fort Garry, had resigned his seat in the provincial House, as required by law, in order to run against Lloyd in the federal election of 1984. Premier Howard Pawley used the dying days of the federal campaign to announce a by-election in the provincial constituency of Fort Garry. He knew the NDP would probably lose, as it was a PC seat provincially, but hoped there would be little attention paid because of the excitement of the federal campaign. I had worked flat out during the federal campaign and, like everyone else, was tired. However, I knew it was not fair to ask anyone else to be the Liberal candidate and decided to run myself.

I called a press conference to announce that I would be running. And then I did the unthinkable. I announced that we would come second. It was a gamble, but an important one. The provincial Liberal Party had only 9 percent of the popular vote in the 1981 election in this constituency. Although the provincial constituency of Fort Garry was about one-fourth the size of the federal constituency of the same name, it was not one of the areas in which Axworthy had strong voter support. The chances of us winning were probably nil. It was also clear that the federal Tories were going to win nationally, although probably not this constituency, and this would have a spill-over effect on the provincial scene.

The party "bigwigs" in the party were flabbergasted by my statement. The media were intrigued. Never before in their experience had a candidate announced that he or she would run second. When I did I established two things. One, that I was an interesting politician; and two, that when the time came for me to tell them I would win (which I did two years later) perhaps they should sit up and take notice.

The campaign was one that once again depended primarily on John and me. John took his holidays and he and I knocked on every door in the riding—one poll in the morning, another in the afternoon and a third in the evening. Sundays we rested! Lloyd and his supporters were conspicuously absent from the campaign. Adrian co-chaired the campaign along with Sheldon Fulton, and she finally became angry enough with Axworthy's passivity to demand that, for her sake and the efforts she had put into the federal campaign, Lloyd should hit the streets. He did, for one afternoon. He arrived, perhaps deliberately, after John and I had left the campaign headquarters and chose a poll other than the one we were in. I was not to be easily forgiven for my work for Chrétien.

Hillaine Kroft looked after the finances, and many of the Chrétien supporters throughout the province came to my aid, as did many of the Donald Johnston supporters (Adrian had chaired the Johnston campaign in Manitoba). Our popular vote in this campaign increased from 9 percent to 27 percent and we indeed ran a strong second. Because of the announcement I had made at the start of the campaign, our workers were jubilant. I announced that night that in my next campaign we would win.

It was during the by-election campaign that Pope John Paul II arrived in Winnipeg as part of his cross-country tour. I received an invitation from the St. Boniface Hospital Research Foundation to attend their award presentation at St. Mary's Cathedral. The Pope was to receive the Foundation's Humanitarian Award. Adrian, my campaign manager, insisted not only that I go to the presentation but that I wear a hat! I would probably have gone to the ceremony in any case, but I was not pleased about the hat. To me hats were something wives wore, not politicians! Finally, and only for Adrian because she was working so hard on the campaign, I went off to Maria's Hat Shoppe, *the* place to buy hats in Winnipeg, and bought a black-and-white model which I still have, after wearing it that one and only time. It rests on one of the shelves in my closet that only someone six-foot-six could reach. John affectionately calls it my "Popey hat."

Several weeks before his arrival in Canada, the Pope had made statements to the effect that he preferred nuns to wear their habits and, in particular, their veils or other head coverings. I arrived at the Cathedral, complete with hat, and observed that all the women there were decked out in similar finery. All, that is, except the nuns! As I looked up to the altar there were members of the Grey Nuns, the administrators of the St. Boniface Hospital, and not a single one of them had a veil or hat on her head! I was delighted with their statement and wanted to join them. More independent action like this on the part of nuns, and also priests, could reform the Catholic Church and bring it into the twentieth century, and once again make me feel a part of a Church that will always remain a part of my being.

Lloyd Axworthy was deeply depressed, as were most of his colleagues, following the federal campaign. As someone who has only been an opposition politician I can only imagine what it must be like to go from government to opposition. My observation at both the provincial and federal level is that most cannot cope. They have had enormous power as cabinet ministers, and to lose that overnight requires an incredible adjustment. Lloyd dealt with his unhappiness by remaining out of Manitoba for large stretches of time. He had recently remarried, in the midst of the campaign, and his wife worked in Ottawa. Lloyd gave up his apartment in Winnipeg, and when he returned on constituency business he stayed with family. There was even public speculation that he would resign and return to academic life. However, after a two-year funk he decided to remain in politics.

I used his absence from the province and the disillusionment that surrounded many of his supporters, who were no longer the beneficiaries of his very generous patronage reward system, to continue to rebuild the party from a provincial base. I knew there would be a provincial election in two years or less, and I wanted the Liberal Party to make a strong showing.

Richard Good stepped down as federal affairs chair to be replaced by David Unruh, who had neither Richard's expertise nor penchant for hard work but did have a deep and abiding dislike of me. Little work was done federally by the Manitoba Liberals over the next two years. Al Munroe was let go by federal affairs and arrived in my office saying, "Have car will travel." I told him I had no money to pay him. He replied that as long as I could pick up his car expenses we would be a team and he would take me anywhere in the province I wanted to go. He explained later that having travelled with me throughout the election he knew I was prepared to rebuild the party from the grass roots, and he wanted to help.

Over the next eight and a half years Al and I put 750,000 kilometres on four cars. Sometimes he would travel alone but most often we would be together. There are few small towns in Manitoba that we have not visited, most we have visited four or five times.

There are some who have wondered about our relationship. Al Munroe was sixty-seven in April of 1993. He has white hair, as does my husband, and he has been so often seen with me that many Manitobans think he *is* my husband. Our relationship is filled with the many kindnesses he has shown to my children and to John. He was always paid inadequately, for a long time not at all, never took a holiday and worked eighteen-hour days. He is devoted to me and the Liberal Party. Yet we are not always philosophically in tune. He is far tougher than I, and many in the party are afraid of him. I suppose I could have softened his image, but he and I both knew that it was to my advantage that he play the tough guy and I be the softer one.

I believed it essential that if the next general election in Manitoba was to show an increase in popular support for the Liberal Party we had to run a full slate of candidates. To do this we had to reorganize all of the constituencies, but particularly those in rural Manitoba. There are really two campaigns fought in Manitoba. The city of Winnipeg in those days had twenty-nine constituencies. There were twenty-eight spread throughout the rest of Manitoba. In 1990 the numbers were thirty-one and twenty-six. While it is possible to run candidates in the city in all ridings, whether or not they live there, that is not possible in the rural ridings. We felt confident we could find twenty-nine Winnipeggers to fill the urban seats, so we began our rebuilding of the party in rural Manitoba. It was bleak terrain.

My favourite constituency quickly became Turtle Mountain, in the southwestern corner of Manitoba. Our first meeting there was held in the back of Al's car. We had agreed to meet Liberals in Killarney but the only ones to show were Helen and Gerald Rigby. The coffee shop where we planned to meet was closed, and it was pouring rain. Helen and Gerald climbed into the back of Al's car and he began his pitch about how important they were. After an hour Helen and Gerald had agreed to help reorganize the riding and to chair a meeting to be held within the month. Our next visit brought out eight people. Ross MacMillan was the last person to arrive and, as a result, was made the president and future candidate (he ran in 1986 and again in 1988). The following meeting saw twenty-five show, and our popular vote in the riding soared to 17.4 percent in 1986.

No one would run for us in 1981, but in 1988 the Liberal vote in Turtle Mountain climbed to 33.8 percent and to 35.8 percent in Manitoba. All because of efforts like these.

We had no money. It was a perennial problem. Al and I used to tell people we couldn't stay overnight in their communities because I couldn't sleep in strange beds. In fact we didn't have the money to stay overnight and would often drive back to Winnipeg, arriving at three or four o'clock in the morning, to save the expense. In those days if I did stay over it was usually in the home of a Liberal. In Brandon it was at the Fjeldsted home, which we jokingly called a hotel, until my violent allergy to cats drove me to Margaret Workman's place. In Thompson I would stay at the Murchie "hotel." Alex Murchie, an engineer with Inco, and Grace, in the early days a city councillor, were active Liberals, originally from Ontario. They put me up on numerous occasions, because even if I could find the money for the flight to Thompson

I could not manage the hotel accommodations. Constituency by constituency we rebuilt the party.

All too often in the past those who ran for the party were not only defeated but also lost financially since the party was unable to adequately fund the campaigns. I decided we had to come up with a strategy that would have Liberals give of their time to be candidates, but would not have them also sacrifice their own money.

Enter Ernie Gilroy. Ernie had been born and raised a Liberal in Portage la Prairie, where his parents still live. He owned a small insurance business in Winnipeg and loved politics. I asked Ernie to chair the provincial campaign expected in 1985 or 1986. Once again I was accused of bucking the system. He and his wife lived moderately and he was certainly not an establishment Liberal. He was also not part of the Axworthy organization (and that, for me, was part of the attraction). He had supported John Turner, but I didn't hold that against him! I knew he would work hard and he would be completely loyal. He, too, was part of a very special group that made my leadership completely worthwhile.

We agreed we had to provide each candidate with a free package of materials. The package was to include a two-colour pamphlet for each household, fifty large signs and one hundred lawn signs. The pamphlet was designed so that the inside was identical for everyone. Only the front and back changed, but they, too, had a standard format. The pitch to the potential candidate was that they were not to go into debt. Their only obligation was to deliver the pamphlets door to door using local Liberals and friends, and to put up the signs as voters requested, or on public property if possible. If they raised more money they could spend it as they liked. If not, they were to consider their obligation complete. We spoke about the candidates as a family. This was to be their gift to the party. Throughout 1985 we nominated candidates.

The first to declare himself was Dr. Laurie Evans, a plant scientist at the University of Manitoba, who indicated he would run in the rural constituency of Springfield where he lived. His nomination was greeted with great enthusiasm. Here was a candidate who was bright, well educated and highly presentable. He, like all the other candidates, knew his principal function was to make the campaign viable and, with luck, to elect the Liberal leader to the legislature. Laurie was eventually elected in the Fort Garry constituency in 1988. His loss in the 1990 campaign was one of the more difficult ones for me to understand because he had been such a fine MLA. He remains an active Liberal and was the chair of the Avis Gray campaign when she won the Crescentwood by-election in 1992.

The work at times seemed never-ending. A provincial by-election was called in 1985 in the riding of Kildonan. Mary Beth Dolin, a popular NDP cabinet minister, had died of breast cancer, and her husband Marty ran on the platform that he wanted to finish her term. We knew he would be unbeatable; it was another hopeless cause. I decided not to run, since I had already established my credibility in the by-election in Fort Garry in 1984. We nominated a young Liberal, Chris Guly, to run against Dolin, spending a minimal amount of money. John and I campaigned with Chris each day in the riding, and the end result was that we increased our popular vote in Kildonan. But no wonder I was tired, after nine years and seven election campaigns!

I had to choose my own constituency. I lived in River Heights, which had never elected a Liberal in its history. However, I was just outside the boundary of Fort Rouge, and my house had been in the Fort Rouge constituency during the 1977 election, only to be drawn out in the boundary changes prior to the 1986 campaign. Fort Rouge had been a Liberal riding for some years and, although we lost it in 1981, it had, by Manitoba Liberal standards, a relatively high percentage of popular vote at 24 percent. In the by-election of 1979 and the general election of 1977 the Liberal portion of the popular vote had been even higher at 39 percent. In River Heights in 1981 it was 23.4 percent.

However, Fort Rouge had been Lloyd Axworthy's provincial constituency, and I had a fear that, were I to win, the victory would not be considered mine. There would be those in the party who would say I only won on Lloyd's reputation. It was important, I believed, for me to put my own stamp on a constituency. The demographics of River Heights, on the other hand, were interesting. It had the highest percentage of professional women of any constituency in the province. I believed they would be predisposed to vote for a woman if she was the best-qualified candidate in the riding. The PC incumbent, Warren Steen, had a poor reputation both in and out of the House. However, the NDP, who had run second in the riding in 1981, were running Murray Smith, former president of the Manitoba Teacher's Society and husband of Muriel Smith, a cabinet minister in the Pawley government. I believed he would be a tough opponent, as the NDP had received 30 percent of the vote in 1981. However, if I could keep the Liberal vote and persuade the PCs to vote for me, I could win. I chose to run in River Heights.

Ernie Gilroy went off to Ontario to visit the provincial Liberal Party, which gave us invaluable advice. They shared their campaign strategy with us and helped us put together a professional look. We knew that we had to impress the media with a well-run, competent campaign if we were to be taken seriously. This meant a fully developed policy, regular press conferences carefully staged, a leader's tour and television and radio ads. The budget was carefully prepared and monitored daily; it was never exceeded. Indeed, by coincidence, Ernie had arranged a meeting with the bankers with respect to extending a line of credit on the very day the election writ was issued. As I was holding the opening press conference on the second floor of Campbell House on that day somebody passed a note to me. It read curtly, "We have the money—Ernie."

One of the inexpensive gimmicks that we produced in advance for the press and gave out on writ day was a set of notebooks with a history of each constituency, including voting patterns. We knew they were successful because they kept showing up on newsroom desks and in reporters' briefcases. They were bright red and easily identifiable.

When the writ was dropped in early February 1986 with the election called for March 18, 1986, we were as ready as we were ever going to be. Not all of the candidates had been nominated, but they were falling into place. Ernie was ensuring the urban candidates and Al was bringing in the rural ones. I was in Brandon at the nomination of the two candidates there, Kerry Auriat and Eileen McFadden, when Al phoned to tell me that Brian King had agreed to be the candidate in Flin Flon. I knew that he was our fifty-fourth candidate and I teased Al that he was now finished. "No," he said in a tone suggesting that he thought I had lost my wits, "I have three more to go." I told him, laughing, that they could be easily found; after all, there was my husband John, my executive assistant Bob Hanks and Al himself. He told me he'd find the other three! Some of them were very close calls. In The Pas they still did not have a candidate at 7:00 p.m., with the nomination scheduled for 7:30. Al was having dinner with Scott Gray and Lore Mirewaldt, law and marriage partners. Al said he would have to go in and inform the media that the meeting was being delayed because "the candidate" was unavailable that night. Scott said, "It's okay Al, you have a candidate," and half an hour later Scott accepted the nomination, with Lore agreeing to be his campaign manager.

In the Churchill constituency the story was even more absurd. Mildred Wilkie, editor of *The Northern Breeze* in Lynn Lake, called campaign headquarters to ask who the candidate was in Churchill. Al answered that we didn't have one, but by the end of the conversation he had talked Mildred into running, with the caveat that she would give her final agreement at eight o'clock the following morning. Al placed the call at eight with some trepidation. Mildred picked up the phone after the first ring, saying, "You sweet-talking bastard." Mildred became the duly nominated candidate for Churchill after Al wired the bus fare money for her to travel to Leaf Rapids to register with the returning officer. We had our gang of fifty-seven!

McLaren Advertising in Toronto, as a result of their work on the Ontario Liberal campaign, offered to give us some help on our advertising strategy. As it turned out, our advertising was limited by our financial constraints and they were responsible for all of it. The campaign had to be debt-free. This was Ernie's and my undebatable goal.

For many years the favourite media remark about the Manitoba Liberal Party was that all of the members could be squeezed into a phone booth. We decided to play on this and bring some humour to the campaign. The public loved the ad that showed me coming out of a phone booth in front of the legislature saying, "They used to say you could fit all of the Liberals into a phone booth. Not any more!" This and two other ads were taped one Sunday in the first few weeks of the campaign. The night before, Paul Walsh, the co-chair of the River Heights campaign, had arrived at my home to tell me that the reason the constituency campaign was not going as well as they had hoped was because I didn't have any friends. Paul has never been known for his tact. What he was trying to say was that, because I had no real roots in Winnipeg, I couldn't call on the childhood, high school or college friends who are so often a significant part of the campaign. He left me extremely upset. This, coupled with the fact that no scripts for the ads had arrived that evening as scheduled, meant that I spent a sleepless night. When the production team arrived the following morning, expecting to find me well rested with the scripts memorized, they had a bit of a shock. But although it took us twelve hours, the commercials were different and fun and caught viewers' attention.

Meanwhile, my River Heights campaign required constant attention. I asked Lynne Axworthy, an educator and ex-wife of Lloyd, to chair the campaign along with Paul Walsh, the president of the River Heights constituency and a local lawyer. (It became clear eventually to everyone in the campaign that the work was being done by Lynne, and Paul, like so many men in politics, was claiming the glory. In future campaigns Lynne was completely in charge.) My schedule was set in such a way that I spent hours, on at least five days a week, in River Heights. It was essential that I take my message to the voters in my riding first and foremost.

It was a bitterly cold election campaign. Because I was concerned with image I didn't wear slacks. I wore long skirts over two sets of long underwear, work socks in my boots, a hat and a scarf to protect my face. I am a mild asthmatic, and if my mouth wasn't covered I had trouble breathing. I had an additional problem with my glasses. Knocking on doors was a hoot. As the door would open a gush of hot air would escape, my glasses would immediately fog up and I'd have to take them off. This meant that, other than a vague impression of the person at the door, I saw very little of them. For the most part I could distinguish the men from the women, but not always. I would blindly give my pitch and move on to the next house. John was always across the street doing the same thing and having some of the same problems since he, too, wears glasses.

One day we decided to do a "burmashave"—this is a political technique used to attract people going to and from work (the origin of the term is the Burmashave roadside billboards of the 40s and 50s). Politicians and their supporters stand on a corner waving to voters as they go by. On this particular occasion it was −40 degrees with a wind-chill factor of 2200, which means that exposed skin would freeze in less than one minute. We took the burmashave a step further; when the cars were stopped at a light I would run from car to car knocking on the drivers' windows and handing them pamphlets. One driver said if I was this crazy to win I had his vote! Needless to say it got us pictures all over the media, which was the point of the exercise.

Senator Gildas Molgat, himself a former leader of the Liberal Party in Manitoba who, along with his wife Allison, has been among my strongest supporters, arranged for a number of federal MPs to come out to campaign. They were primarily Chrétien supporters, and it was their way of saying thank you to me for having backed him in the leadership race. They included David Dingwall from Nova Scotia, Charles Caccia and Sergio Marchi from Ontario and David Berger from Quebec.

We decided to hold a press conference in Campbell House and then send them out to a variety of constituencies. Since they were all colleagues of Lloyd Axworthy's, and because we wanted the media to have the impression of harmony in the party, we asked Lloyd to chair the press conference. It was hard for all those assembled to believe, but Lloyd chaired the conference, introduced the MPs and told the media that they were now going to hit the streets—all without once making reference to me, the leader! The media fortunately thought it was merely an oversight. The MPs were so shocked that as I was heading out the door with Dingwall he said, "Does he always treat you like a piece of shit?" Needless to say, I replied in the affirmative.

Fortunately I had other, more friendly allies in high places. Jean Chrétien had been asked to help me during the campaign and agreed to come to Winnipeg. Early one morning about two weeks into the campaign he called me to say he was going to resign from the House of Commons and his only concern was how it might affect me. I told him that he should do what he thought was best for him. He explained that he was in an intolerable situation. If he gave a speech and it received national publicity, he was accused of trying to upstage the national leader, John Turner. On the other hand, if he didn't accept speaking engagements, he was accused of being disloyal.

That night John and I returned to our home in time to watch the coverage of Jean's resignation on "The National." During his interview he said he had one task left, and that was to go to Winnipeg to campaign for Sharon Carstairs, a great woman. Is it any wonder I remain loyal to him and hold him in such high regard? To receive national coverage in a provincial campaign is almost impossible, especially if you are a third party with no seats. But Jean is a political animal and knew exactly what he was doing. He honoured his promise to come, flying in from Florida for a weekend of activity.

Jean was enormously popular with Manitobans, and justifiably so. By the time of the federal leadership convention in 1984 he had become the people's, if not the delegates', favourite. Iona Campagnola summed it up well at the conclusion of that convention when she said Jean had won the hearts of the Canadian people. I doubt John Turner was impressed with that remark, having just won the leadership, but she was right. John and I will never forget leaving the Ottawa Civic Centre feeling terribly down after the results were announced and hailing a cab. When we climbed in the driver was in tears. He noticed our convention regalia and, through his tears, said, "How could you have done such a thing?" We pointed to our Chrétien buttons and said, "*We* didn't," and we all cried together.

Jean was an instant hit in the campaign, and the media covered us from the moment of his arrival until he left. We met him at the airport on Friday night. Saturday was spent mainstreeting all over the city, resulting in a picture in *The Globe and Mail* of Jean in a beauty salon pretending to cut someone's hair. I was also in the picture since he wouldn't let me leave his side. His job was to promote me, and that is exactly what he did.

We planned a rally in my constituency for Saturday night. It was then that I learned of Jean's penchant for detail. He wanted to know everything about the arrangements. He was particularly concerned that the room not be too large. We explained that it was divided into sections and as the crowd got larger—if indeed it did—we could make the room larger, always keeping it small enough to look jammed. We had dropped the riding with invitations and had asked all the other Winnipeg candidates to bring their supporters. Seven hundred people showed up for a fun, noisy evening, and the next day as John and I went door to door, we saw signs in windows and on lawns taken from the rally. They were easy to recognize because we hadn't wanted to waste the signs printed for the campaign at the rally, and had instead used my leftover signs from the 1984 leadership campaign! It was Jean, combined with the leaders' debate, that put me over the top in River Heights.

There were two principal objectives to the 1986 campaign. The first and most important was to elect the Liberal leader to the Legislature for the first time since 1973. The second, and inextricably linked, was for me to appear on the televised debate. The debate was to be held on Saturday, March 8, and it was scheduled to feature only Howard Pawley, the premier, and Gary Filmon, the leader of the opposition. CKY, the Winnipeg affiliate of CTV, was making the arrangements since it would be in their studio, the largest in the city. We argued that since we were running candidates in all fifty-seven constituencies we could not be denied participation. With some reluctance it was granted.

David Bowman, a Winnipeg lawyer, negotiated the terms and the draws in the debate, as he was to do so superbly for all three of my provincial campaigns. Luck was with me, and I won all the important draws—I opened and I closed the debate. On the Saturday morning, as we were getting ready with last-minute instructions and strategy, Moishe Kaufman, the policy chair of the provincial campaign, said he was convinced that at some time during the debate Filmon and Pawley would do what they did so often in the legislature. They would start to scream and shout at one another and point their fingers. I was appalled and said I couldn't believe they would be so foolish since it made for such poor television. However, the consensus of the meeting was with Moishe. We decided on a strategy to deal with this situation if it should arise—and incredibly, it did!

The debate was like having *déjà vu*. About halfway through Pawley and Filmon began to yell and scream and point at one another. I interjected and said, "Gentlemen, gentlemen." Then I went on to say to the audience that this was exactly why they needed me in the legislature—to referee! As I walked from the studio I was mobbed by the media, all of whom wanted to know what it felt like to win the debate. In my own mind I wasn't sure I had, but the media certainly gave it that spin.

On Sunday afternoon, when we were again knocking on doors, it was clear that the public, even though most of them hadn't seen the debate, were convinced I had won. The CBC had conducted a River Heights poll the week before showing the PCs with 33 percent, the NDP with 32 percent and the Liberals with 31 percent. Election night results showed an entirely different picture. I had received 45 percent of the popular vote, with the PCs trailing at 30.5 percent and the NDP dropping to 24.5 percent. The province-wide popular vote for the Liberal Party had climbed from 6.68 percent in 1981 to 13.88 percent in 1986. We were on the move.

I have always loved cartoons, and the 1986 campaign produced, to my mind, some of the best. My all-time favourite is one of me sitting in a tree as the Cheshire cat from *Alice in Wonderland*. The caption reads, "Nervous, boys?" The second of that campaign to tickle my fancy was one depicting all three leaders; the two men are finger-pointing and saying "My bus is bigger than your bus" while I say "Tsk, tsk gentlemen!" For me they summed up the campaign.

Vestiges of the federal wing's disapproval of my leadership remained during that campaign. John Turner had come into the province for the annual general meeting of the Liberal Party in Manitoba and had campaigned with me. A poll released the night of his dinner actually showed the Manitoba Liberal Party lower than it had been in 1981, and there was some gloating from those Liberals opposed to my leadership. Some of the Manitoba federal people had even begun grooming the next leader, since it was clear to them that I was not going to win my seat and the popular vote would decline.

They persuaded Jim Carr to run in the constituency of Tuxedo. Jim was a well-known Liberal with deep roots in the party. He had been an assistant to Jim Richardson, a Trudeau cabinet minister, was a close friend of and worker for Lloyd Axworthy and had been appointed by Lloyd to the board of the CBC. He was a journalist, and I was deeply appreciative of his philosophical base as well as his public-speaking ability.

I had wanted Jim to run in Fort Rouge in 1986, but his argument against this was that he was a friend of Roland Penner, the sitting NDP member and attorney general of the province. This didn't prevent him, however, from running against Penner in 1988. Clearly he balked because he didn't think he could beat Penner but might be expected to since it was Axworthy's old provincial riding. It was obvious that he couldn't beat Gary Filmon in Tuxedo, always a Tory stronghold, but no one would really expect him to win this constituency. However, if he improved our vote and raised his political profile by running against the leader of the Conservative Party, then his stock would increase for the next leadership race.

He did improve our vote from 12 percent to 33 percent. Unfortunately for his federal friends, I won in River Heights, and that put an end, at least for the time being, to his leadership plans.

ten

Life as the Only Liberal in the House

I was now the MLA for River Heights as well as the leader of the Liberal Party in Manitoba. Indeed, I was the only Liberal leader with a seat in western Canada! For over a decade legislatures in western Canada had been sitting without Liberal participation. The last Liberal leader to hold a seat in Manitoba had been Izzy Asper in 1973.

Howard Pawley and the NDP had been re-elected, although their majority was small. They held only thirty seats. The Tories, under the leadership of Gary Filmon, had twenty-six. I held the remaining seat.

It was a time for celebration, but I did not have much time to bask. It didn't take me long to learn how much pettiness is part and parcel of our political system. Shortly after I was elected, I was told that my office would be Room 167 in the Manitoba legislature, but it would be a while before I could move in. That was because Sterling Lyon, the former Progressive Conservative premier, who had resigned the leadership of his party in December 1983, still occupied the office. He simply wouldn't get on with moving out, and it was only after several weeks had passed that Government Services finally packed his belongings and made room for me.

When I arrived in the office, I found there was only one phone. Since I was now accepting only $15,000 from the party instead of $35,000, I wanted to use some of the extra money to hire a secretary. The only money I was to receive from the legislature in addition to my salary, was $3,500 per year to run my office and that would not buy an assistant. As I was a lone member, there were to be no funds for caucus or research. In any case, I asked Government Services for another phone for my forthcoming secretary. You would have thought I had asked for the moon! I had to write a letter to the Legislative Assembly Management Committee (LAMC) requesting the additional phone line. I was told by the clerk of the House that they would meet within the next six weeks and, although I could ask to appear before them, I could not remain for their deliberations. I quickly learned that this group had enormous power since they established the budgets for all MLAs. I told the clerk that the party was prepared to pay for the additional line, so I was not asking for an expenditure. I was again informed that the decision could only be made by the LAMC. Six weeks later my second phone was installed, and the LAMC magnanimously agreed the costs would be paid by the legislature!

I hired Marguerite Martin, a fluently bilingual secretary who had earlier worked for Bob Bockstael, for the magnificent sum of $12,000 per year, paid for by the party. In theory she was supposed to work short hours, but she always arrived at about 7:30 in the morning, worked through lunch and well into the afternoon. She is another of that wonderful group of women who have been so loyal and supportive. She alone has known of many of the hurts and disappointments I have felt. She was always there to support me but not, I might add, to forgive those who trespassed against me. She had her list, and those individuals often had a hard time getting past this five-foot tall, ninety-five-pound dynamo.

Premier Pawley called the House back into session on May 8, 1986. It is hard to express the awe I felt on that very first day. The Legislative Assembly of Manitoba is one of the finest buildings of its kind in Canada. David Peterson once remarked that my office as leader of the opposition was far grander than his as premier, and indeed it was. Built in 1916 of Manitoba tyndall stone, it has marble floors and high cathedral ceilings. The chamber itself has a domed ceiling and walls with mosaics depicting events in ancient history. I still feel that sense of awe every day I walk into the building.

By tradition, on the opening day of a new legislature, a Speaker, appointed by the government of the day, is led to the chair. Howard Pawley announced that his choice for Speaker would be Myrna Phillips, only the second woman in Manitoba to hold this office. Myrna was an extremely partisan NDP member and was held in low regard by the Tories. Gary Filmon, contrary to all tradition, refused to second her nomination, so Howard Pawley phoned and asked me to do it. I was happily incredulous. There I was, opening day, my first time in the legislature, escorting the Speaker to her chair. Not only had Filmon lost the election, he seemed bound and determined that I would get a disproportionate amount of positive publicity.

My role in her nomination led Myrna to recognize me every day in Question Period, which resulted in my getting media coverage pretty frequently. I used Question Period to great advantage, furthering my reputation for being different. Instead of always attacking government policy (although I certainly could on occasion), I tried to focus on why and how a program or initiative could be better. Since I wasn't in the official opposition, the onus wasn't on me to counter policy initiatives. The public viewed me as a politician different from the mainstream and respected me for it.

Several incidents in that session truly reflected how very mean-spirited politics could be. Jim Walding of the NDP had been the Speaker during the previous legislature, 1981 to 1986. Foolishly he challenged the premier to make him a cabinet minister this time round, or, failing that, to return him to the Speaker's chair. No premier takes kindly to being told who to appoint, and Howard Pawley was no exception. He refused to give Walding a cabinet post. Walding had angered the NDP in the previous legislature because as Speaker he had refused, during the French-language debate, to call for the vote as long as the Progressive Conservatives were not in the House. The bells had rung for days. He became a chastised backbencher during my first session. He was, to all intents and purposes, a loose cannon and dangerous for the NDP, who had only a three-seat majority—really two, with the Speaker in the chair.

I realized that Jim had acted unwisely in demanding a cabinet post, but I felt some sympathy for him. He had helped me learn the ropes, which very few others had done. In August I had an opportunity to help him in return. I was invited to attend the Canadian Parliamentary Conference. Traditionally Manitoba sent five representatives from its legislature, three government and two opposition, but because of their slim majority, and knowing someday they may want a favour from me, NDP House Leader Jay Cowan offered me the fifth spot. I turned the offer down because if I was not in the House then the Liberal Party was not in the House, and I could not take a chance of losing publicity. Instead I spoke with Jim Walding about "pairing," a procedure whereby a government member and an opposition member both refrain from voting if either one of them is not in the House, thereby not changing the overall numbers distribution in the legislature. I told him I would not pair with anyone else, but he could go to Cowan with a signed pair for himself from me. I thought that by making it possible for Jim to attend the Parliamentary Conference it might help him get over his sense of rejection. Unfortunately Cowan refused.

The NDP continued over the next two years to treat Jim Walding with disdain even though he was one of their members. No one, therefore, should have been surprised when Walding rejected the NDP in 1988 and brought down the government by voting against their budget.

Another incident occurred the day after the session opened. Gerry Mercier, the PC House Leader, came to my office to tell me that the following Monday would be "Opposition Leader's Day." By custom, he told me, we would forgo Question Period and adjourn following Gary Filmon's speech. Out of courtesy, he asked me if I would be prepared to follow custom. I agreed I would, but although I am polite, I am not stupid! I immediately went to the Legislative Library and checked *Hansard* for the normal activity on the Monday following the opening day of a session. I learned there was no such thing as "Opposition Leader's Day." Mercier was simply trying to get publicity for his leader at my expense. I went back to him and said I would abide by my word, but I would never agree to anything again before I had checked it out. Howard Pawley even called me to tell me I had been taken in, and while he said I should have exercised my rights in Question Period, he was amused that I had actually researched the issue. I cannot abide liars. My children always knew that telling the truth was always far easier than being caught in a lie. The infraction was easy to forgive, the lie wasn't! I never trusted Gerry Mercier as long as we sat in the House and was not unhappy when John Angus, the Liberal candidate in St. Norbert, defeated Mercier in the 1988 provincial election.

Casting my vote as the lone Liberal wasn't always easy. Our rules now allow for the bells to ring for a maximum of one hour. However, at any time during that hour the whips can indicate that all their members have arrived, or at least all the members they expect, and the bells will be stopped. At this point the doors are locked and no additional members can enter. Since the Liberals had only one seat, there was no whip. Twice I went briefly to my office at the beginning of the bells only to have them stop before I could get back. Both times I lost my opportunity to vote. My only choice was to remain in the House until the vote was taken. Finally, Abe Kovnats, the PC member for Niakwa, a former referee for the CFL and an obvious believer in fair play, took pity on me. He told me that he would phone my office before he entered the House when a vote was called and wouldn't go in until I arrived. I didn't take advantage of his offer very often, but it was handy when nature called. I was sorry we defeated him in 1988, not because I wasn't delighted with the win, but because of his kindness to me.

At some point during this session the government agreed to pick up Marguerite's salary—but not without a struggle. I was asked one day during the session to go to a meeting with House leaders Jay Cowan and Gerry Mercier. They had decided between them to increase the staff in both the NDP and PC caucus rooms and wanted to introduce a change to the LAMC Act that would make this possible. Again by tradition, they wanted to do it with unanimous consent, meaning that the change would go through with little or no debate. At this point I began to wonder if they treated me the way they did because they thought I was stupid, naive or just because I was a woman! I told them I would not give consent. They seemed genuinely shocked. I stated as clearly as I could that they seemed bound and determined to be generous to themselves, but I couldn't see anything in the package to benefit me or the Liberal Party. After mutterings about all of them having to do their work properly and the importance of the people being represented, they asked what I wanted. I asked for Marguerite's salary and got it. But it was written into the act that staff monies could only be received by a leader, not by an Independent MLA. Obviously Jay Cowan was not going to make this an option available to Jim Walding!

It was also during this session that I had an extremely strange lunch with John Turner. He was in Winnipeg in July 1986, securing support for his leadership review vote that fall, and he asked me to have lunch with him. I had not made up my mind how I was going to vote at this point, although I was disturbed about the position he had taken a month earlier during an interview for *Le Devoir* in which he proposed a constitutional package recognizing "the distinctive character of Quebec." To me this smacked of the *Deux Nations* theory of Robert Stanfield and was contrary to the Trudeau vision of Canada to which I subscribed.

We had lunch at Dubrovnik's, at that time the best restaurant in Winnipeg. After chewing the usual political fat, John, a Catholic, asked me why I was no longer a practising Catholic. I was surprised at the question since I wasn't sure how he would even know such a thing, but I tried to explain to him that I had left the Church primarily because of its attitudes towards women. I told him that since I had daughters I was not prepared to have them raised in a Church that treated women as inferior human beings. Since my husband is an agnostic, I knew any religious instruction my children received would come from me and, while I had them baptized in the Church in case they felt they needed the documentation at some time in their lives, that was as far as I was prepared to go. He then proceeded to tell me that I was making a serious mistake. I should go back to Halifax, get in touch with my roots, go into retreat and reunite with the Church! I couldn't believe my ears. This was supposed to be a conversation between two leaders—neither one of whom liked the other very much—and I was being subjected to a Father Confessor lecture!

When I got back to the legislature that afternoon, I tried to analyze just what had happened. As so often in my political career the question I asked was, would this conversation have taken place if I had been a man? I think I know the answer. Perhaps John Turner proselytizes with everyone, but I somehow doubt it.

The last memorable episode of the session, and one that left me dumbstruck, was the closing night. We had spent the afternoon and evening debating and passing the last of the bills. As the hours passed midnight and moved gradually towards the morning I noticed MLAs stockpiling crumpled-up balls of paper. After Royal Assent had finally been granted the bills, a free-for-all broke out. The MLAs started pitching paper across the floor at one another. Apparently in earlier years they had also thrown books, but that had been banned after a reporter was hit near her eye while seated in the press gallery! I watched dumbfounded and, slowly shaking my head, I left the chamber. Such activity was banned from the Liberal caucus, and it has pretty well died out.

Another habit that truly appalled me was pre-session drinking. I suppose I should now admit—if you haven't already guessed—that I am a fuddy-duddy. In those days the legislature met three evenings a week. It was not unusual for the members to be well into their cups during these sessions. I decided that there would be no liquor in my office or in the caucus room, should I ever have one. If the majority of the public only knew that bills are frequently passed in the wee hours of the morning, not having been read by the majority, some of whom are too drunk to read them at that stage even if they wanted to, we would all be thrown out of office. These are the stories that are not told by the media. I think they should be. Just this year two of the pages went public, saying that there was Jack Daniels in the cup of one of the MLAs while in the House. They nearly lost their positions for their courage in telling it like it is.

At the end of the legislative session John Harvard, now the Liberal member of Parliament for Winnipeg St. James but then a hard-nosed reporter for the local CBC, did a feature interview on my performance. Using the Leo Durocher "nice guys finish last" scenario, he built a case for my not being tough enough for this business. I was hurt because I was trying so hard to live up to the standard for an MLA set by my father. I think what Harvard missed, and what I forgot myself, was that my popularity was derived from my being different. The public was looking then, and even more so now, for the non-politician politician. If politicians are not prepared to change to meet new expectations, then our whole parliamentary system is in peril.

During the time between the closing of the 1986 session and the 1987 session, Al and I travelled the province. Yet again, according to my diary, we were in Ste. Rose, Winkler, Teulon, Gimli, Neepawa, Minnedosa, Selkirk, Deloraine, Flin Flon, Thompson, Dauphin, The Pas, Treherne, Brandon and Hartney. In addition there were trips to Saskatoon, Toronto and Ottawa, all on behalf of the Manitoba Liberal Party. But it was the Canadian Liberal Party that was holding our attention at the time. Things were heating up for John Turner.

In The Pas on November 19, 1986, I received a phone call from Jim Coutts. He was disturbed, he told me, by a resolution being proposed on behalf of John Turner at the policy conference scheduled for November 27–30. The purpose of the national convention in Ottawa was, ostensibly, policy formulation. But the media and most of the delegates were focused on the leadership review vote scheduled for Saturday. I was not convinced that Turner was the best leader for the party, even though following his election as leader I had worked for him in the 1984 federal election and had been supportive since then. Our lunch the previous July had turned me off him permanently, and this policy initiative just added fuel to my ire.

Turner was proposing that the Liberal Party recognize Quebec "as a distinct society." As I've said, this went against my vision of Canada—not to mention the vision held by other Liberals, such as Marc LaLonde and Senator Keith Davey. Jim wanted to talk to me about an article written by George Radwanski which *The Toronto Star* was prepared to print the following week. It was a consideration of the meaning of "distinct society," among other things. George, a biographer of Trudeau, was unable to put his name to the article because he was working for the Ontario Peterson government writing their white paper on education. Jim wanted me to put my name on the article. I asked him to fax it to me and, after I made some minor edits, it was printed in *The Toronto Star* on Wednesday, November 26, the day before the convention was opened. It was later distributed to all delegates at the convention.

This was really the beginning of the Meech Lake debate, although we didn't know it then. The article outlined what were to be my major concerns throughout the Meech Lake and Referendum debates. It discussed the true meaning of the distinct society clause, which was apparently intended to give additional, special powers to Quebec. Why else, I asked, would it be there? In addition, it spoke of the need to keep Canada from becoming two solitudes. It is only in helping all Canadians to feel truly at home in this country that we will be able to keep them united, the article said.

At the convention I voted against the distinct society resolution and got involved in a debate with Lloyd Axworthy on the floor of the convention hall. Needless to say I lost the debate, the resolution passed, and so did the vote on Turner's leadership. But the die was cast for my position on the Meech Lake Accord. Although Manitoba Liberals supported Axworthy in this round, they were to reject his position unanimously at the Manitoba convention held in March of 1988 during the provincial election, when all delegates voted in favour of a resolution rejecting the Meech Lake Accord.

This was a most uncomfortable convention for me, and not only because of the Turner resolution. I knew that Young Liberal support was being bought and paid for by the Turner camp. Most Young Liberals had their airfare paid and were given spending money. In return they were to support Turner and work the convention. Gwen Charles, who had run provincially for me in 1986, wanted her son to attend, but he didn't know how he wanted to vote on the leadership question. He was told he could have his way paid by the Turner organization for "doing the right thing" (which was, of course, supporting Turner). I offered to help send him with no strings attached. He accepted my financial help and to this day I don't know how he voted. The Turner approach was another example of the abuse of youth which I find so offensive but which the party has created by giving almost 33 percent of the delegated spots to people aged fourteen to twenty-five. It is a youth-craze movement that has caused us nothing but problems. Far too many of these young people are easily manipulated by the money and the smell of power. It is a dreadful way to introduce them to our democratic practices.

As I walked around the convention I wore no buttons declaring myself for or against the vote on Turner's leadership. I was repeatedly swarmed by throngs of youths who would drape me with Turner scarves, which I promptly removed. Even though I had Al and John on either side of me they would chant and crowd around. Members of my own delegation also tried to put pressure on me, even though I had made it perfectly clear that I would vote as I believed was in the best interests of the party, and they could do likewise.

Some Manitoba Liberals feared that because I had supported Jean Chrétien in 1984 I would vote for review. In fact, I did vote for review, but I did not disclose that choice to the media. Invariably the conversation about how I would vote would turn to the topic of my own leadership review, which was expected in six months' time. The implication was that if I did not support Mr. Turner then they would not support me.

The circumstances were somewhat different though. Mr. Turner had led the government to defeat in 1984, a defeat that should have been more clearly laid at the feet of the government of Pierre Trudeau, of which Mr. Turner had not been a member since the mid-1970s. On the other hand, I had been elected in March of 1986, the first Manitoba Liberal leader since 1973 to be elected to a seat in the Manitoba legislature. However, the threat from these Manitoba Liberals was palpable. If I did not vote for Turner, they would not vote for me when the time came.

The Manitoba party had rented a hospitality suite for the convention and I was asked, as the leader, to open it on the first day at four o'clock. But when I arrived at the appointed hour I walked right into a pro-Turner meeting. It was a set up to suggest that I was supporting Turner, even though I had refrained from publicly announcing my intentions. I was livid and stormed out, informing them that it was an affront to all those Manitoba delegates who had made the choice to vote "No," and since their donations were also paying for the suite they had no right to hold partisan meetings there. Ernie Gilroy, the provincial campaign chair, and Karin Kuhl, the wife of the Liberal president, came back to my room to try to calm me down. However, I remained angry with the executive and refused to visit the suite for the duration of the meeting.

To me these kinds of threats and intimidation tactics are the classic techniques used by the child-abuser. I have spent a lifetime rejecting these initiatives, and I was simply not going to accept behaviour of this kind from anyone in my party. They could have my hard work and loyalty but they could not control my mind or my actions.

I rode up a crowded elevator one morning of the convention with Quebec MP Jean LaPierre, who told all on board who would listen that I was a bigot. I was furious. I told him it wasn't the people of Quebec who defended the rights of francophones outside of Quebec, it was people like me. After the votes on Saturday, both on the leadership question, which Turner won with a resounding 73 percent, and on the distinct society vote, which he also won, John, Al and I went to dinner in the dining room of the Westin Hotel. LaPierre came up to me as we were going in and said all was fair in love and politics. I turned away but he insisted on following me to my table. I continued to ignore him and eventually the head waiter came to the rescue and physically removed him!

On our return to Manitoba, Al and I continued to crisscross the province, and once again the trip revived my faith in the political process. It became clear that more and more people knew who I was. The response from women was particularly heartening. They seemed to like having a woman politician to look up to, and, as a result, in Manitoba a significantly higher percentage of women vote Liberal than men.

The 1987 session was a particularly significant one for me. The provincial government of the day introduced a human rights amendment, and Meech Lake became a buzzword in Canadian politics.

We were called back into session on March 26, 1987. The government announced in its Speech from the Throne that it would be introducing an amendment to the Manitoba Human Rights Act that would prohibit discrimination on the basis of sexual orientation. As I was leaving the chamber the day the bill was introduced, I heard Gary Filmon announce to the media that he would be voting against the bill, as it was a moral issue. When they asked me I said I would be voting for the bill, because it was a human issue. It was one of my proudest moments as a Liberal because throughout the debate I heard from only one Liberal who challenged the way in which I intended to cast my vote. This was my party, and once again it would stand tall for the protection of individual freedoms.

However, the ensuing debate was a low point for me in terms of any kind of respect I had for members of the Tory party. I couldn't believe the venom that spewed from their mouths. Denis Rocan, who would become the Speaker in 1988, announced that if his son came home wearing an earring (an obvious sign to Denis that he was a homosexual), he would cut off his ear. All I could think of during this speech was that my daughter Cathi's boyfriend wore two earrings and he was not a homosexual. And why did this member feel he had the right to gay-bash, even if the victim was his own son! Gerry Mercier, later appointed by Mulroney to the bench as a family court judge, got into the act by suggesting that all of us who supported the bill were immoral. Don Orchard read nauseating materials in the House, including sections from a book declaring that homosexuals had unprotected sex in order to deliberately spread the AIDS virus. He asked us all if we wanted Winnipeg to become the AIDS capital of Canada. Gary Filmon, while announcing that the Tories had a free vote, allowed such intimidation to go on in his own caucus that even though two of them wanted to vote in favour of the bill they didn't dare break ranks. Gilles Roch, then a PC member but later a Liberal, once told me that the pink postcards we all received from the gay and lesbian communities in favour of the bill were all placed, with lots of snide comments and laughter, in the mail boxes of those who indicated they wanted to support the legislation.

There wasn't complete harmony in the NDP caucus either. Don Scott, Harry Harapiak and Larry Desjardins all had problems with the bill. Harry Harapiak, a devout member of the Ukrainian Orthodox Church, had problems on religious grounds but apparently spoke to no one in the chamber about it and quietly voted for the legislation. Larry Desjardins was quite amusing. On the evenings when the legislature sat, after the media had left, Larry would come and sit beside me on the opposition side. He would always make jokes about his really still being a Liberal at heart and he would ask me again and again why he should support this bill. Larry was never a socialist, and he was a good Catholic. Certainly the Church had entered the debate in the beginning, raising concerns as to whether Catholic schools would be forced to hire homosexual teachers. Religious schools were excluded from the bill, and once the Roman Catholic Arch-bishop, Adam Exner, understood this, he kept quiet. But he had made presentations to both Larry and me, and probably to oth-ers. Larry knew I was not a practising Catholic, but he and I shared similar views. The arguments I made in support of the bill were always the same, and he would always get up to return to his seat saying, "That's right. It is a human issue." Don Scott simply didn't understand the issue. He seemed more comfortable voting for the bill when I convinced him that homosexual acts in prisons were usually performed by frustrated heterosexuals!

Finally, after hours of public hearings, most of which included public presentations that were homophobic and outrageous, the bill passed. It was one of the finest things the NDP did, and I was glad to have been able to do my part.

I now had two legislative sessions under my belt and was beginning to have a better understanding of the rhythm of the legislature. With an election thought to be about two years away, it was time to focus on choosing candidates and a campaign team.

Little did we know that this election would take place far sooner than anyone anticipated. Nor could I have anticipated that the next five years of my life would be dominated by the Constitution!

eleven

Meech Lake Is the Pits!

One of my proudest moments as a Liberal came in 1982 with the enshrinement of the Charter of Rights and Freedoms in the Canadian Constitution at the time of its patriation. I have been interested in the Constitution since 1960 when I took a course in constitutional law at Dalhousie University as part of my political science major. I loved it, and had I ever gone to law school, it would have been my area of concentration. Like many avowed Charterists I hated (and still hate) the notwithstanding clause, but I understood the political reality: the Charter would not have met with the approval of the premiers in 1982 without its inclusion, because they were unwilling to give up political control of individual rights.

Canada's human rights record is, to my mind, quite dismal. Canadians have betrayed the rights of both Aboriginals and other Canadians since Confederation. The internment of Canadians of Japanese origin during the Second World War and, to a lesser degree, Canadians of German and Ukranian origin during the First World War are only two examples. There was also the imposition of the War Measures Act in 1970 (which I supported at the time, to my subsequent shame). These "measures"—these rights violations—were always supported by the majority of members of the House of Commons. Given our history I can only conclude that if we look solely to our elected representatives to protect minority rights, then we do not do the minorities justice. Politicians want to be re-elected. They do go against the perceived will of the majority, but only very infrequently, and only when they think they will be forgiven in time for the next election. In my opinion, it is necessary to allow others, who have no electoral interests, to protect minority rights. I mean, of course, the Supreme Court. I don't always agree with the Charter decisions of the Court, but I have more faith in its judgment than I do in the vagaries of electoral politics.

It was with great excitement that I received my copies of the Charter after its official proclamation. I was teaching junior high at the time. I gave my poor twelve- to fifteen-year-olds each a copy, and we read it aloud in class. I am sure they thought it was just one more silly thing a teacher asked them to do, but I believed it incumbent upon me to show them this document, the embodiment of their Canadian value system. That same year I remember watching a young Sikh boy being taunted by fellow classmates as he walked down the corridor. They were chanting "Gandhi, Gandhi," because of the movie so popular that year. I called them all into my room. After explaining that he was not a Hindu as Gandhi had been, I made them examine why they were taunting him. Was it because he was different and was wearing a *phatka*, worn by young Sikh boys before they wear a turban? Was it because of his brown skin or his accent? When caught at their racism all children are embarrassed—much more so than adults— but to me it was a graphic case of why we needed a Charter.

I was not naive. I knew the Charter would not end discrimination, prejudice or racism, but it was an important first step and one that all children should understand. It of course also spoke eloquently of the rights of women, rights long unrecognized in this so-called advanced country. I did think these rights were, now, forever to be protected. I was soon to learn that nothing, despite the rhetoric of election campaigns, is ever sacred to politicians. This was the lesson of Meech Lake.

The premiers met, at Mulroney's instigation, at Meech Lake on April 30, 1987, to recommend revisions to Canada's constitution. Their "deal" was greeted with enthusiasm across the land. The agreement called for a recognition of Quebec as a distinct society, gave the provinces a role in the appointment of senators and members of the Supreme Court, gave the provinces new powers over immigration and allowed provinces who opted out of national social programs, in areas of provincial jurisdiction, to receive compensation. It also gave Quebec a veto over future constitutional changes to institutions by imposing unanimity—whereby no further changes could be made without the consent of every province—and constitutionalized in perpetuity First Ministers' Conferences. My first reaction was that it was worthy of study. My second was that it was the pits!

I identified those parts that weakened the Charter and those that led to a further decentralization or weakening of the federal government as of significant concern to Canadians. John Turner and Ed Broadbent announced their full support of this "historic achievement." To me, the only achievement of note was that they had all given approval, as though their unanimity was enough to make it good! No one in the NDP caucus in Manitoba broke with the premier, who supported Broadbent's position, and Gary Filmon and the Tories gave it their full support. There was I in the Manitoba legislature, the lone member opposing—and proud of it.

Because of changes made to the amendment formula in the 1982 Canada Act, it was necessary for the House of Commons, the Senate who had a suspensive veto only and all ten provinces to approve this package within three years. Quebec started the clock by passing the bill in its National Assembly on June 23, 1987.

In late May Lloyd Axworthy called a group of Manitoba Liberals together to discuss the Accord. Izzy Asper, Bill Ridgeway (at this time the federal policy chair), Una MacLean Evans (president of the Liberal Party of Canada in Alberta) and others gathered in the Charterhouse Hotel. Lloyd, like many of his colleagues in Ottawa, didn't like the deal but was caught between his vision of the country and loyalty to his leader. I viewed the meeting as one in which we were all supposed to make Lloyd feel better about going against his conscience, but it was clear that Izzy and I were adamantly opposed. The others, like Lloyd, were unable to break with Turner. At about 11:45 p.m., when it was clear that Lloyd was going to vote for the package despite his pangs of conscience, I left in disgust. I told him he could do as he damn well pleased, but I was voting against it—even if I turned out to be the one no vote in our legislature.

I drove home in a rage. That afternoon I had purchased several flats of petunias at the garden shop, anticipating planting them around our pool in the backyard that weekend. John heard the garage door go up, but I never came inside. He finally came looking for me and found me out back furiously planting petunias at midnight. Each hole I dug represented those unwilling to stand up and be counted for the Liberal principles we were supposed to uphold.

Later that summer John and I attended the Canadian Bar Association Convention in Ottawa. While we were there several significant things occurred. Frank McKenna, then the opposition leader in New Brunswick, made a presentation to the Special Joint Committee of Parliament on the Constitution. I went up to Parliament Hill to hear him. Frank raised many of the concerns I had, although he refrained from giving a definitive answer as to how he would vote in the New Brunswick legislature. After his speech he turned to me and asked, "How did I do?" I told him I was delighted, but then I had to act as his press aide since all the reporters wanted to speak with him. I urged him out to the corridor to face the scrum. If only he had stuck by the principles he espoused that day, the scenario in June of 1990 would have been significantly different.

The next day Trudeau issued his scathing attack on the Accord, which for the first time made Canadians sit up and take notice of how the politicians were dealing with the constitution. And this was also the week in which Larry Desjardins announced his resignation from the Manitoba cabinet and gave hints of his resignation from the legislature, his forthcoming heart bypass surgery being part of the reason.

Desjardins's move was highly significant for two reasons. The people of the St. Boniface riding had supported Larry as both a Liberal and a New Democrat, so the seat belonged to him, and not to any party. In spite of his enormous popularity as a New

Democrat, winning 60.5 percent of the popular vote in the St. Boniface constituency in the 1986 election, the Liberal Party had also managed an encouraging 24 percent. The Tories were out of it with only 13.5 percent. Those figures made me confident that it was a by-election we could win. I also knew the NDP government would not be anxious to call it. As it turned out, Larry told me they begged him to remain at least as an MLA, offering him any position he wanted. Howard Pawley even visited him in the hospital days after his bypass, urging him to remain. Larry was determined to retire, though, and was equally determined that he would not lend his active support to ensuring that he was replaced by an NDP member.

Desjardins's leaving was an enormous blow to the Pawley government—in fact, the government was ultimately defeated in 1988 because of it. Most analysis of the NDP defeat focuses on Jim Walding's vote with the opposition on the budget, but if Larry Desjardins had remained as part of the NDP caucus, then Walding's vote would not have resulted in a defeat but a tied vote —a tie that would have been broken in the NDP's favour by the Speaker. Larry Desjardins's resignation sounded the death knell for the NDP in Manitoba.

In October 1987, a poll was released that was music to the ears of the Liberal Party in Manitoba. For the first time in twenty-five years it appeared that Manitobans were seriously looking at us as an alternative government. The poll projected a popular vote for the Liberal Party of 23.5 percent. This meant we would probably win additional seats in the legislature and possibly have the four seats needed for official status after the next election. It also represented a significant chance for us in the by-election in St. Boniface, which we anticipated would soon be called.

Liberal fortunes were also helped by the Autopac issue. In December the Manitoba Public Insurance Corporation (MPIC) announced that car insurance rates, known in this province as Autopac rates, would increase by 24 percent. Manitobans went wild, particularly when they learned that the government had deliberately held back the rates in 1985 and 1986 anticipating that these would be election years. Manitobans protested en masse, and the minister in charge, John Buklaschuk, made a complete fool of himself both in and out of the legislature. The government tried everything from removing the minister to replacing the administration of MPIC, to no avail. When the government called us back into session on February 11, 1988, things were in rough shape.

The Speech from the Throne was introduced and everyone waited with anticipation to see what the loose cannon, Jim Walding, was going to do. Would he support the government in the vote required in eight days or would he vote against them? The debate began. Gary Filmon, observing the traditional role of the opposition, introduced a non-confidence motion at the end of his speech. Walding's own speech was negative, and the press gallery was filled on February 23, 1988, when the vote was taken, anticipating a defeat for the NDP. But Walding voted with the government and they survived their first non-confidence vote.

The budget was introduced next, and it was actually a "good news" budget for the NDP. Their budget in 1987 had imposed so many new taxes that this one showed tremendous growth in revenue and really no new taxes. The deficit was projected at a record low for the NDP. However, it was clear that the public was out for blood and would interpret a vote against the budget as a vote against the Autopac rates. The Tories could barely conceal their eagerness to form the next government. For my part, I was delighted at the prospect of an early election and no longer being alone in the legislature.

On March 7, the day before the budget vote, in an interview with the media Jim Walding implied that he would vote with the government. The letdown was tremendous. At lunch on the day of the vote I gave a speech to the Tourism Association meeting in Portage la Prairie, and someone asked if the government could fall. I replied in the negative on the basis of Walding's statement. On the drive back to Winnipeg, Al asked me if I wanted him to remain at the legislature for the 5:30 vote. I told him to go home, as the vote would be all form and no substance. The media had also gone home, assuming a non-event.

I was sitting in the legislature at 5:30 p.m., as were all the

members, for the scheduled vote. I rose to vote on the opposition's non-confidence motion and went back to signing letters.
Jim Downey, a Tory member who sat in front of me, turned
around to yell, "Walding voted with us!" It took me a few seconds,
as it did everyone else in the chamber, to realize that the government had been defeated. I looked across the floor to Howard
Pawley, who was ashen-faced. The Tories were jubilant. The
Speaker adjourned the House and I went to my office. I called Al,
Marguerite, Ernie Gilroy, Moishe Kaufman (then the president of
the Liberal Party in Manitoba) and other members of the campaign committee, asking them to come to my office as soon as
possible. I knew the media would be arriving within minutes, and
their first photos of the Liberal campaign would be of my office
crowded with people. This wasn't difficult to achieve since my
office looked crowded with more than ten people in the inner and
outer offices combined! However, impressions are everything in
politics.

During that meeting I had a phone call from Jay Cowan, the
Minister of Northern Affairs and the NDP House leader. He told
me that he and Wilson Parasuik, the Minister of Health, wanted
to meet with me that night, but not at the legislature. He suggested Wilson's office, since it was the only ministerial office not
located in the legislature itself. I said no, I wanted the meeting on
my turf, and asked them to come to my home at 9:00 p.m. I also
told them that, since there were two of them, I would have
Moishe Kaufman with me. There was only one possible reason
for the call and that was that they wanted to cut a deal. I told the
assembled group and we talked about the deal-making I should
expect from Cowan and Parasuik. We adjourned after everyone
was assigned duties for the campaign, and a second campaign
meeting was called for the next day.

Wilson and Jay presented me with the following scenario: they
would write a new budget to be presented to the House with my
approval, and they would inform the lieutenant governor that
they had my support. In return I could cut the deal I wanted.
Presumably I could become a cabinet minister in the NDP government in whatever portfolio I wished. Jay told me that if I did

not cut a deal I would lose my own seat, no Liberals would be elected, and Medicare as we knew it would be destroyed by Don Orchard, who would become the Tory Health Minister. I informed them that I was not interested in the deal and that I would take my chances with the electorate. However, I did say after much prodding that I would sleep on it and give them my final answer in the morning. After they left I told Moishe that I had no intention of changing my mind and that we should get on with planning the election campaign. I called Jay the next morning, and he was not surprised by my reply.

Later that day Howard Pawley announced that he was resigning as leader of the NDP, and a leadership campaign would begin immediately. Ed Schreyer had been elected NDP leader in the middle of the 1969 campaign, and the current NDP group obviously hoped that this strategy would reverse their negative position in the polls. The provincial election would be held on April 26, 1988, my forty-sixth birthday. A wonderful birthday present, I announced later to the media.

The 1988 campaign was pure magic. Everything seemed to go in our favour. By chance, the annual general meeting of the Liberal Party in Manitoba was held two days after the election was called. With the other parties busy behind closed doors, one trying to plan a leadership race and the other planning strategy for the campaign, we were the centre of all the media attention, and we used every bit of it to our advantage.

My husband John, who was in Toronto when the government fell (and ruefully says he is always away when I need him, which is not true), returned during the opening ceremonies on Friday night. After I kissed him, noting that he looked a little pale, I saw that his hand was bruised and swollen. He admitted to having fallen the night before, having missed a step coming out of a room. I was sure his wrist was broken, but he refused to go to the hospital until after my speech to the convention on Saturday, just before lunch. He also insisted on going alone since he was sure his wife was being overly solicitous. When he returned to the convention on Saturday afternoon, complete with cast, it was to tell

The Connollys, 1943. Back row, from left: Catherine, Sharon, Mum, Dad, Dennis. Front row, from left: David, Maureen.

My crowning glory at age four, "the ringlets."

From left: Patricia, David, Sharon, Dennis. By 1951, when I was nine, the ringlets were no more. This was about the time of the abuse.

At seven, the only time in my life I have looked good in a bathing suit!

The uniform in all its ugliness! But it freed our minds to concentrate on our development.

Graduation from Dalhousie University, 1962—already an activist.

Sharon and John,
August 6, 1966.
A formal affair.

Politics from the
beginning: best man
Jim Coutts, then
appointment secretary
to the Rt. Hon. Lester
B. Pearson, Prime
Minister of Canada,
reads a telegram from
Mr. Pearson, a well-
wisher.

Leadership campaign, 1984. The glasses had to be replaced immediately because the TV cameramen couldn't get clear shots with them!

I declared for Jean Chrétien in 1984, causing dismay in Manitoba Liberal circles.

I wasn't supposed to win in 1986, but did, thanks to the campaign team shown here in my first legislature office.

From left: Cathi, Jennie, Sharon and John at the swearing-in ceremony, 1986.

His Holiness Pope John Paul II during the Papal Visit in 1986. I wore my one and only hat for the occasion, but the Grey Nuns didn't wear their veils!

Marguerite Martin and Sharon. Marguerite's hard work, dedication and friendship made much of what we accomplished possible.

Peter Johnston and Sharon during the 1988 campaign. He got the best from me.

From one seat to twenty: a miracle deserves some celebration. On election night, April 26, 1988, we celebrated—our win and my 46th birthday.

The 1988–1990 caucus, neophytes all, but we tried despite incredible obstacles. Back row, from left: Neil Gaudry, Gulzar Cheema, Al Patterson, Richard Kozak, Giles Roch, Jim Carr, Reg Alcock, Paul Edwards, Mark Minenko, John Angus, Harold Taylor, Harold Driedger, Laurie Evans, Kevin Lamoureux. Front row, from left: Ed Mandrake, Bill Chornopyski, Gwen Charles, Sharon, Iva Yeo, Avis Gray, Bob Rose.

Premier David Peterson with Sharon, 1989. I tried to explain Manitoba's position on the Meech Lake Accord, but to no avail.

Lloyd Axworthy and Sharon, 1990. Appearances can be deceiving. We did not work together—to both our disadvantage.

Perry Diamond

Campaign rally, 1990. As always, Jean Chrétien gave his support and encouragement. Paul Edwards went on to be the new provincial leader in 1993.

A composite photo for the 1990 campaign poster, made up of the head from one photo and the body from another. Like the campaign, it was disjointed!

My faithful sidekick, Al Munroe. Al and I went through four cars covering Manitoba.

Now we are seven, September, 1990. Back row, from left: Paul Edwards, Kevin Lamoureux, Gulzar Cheema. Front row, from left: Neil Gaudry, Reg Alcock, Sharon, Jim Carr.

The wind beneath my wings. John and I on our 25th wedding anniversary, August 6, 1991.

My staff on my retirement. Back row, from left: Sherry Wiebe, Al Munroe, Barbara King, Derek Boutang, Judy Edmond. Middle row, from left: Darrell Neufeld, Marcelle Balcaen, Mary Ellen Dunn, Kim Morrison. Front row, from left: Marguerite Martin, Sharon, Leanne Matthes.

Some of my favourite political cartoons:

THE CAMPAIGN RAGES ON INTO IT'S FINAL DAYS!

GENTLEMEN! TSK! TSK!

...OH YEAH!

MY BUS IS BIGGER THAN YOUR BUS!

1986 campaign, "After the Debate."
Phil Mallette, *Winnipeg Free Press*

JEAN

SHARON

LLOYD

Chocolate

1990 federal Liberal leadership
campaign. Jan Kamienski,
Winnipeg Sun

A GATHERING OF MANITOBA LIBERALS —

After the 1988 campaign. Del Cummings, *Winnipeg Free Press*

us all that he had broken his wrist. It didn't keep him from campaigning, or even shaking hands with potential voters, since it was his left hand. He has always been so considerate! Indeed, I suspect it got him, and therefore me, some sympathy votes.

The annual general meeting, held during the first week of the campaign, was a love-in with the party, the media and the public all participating. While in 1986 it had been difficult to find candidates, this time we seemed to have them coming out of our ears, even in rural Manitoba. We arranged to have a photographer at the convention and all of the "potential" candidates had their pictures taken, both alone and with me, for future campaign materials. Few of the pictures went to waste!

During the meeting I announced that the Liberal Party in Manitoba would gradually eliminate the payroll tax. This tax had been imposed by the NDP in 1987 and was detested by the business community, who considered it a tax on jobs. Since at this time we were the only province other than Quebec to have it, the Chambers of Commerce and others argued that it was keeping business from both coming to and expanding in this province. Luckily for us, Gary Filmon, in his opening foray in the Tory campaign, stated that he didn't think a government led by him would be able to change the tax. This policy was to be amended later in the campaign, but the damage was already done. The business community, which had, to this point, looked favourably only on the Tories, started to look at the Liberals. The donations poured in, enabling us to spend twice what we had in 1986. We still spent less than the other two parties and made a profit on the campaign of $110,000. Rick McKay, our wonderful auditor, Ernie, who was still chair of the campaign, and my husband, the fund-raiser, continued to moan and groan about money throughout the campaign, but they knew everything was going just fine. I think, to be fair to them, that having had to fight for every cent in other campaigns, they just didn't want to jinx this one.

I received a number of standing ovations during my speech to the annual general meeting (Ian Gillies, in my opinion the best speech-writer in Canada and presently a senior officer with

Cargill Grain, wrote it). But none of the ovations was more sustained than the one following my comments on the Meech Lake Accord. It was clear that Liberals in Manitoba disliked this deal and special status every bit as much as I did.

I even insisted that a statement of our rejection of the Meech Lake Accord be included in the generic candidates' pamphlet. Donald Benham, who is, I believe, the best political reporter in Manitoba (even though he is a Tory), thought I harped on Meech too much during the campaign. "No one cares," he said. I responded that I cared, and I saw it as my responsibility to inform Manitobans about its fallacies. And Manitobans cared too. Many for the wrong reasons, but lots for the right reasons. The people of Manitoba believe devotedly in the equality of all Canadians, and they reject special status for anyone. Above all they believe in a strong federal government. As a small "have-not" province they know we need the federal government to ensure a level of service to our citizens at least somewhat equivalent to that in other provinces.

No matter what we did in the campaign we seemed to generate publicity. We even turned the production of our signs into a media event, with all three stations showing our signs coming off the assembly line on their six o'clock news programs.

The campaign had some funny moments. Olva Odlum, a close friend, was waiting for a bus one day in the midst of the campaign. She struck up a conversation with another woman and asked what she thought about the campaign. Her reply was, "I think I will vote for that woman, even if she is a rich bitch and lives on Wellington Crescent."

The exchange was funny, but it is unfortunate that this image is still borne by female politicians. During the Liberal nomination battle for the federal constituency of Winnipeg South in March of 1993, the word "bitch" was prominent. The major contestants were Reg Alcock, a member of my caucus and the eventual winner, and Linda Asper, Izzy's sister-in-law and a candidate for me in 1990. I couldn't get involved. However, I was furious that this bright, well-educated, fluently bilingual woman with a Ph.D. in Education Administration was being called a bitch by those working for her opponent. I am sure there were some of her workers referring to Reg as a bastard, but that is seen almost as a badge of courage for a male politician. It shows he is tough. For women, the term bitch is completely negative!

As per usual, there were those within the party determined to undermine and control me. Ed Coutu, Alain Hogue, Guy Savoie and Renald Guay decided that they knew best how to run the campaign in the provincial constituencies comprising the federal riding of St. Boniface. Indeed, each one had chosen a constituency and they wanted me to endorse them and to push away all opposition. I refused, and told them if they wanted the nominations in St. Vital, St. Boniface, Niakwa, Riel and Radisson, they could fight for them like everyone else. They were furious and decided none of them should be treated this way by their female leader. They tried their best to intimidate delegates and potential candidates at the annual general meeting. None of them became a candidate, and we ultimately managed, without their help, to win four of the five constituencies! (Riel was held by Gerry Ducharme, a Tory who had taken it from the NDP in the 1986 campaign.)

I also received a visit early in the campaign from the leadership of the Winnipeg Sikh community. Provincially they had traditionally voted NDP. However, they were very angry with Howard Pawley, Gary Doer (who was to replace Pawley) and Marty Dolin, the NDP member for the constituency of Kildonan, where the majority of them lived.

After the Air India crash of June 1985 (alleged to have been a deliberate sabotage by a group of militant Sikhs), Joe Clark, then the External Affairs minister, had written to the premier indicating that the government should be very careful of associating themselves with members of the political group, the World Sikh Organization. As a result, Doer and Dolin had cancelled plans to attend a dinner in the Sikh community. John and I had been appalled by what we believed to be the abuse of this community by the NDP during the by-election in 1985, when Sikhs had been brought to the polling stations by the NDP, many of them not fully understanding what was expected of them. The NDP's subsequent rejection of them was considered by the community as a slight, and one they did not intend to take lightly.

They asked me if I had any objections to a Canadian of Sikh origin running as a candidate for my party. "Of course not," I replied, which was obviously what they wanted to hear. I told them the rules for the nomination process, making it clear that there would be special rules for no one. They agreed, and said that as long as the rules were the same for everyone they would abide by them and take their chances. I must admit to some trepidation when they left my office, wondering who they would come up with as a candidate. I knew nothing of the Sikh community. I was soon to learn that they were politically sophisticated and had a great capacity to support the candidate of their choice. Their candidate, Dr. Gulzar Cheema, turned out to be so outstanding that any party would have been delighted to claim him.

A physician with advanced training in pediatrics, geriatrics and psychiatry, Dr. Cheema had been in Canada only since 1979. However, his wife, Harinder, who is an incredible political organizer, had been here since she was nine years of age. They are practical, hard working and philosophically Liberal. I would have liked to have seen him in the race to replace me as leader, since his intellectual capacity is equal or superior to everyone else in caucus. However, he is also a realist and believes, as, unfortunately, do I, that Manitobans are not yet ready to accept a brown-skinned Canadian as the leader of a political party and as a potential premier! Some might question whether someone from his community would support a female leader, but his loyalty to me has never been a question in his mind or mine.

Jean Chrétien again came into the province to help out, and this time we took him up north. This visit generated the only bad publicity of the campaign. When we arrived at a scheduled plane stop in Norway House, a native community, no one was there to meet us. We had media on board, and both Jean and I were dismayed. When we arrived at the Band Council offices we were told that the leaders were away but would return at some point. One of the Aboriginal staff persons, hearing this, made a passing reference to "Indian time." Eventually the meeting was held and we reboarded the plane for the return trip to Winnipeg.

Gerald Flood, who had not been on the plane, was told by the *Free Press* reporter on board that I had blamed the fiasco on "Indian time," and wrote a story implying racism on my part. The Indian leadership, always sensitive (and with great justification), asked for an apology, which of course they got. It is one of the pitfalls politicians can easily fall into since many communities—Aboriginal, Filipino, Latin American—often poke fun at themselves for the way in which their sense of time differs from the establishment norm. While it is okay for them to make jokes, it is not acceptable for a politician, no matter what community he or she hails from!

On the plane home we received a message from the campaign committee that Lloyd Axworthy and Sergio Marchi were attending the Winnipeg rally for the ethnic communities that night, where Jean Chrétien was to be the guest speaker. Out of courtesy to their leader, John Turner, they would not sit on the same platform with Jean. I passed the message on to Jean, and he said that if that was the case, he wouldn't speak. I told him that was not the issue. If Lloyd and Sergio would not sit on the same platform, then they would sit by themselves, since I was sitting with Jean. Needless to say they decided to share the platform with Jean. I suspect that Sergio didn't even know that his name was being bandied about in this manner.

The following night we held another rally after visiting all of the shopping centres during the day. We actually charged admission, and two thousand people showed up at the Convention Centre, certainly the largest rally in provincial politics for any party that I can remember.

Polls kept coming out showing us with a larger and larger percentage of the popular vote, but none of us closely tied to the campaign could identify the seats. We were pretty sure that Jim Carr would win in Fort Rouge, Reg Alcock in Osborne, Neil Gaudry in St. Boniface and me in River Heights, giving us the four seats we needed for official status, but where, we wondered, was all the other vote going? Neil Gaudry, for example, was not

even supposed to have been the candidate in St. Boniface, according to the self-proclaimed experts. It was supposed to have been
Guy Savoie, and that in itself was one of the most interesting
stories of the campaign.

Guy Savoie was the City of Winnipeg councillor for St. Boniface. He had run for us in 1981 and received the highest percentage of the popular vote of any Liberal candidate. Indeed, he had
been touted as a potential leadership candidate in 1984, and he
would have been hard to beat. However, he'd decided not to run,
supporting Bill Ridgeway instead. Unlike many of his cohorts,
such as Eddie Coutu, who had told me the week I was elected
leader in 1984 that he could never support or work for a woman,
Guy had come to see me in 1986 after the election to tell me that
he had supported the wrong candidate and was impressed by my
efforts to rebuild the party. He said he was seriously considering
running again in the next election. Unfortunately, his popularity
in St. Boniface was declining. He had angered residents by his
support for a development project owned by Alain Hogue, a local
Liberal, which they thought would ruin the character of old St.
Boniface.

A group of Liberals decided that they wanted Neil Gaudry, the
president of the St. Boniface Provincial Liberal Constituency, to
be the candidate. Neil was an accountant, very active in the
francophone community, who had been the Official Voyageur
for Festival du Voyageur during the mid-1980s. I had wanted Neil
to run in 1986, but he didn't think the timing was right for him.
Now he was prepared to go. Guy was furious. In order to maintain
peace in the family I asked them both to come to a meeting at my
house one Friday afternoon. Guy was sure he would have the
support of the party, but I knew that Neil and his supporters had
already sold over three hundred memberships, which they hadn't
yet turned in to the party offices. Even without those membership votes, Neil was prepared to take his chances on the names
already registered.

I suggested that membership lists close that afternoon. Neil
agreed. Guy did not. He argued that his family had not even
renewed their memberships and he had to have some time. It was

decided that the cut-off would be Saturday morning at noon. Neil and his supporters arrived with nearly four hundred memberships. Guy and his supporters arrived with slightly more than one hundred. When he saw the handwriting on the wall, Guy withdrew from the race. Several days later, having accepted the poor advice of Eddie Coutu and others, he announced that he would be running as the Tory candidate in the St. Boniface constituency. Before he made the official announcement he called me. He was in tears as he told me what he planned to do. I wished him well, and he said, "You are quite the lady." He was defeated, badly. Neil received 5,743 votes, 60 percent of the popular vote; Guy received 1,586 votes, 17 percent of the popular vote. The NDP candidate was able to get only 22 percent in a seat formerly held provincially by New Democrat Larry Desjardins.

Even on the day before the election Ernie and I were unable to tell which ridings we were winning. By this time the polls had us with as much as 35 percent of the popular vote, and we were beginning to anticipate that John Angus would win in St. Norbert and Laurie Evans in Fort Garry, but even our best estimates gave us only nine or ten seats.

In 1986, I started a custom of delivering to all of my urban candidates a red rose the day before the election and phoning each one of my rural candidates to wish them luck. On April 25, 1988, I spent all day visiting the twenty-eight city headquarters, leaving the twenty-ninth, my own, until late in the evening. I was with Al, who knew which candidates I was most concerned about (in terms of handling their potential defeat), and he was going to take special care to be by their side on election night. In the Inkster constituency, Kevin Lamoureux and his wife Cathy told us they were convinced that Kevin was going to win. Kevin had run in 1986, but realizing that he could not win, he had distributed his pamphlets in his Logan constituency and came to work on my campaign in River Heights. I told Al they were number one on his list because I didn't see how they could possibly win this time either, and he had to help cushion their fall.

When we arrived at Ed Mandrake's headquarters—his house, actually—in Assiniboia, he too told us he was going to win. He had just returned from putting up his last sign. I knew Ed had spent less than $3,000 and had no workers, but he was sure he was going to win. He became number two on my attention list for Al.

I always go to my own constituency office to watch the election results, and 1988 was no different. I arrived at about eight o'clock, just as the polls closed. The place was jammed with media, who were obviously anticipating something. The first results, all rural, showed only NDP and PC potential wins. Lloyd Axworthy made the comment on CBC that obviously it was not to be the Liberals' night after all. Then the city numbers began to come in. One after another, Liberal victories were announced. My win in River Heights was declared with 59 percent of the popular vote. Even Gary Filmon was in trouble against the Liberal candidate, Dr. Jasper McKee.

At one point the results showed twenty-five Liberal seats to twenty-two Tory seats and ten NDP. At that point I turned to John and said, "What the hell do we do now?" The CBC sound didn't pick up my voice, but it was still easy to read my lips on TV! I thanked my River Heights workers and went to the downtown Holiday Inn to a suite just before the victory party. By the time we arrived it looked as if the PCs would have twenty-five seats, we would have twenty, and the NDP twelve. That was in fact the result, but no one in the suite could tell me which were our twenty seats because they kept changing all night.

I refused to go to the victory party until I knew who had won and, equally important, who had lost. We finally identified nineteen seats: eighteen in Winnipeg, including Ed Mandrake's, and Gwen Charles's in Selkirk. It seemed Kevin Lamoureux had to be the twentieth. I asked Peter Johnston, my incredible campaign manager and Donald Johnston's nephew, to phone and confirm. He asked me what he should say and I told him to tell Kevin he had done a wonderful job, and to just hope Kevin would be forthcoming. Kevin replied that, yes they had, but said nothing more. Peter, with his hand over the mouthpiece, asked me, "What do I say now!" I told him to say Sharon needs the official results. At that point we learned that Kevin was our twentieth MLA, and I was absolutely delighted.

The ballroom at the Holiday Inn was going wild. I went into the crush of media and ecstatic supporters, finally making my way to the podium. It was the most exciting moment of my life. John and I left the party early and went home for a quiet drink together. I knew that there would be hard work ahead, but I had been working hard for four years, and I thought that now that I had some help it would be easier. It wasn't to be. Indeed, the real work of my political life was about to begin.

twelve

Meech Lake Is Dead . . .
I Think

The day after the election I asked all of the newly elected caucus members to join me at the legislature for a press conference. Since we did not yet have a caucus room, we met in the media room. The poor media room staff was in a panic because I managed to put twenty MLAs on a platform built for four; they were afraid we would fall through! I introduced them all since most were virtually unknown to the media.

The press conference was warm and convivial, but not exactly hard news stuff. That is until Jane Chalmers, now a CBC producer in Winnipeg but then a reporter for CBC's "The National" for Manitoba, asked me what would be the effect of the election on the Meech Lake Accord. I said, "Meech Lake is dead." This turned out to be a somewhat controversial statement.

When asked about my comment, Prime Minister Mulroney replied that he understood that Gary Filmon—not Sharon Carstairs—was the new Manitoba premier. I may not have been the premier but on this issue I was holding most of the cards. I was convinced that most Manitobans favoured my position on the Meech Lake Accord. In addition, a number of members of Filmon's caucus were unhappy with the deal. NDP MLAs Maureen Hemphill and Andy Anstett, both of whom had run unsuccessfully for the leadership of their party, had said they opposed the deal during their campaigns. Maureen had been re-elected to the legislature. Len Evans, Jim Malloway, Jerry Storie and Elijah Harper were also thought to be against the deal, although they had not said so officially at this point. I knew that getting this deal through the Manitoba legislature would be tough for Filmon. However, Brian Mulroney was obviously confident, because no one cared to listen to my concerns first-hand until the spring of 1990. Meanwhile I had other problems to worry about.

The morning after the election I asked Al Munroe to start talking to Government Services about our office space. We were told that, since the government was changing, there would be major upheavals and the new Tory government would have to be considered first. It would be several weeks before we could get permanent space for caucus and staff.

The NDP was faced with a major dilemma. It now held third-party status in a minority government situation. Their support was necessary to whichever party formed the government, otherwise Manitoba would be thrown into another election campaign. Their caucus members, ten of whom had been cabinet ministers and all of whom had legislative experience, were divided as to what they should do. Jay Cowan thought that they should enter into a deal with the Liberals, making us the government. Because of our lack of experience, he reasoned, we would fall flat on our faces and the NDP would then be in a position to pick up the pieces, since they could choose the timing of our defeat. They would simply wait until our popularity had declined and vote with the Tories on a non-confidence motion. But Gary Doer believed it was better to cut a deal with the Tories, and this is what they ultimately did. It was a two-year agreement, giving the NDP time to rebuild. The deal, unlike the one struck in Ontario during its minority Liberal government, was never disclosed, but it soon became evident in the budget vote several months later when only Gary Doer and Maureen Hemphill were in the House to vote, leaving the other ten members of the caucus in the caucus room! The following year they actually voted for the government's budget—a rarity for an opposition party.

In any case, when we eventually received our office space, it was inferior to the NDP's. I can only speculate that this was part of the package negotiated with the Tories. Gary Doer was given an extra staff person even though the salary for this position was assigned to the PC caucus. When I questioned the premier about it, he replied that he could use his staff any way he saw fit.

No wonder the public is cynical about politics. Here were the PCs and the NDP, avowed public enemies, cutting deals together, not because they had any ideology in common—both are closer to the Liberals, in the middle of the political spectrum—but because it was the only way one could keep power and the other the hope to rebuild. Power is the name of this game. Public policy issues are irrelevant, and so too are the wishes of the electorate, apparently. Power alone is the altar at which politicians worship.

There we were, twenty elected MLAs with a total of two years of legislative experience among us—mine. And my experience was not even normal since it was that of a lone member and not a member of caucus. We quickly realized that, with the minority government, it was the worst possible scenario. If there had been a majority, we would have had at least three and probably four years to gain experience and expertise. If we had elected more members but had only traditional third-party status, the expectations would have been far less. Even if we had formed a government, we would have had at least the expertise of the civil service to help us find our way. As it was, we had to do the best we could with what we had, and the task was of mammoth proportions.

My first job was to select a deputy leader, House leader and whip. I kept the title of caucus chair for several months, rotated it for several more and, finally, the caucus elected Laurie Evans—a wise choice because he was competent and very well liked by other members of caucus.

I chose Jim Carr as my deputy leader. I knew of his ambitions, but I also knew he was smart enough not to challenge me at this point. Of all the members of caucus I was most philosophically in tune with him. Jim and I had an uncanny ability to answer the same question the same way, often using identical language, even if we were miles away from one another. I knew that whatever he said on behalf of the party I would be comfortable with. This was critical for us at this time since many of the new MLAs didn't yet have the discipline to refrain from making statements if they didn't know what the party line was. Jim is an extremely cautious person by nature, and he rarely goes out on a limb. However, I knew that even if he did I would seldom be at odds with him, and his position would be so reasonable that I could live with it.

The only disappointment I had with him was his desire to live a nine-to-five life as a politician. He and his wife, a physician, have three children, the third born after the election of 1988. He insisted on spending the vast majority of his weekends and evenings with his family. As a result, I was left with a schedule that, for the most part, was excessive and led Gary Doer to remark on the day of my retirement that he knew I had been at more events than all of my MLAs combined. It was probably a mistake on my part to take on so much; it led perhaps to an earlier than necessary burnout. My sense of duty is deeply ingrained and not easily ignored. During my two years alone in the legislature I rarely missed a day or evening session and did three major departmental estimates each year. Normally a critic is responsible for only one department in each session. In the Manitoba legislature the detailed estimates of each government department consume 240 hours of session time. Unfortunately, I was unable to share the burden with Jim.

My second appointment, that of House leader, was Reg Alcock. Reg had been executive director of the Liberal Party in the 1970s, and since then had been a civil servant in the Department of Child and Family Services. I chose him because he at least knew the government from the perspective of a civil servant, and that was more experience than any one else had. He worked hard at learning the ropes, but I had difficulty with him, too. He was far too close to Lloyd Axworthy. I always knew that if he were asked to choose between my position and Lloyd's, I would be the loser. I was livid the day I found out that a press conference had been scheduled for the legislature featuring Lloyd and Reg, who hadn't told me anything about it. Perhaps I was over-sensitive, but I could see the long arm of Axworthy manipulating my MLAs and between the lack of courtesy and the power play I was fit to be tied. It didn't happen again. Was this another example of sexism? I tried not to be paranoid, but I couldn't help but think they would have behaved differently with a man. However, I was careful never to give public vent to such feelings—then I would be accused of whining, which is a behaviour generally ascribed only to women.

I chose Kevin Lamoureux to be the whip. Kevin was and is the youngest member of caucus, having been elected at the age of twenty-six, but his personal loyalty and his capacity for hard work were important to me. He is presently running to replace me as leader, but it is unlikely that he will win, because of his age and because his small stature tends to make him look even younger than he is. However, I anticipate that he will someday be the leader, or will move on to the federal arena. Kevin knew he had my support, but he had some rough times with some of the older members who thought he was a push-over. They gradually changed their opinion when it became clear he was no one's fool. More than any member of caucus, he worked at the top of his talents and abilities.

Having chosen these three, I assigned their offices. The remaining members of caucus chose theirs by drawing from a hat. I didn't wish to participate in the usual bargaining in which the qualities, training and expertise of one is compared with another. Some of the MLAs were dismayed with their offices, but at least they could blame it on the draw and not my favouritism.

Choosing their seats in the legislature was another task. Since no one had seniority, the choices for the front bench were easy. I chose Gulzar because he was the Health critic, a major responsibility, but also because he was the only member of a visible minority community and the first, to my knowledge, to sit in the front row of the Manitoba legislature. I wanted a woman, too, and Gwen Charles was our only MLA from outside of Winnipeg, so that was an easy choice. They were joined by me, Jim and Reg. The second and third rows were more difficult and some people were naturally offended, but for the most part they were excited just to be there. As long as they still felt that they owed their victory to me, they were forgiving. It didn't take some of them very long, however, to begin to think their victory had been solely due to their own talents. Certainly John Angus was one of these and, although according to him I had nothing to do with his victory in 1988, he blamed me entirely for his defeat in 1990. I had been so very thrilled to have been elected at all in 1986 that I found this pettiness disconcerting and quite frankly a waste of time. However, for some of them it seemed to be a way of life!

Politicians have big egos—myself included. You couldn't do the job without one. It gets in the way, though, particularly when you believe the public will never reject you. Most of the MLAs elected in 1988 simply did not build the constituency organizations necessary during their tenure to ensure re-election. Some did, and the results showed it in 1990. Many who narrowly won in 1988 and equally narrowly lost in 1990 can't be faulted, but still others did not even have full executive committees in their constituencies, let alone campaign teams of any size, and very few had raised the necessary dollars to run the 1990 campaign.

One of our first activities as a caucus was to hold a working strategy and training session in Brandon. Most of the MLAs had never been at a Question Period or even watched one on television. They, like most of the public, thought that cabinet ministers were supposed to answer the questions as openly and directly as possible. But the legislature is not a courtroom, and the object of the exercise usually is to phrase the "answer" in such a way as to heap praise on the government while at the same time providing as little information as possible to the opposition members. Some ministers, like Don Orchard, are experts at it and drive opposition members crazy with their obfuscation. My task was to make the MLAs understand that it was not the answer that was important, it was the question. Would the question intrigue the media? If it did, then the media would go after the responding minister in the scrums outside of the House, and the opposition critic would get credit for raising the matter.

We were at a massive disadvantage to the NDP. Since most had been in the previous government's cabinet, and all had experience, we couldn't touch their knowledge of the issues. For example, they knew of all the negotiations on programs with the federal government and their status. They took files and pieces of draft legislation with them when they left cabinet. They had staff, and computers! When we made inevitable errors early in the session the government would blame it on the "Liberal computers." But when we inherited our caucus room and staff offices there was nothing there, not even a pencil! We did not get any computers for months because the government wouldn't finalize our budget.

The session opened on July 21, 1988, with great fanfare. Denis Rocan was the Speaker. A scrupulously fair politician, he often got flak from the government for his efforts. The Speech from the Throne was typical, lots of pious phrases without much substance. But there were two exceptions. The lieutenant governor, George Johnson, announced that the government would repeal Final Offer Selection (FOS), a piece of labour legislation introduced by the NDP in 1987. The lieutenant governor also announced that the government would introduce the Meech Lake Accord to the Manitoba legislature. (Officially, the NDP were still in favour of Meech, but that changed the day after the federal election, on November 21, 1988, when Doer, with no need to worry about being offside with the federal party—Mulroney's Tories had been re-elected after a seesaw campaign—withdrew his support. I was so excited that I phoned Pierre Trudeau. It was our only discussion on the Meech Lake Accord.)

The Final Offer Selection repeal was another example of power triumphing over principle. The original bill had been passed by the NDP government when I was the lone Liberal member of the House. Its purpose was to prevent strikes by forcing both parties to put their final offer on the table and allow an independent arbitrator to decide. The problems with the legislation were two-fold. Only labour could demand it, and then only six weeks before a strike, or six weeks after the strike had begun. Labour did not need management's approval to invoke FOS, but management could not ask for FOS to be put into place without labour's approval. The Tories had promised their supporters in the business community that they would repeal the act as soon as they formed the government, and they introduced the repeal legislation in their first session. The NDP were prepared to go to the wall to protect their legislation and therefore were prepared to defeat the repeal bill.

I had voted against FOS in 1987 because of its inherent unfairness, but also because labour unions had convinced me that in the long run it would not be in their best interests. They were afraid that issues won through hard bargaining over the years could be lost because the management offer might be accepted. As a party in 1988 we were prepared to continue to vote against the measure and in favour of repeal. We were, however, also prepared to end the stalemate in the House. We proposed that the repeal take effect at the end of December 1989, allowing several years of trial negotiations to take place under FOS. The PCs supported our amendment in committee and then took an action unprecedented in parliamentary tradition—they voted against their own bill! Their concern was that, had they voted for the bill as amended, they would be accused by the business community of not honouring their campaign promise of getting rid of it as soon as possible. The result was that the legislation remained on the books even longer than our amendment would have provided. The Tories were not able to repeal it until after they'd won the 1990 election. Politics doesn't always make a great deal of sense.

In an oblique way the FOS situation made me very concerned about the way political parties are funded. Westfair, the owner of Super Stores, which control about 40 percent of the grocery market business in Winnipeg, had given the Liberal Party in Manitoba a $14,000 donation in the 1988 campaign. Like most donations, there was no quid pro quo, or so we thought at the time. However, they did not donate to the 1990 campaign because of our compromise position on FOS. Presumably they considered us sufficiently punished in 1992, because I received a donation of $5,000, personally delivered. Do they and other corporate enterprises think it is that easy to pull the strings of politicians? If they do, then there is something seriously wrong with the system. Most Canadians fail to realize that, because of the system of tax credits to political parties, about 50 percent of parties' costs are paid for by the taxpayers. I believe it would be better for the taxpayers to pay 100 percent of the costs, place tight controls on spending by political parties and thus prevent business and labour from being able to pull political strings. It is the only way to ensure integrity in decision-making.

Premier Gary Filmon rose in the House on December 16, 1988, to introduce the Meech Lake Accord for ratification in the Manitoba legislature. As I told my husband later that evening, the speech was so glowing that Senator Lowell Murray, the federal minister in charge of the Constitution, might have written it! The prime minister was delighted. The premier's timing was awful, however. The day before, the Supreme Court of Canada had ruled that Bill 178, the sign law in Quebec that required all outdoor signs to be in French only, was unconstitutional because it violated both the Quebec and Canadian Charters of Rights. The court ruling did give the Quebec government a bit of an out because it said that there was justification to demand that French be required on all signs, and that it could be the predominant language; it also said that the use of English could not be denied. We all hoped that the Quebec government would be prepared to amend the legislation accordingly, although popular wisdom was that Robert Bourassa, the premier, would invoke the notwithstanding clause of the Charter of Rights and Freedoms. Bourassa said he would make an announcement on Sunday as to what action his government would take.

My caucus and staff and all their children were at my home for a Christmas party during the news conference scheduled by Bourassa. With Jean Paul Boily, my executive assistant at the time, a francophone lawyer who had studied law in French at the University of Ottawa, I went to my den to watch the press conference. It was clear that Bourassa intended to use the notwithstanding clause. But, more incredibly, his reasons for wanting Quebec defined as a distinct society under the Meech Lake Accord appeared to be that Quebec would be allowed to make laws in such a way as to deny the rights of the anglophone community under the guise of the distinct society clause. The battle was on.

Filmon now found himself between a rock and a hard place. He had already lost one caucus member, Gilles Roch, who had crossed the floor to join the Liberals in October, giving as his reasons his opposition to the Meech Lake Accord and the autocratic style of the premier. It was clear that others in his caucus disliked the Accord, and the rumour in the House on Friday was that only Darren Praznik, his legislative assistant and the MLA for Lac Du Bonnet, was prepared to second the constitutional amendment.

The rules of the Manitoba legislature on a constitutional amendment require that all other business of the House be set aside for the debate and that, after five days of such debate, public hearings be held. The House was to open at 1:30 p.m., and, in accordance with the rules, Question Period on Monday would be taken up with debate on the government's stand on Meech Lake. My speech on the constitutional accord would immediately follow, and, if anything, would now be even tougher than I'd originally planned.

Jean Paul and I had monitored the morning open-line radio shows. Invective against the Quebec government's decision filled the airwaves. We were concerned that the anger would soon turn against the francophone community in Manitoba.

The premier called at 1:15 p.m., asking for the opening to be delayed and stating his intention to withdraw the constitutional amendment from the House. It was clear he was extremely worried about the effect this was going to have in Manitoba. I told him he could delay the opening and indeed withdraw the accord subject to the approval of my caucus, which I was sure I would get.

I called the caucus into session and explained what was happening. I told them of my very real concerns about public hearings at this time. It was clear to me that all of the hatred and bigotry of the French-language debate of 1983 would be reopened, and it would be difficult days for Manitoba. John Angus was the only member of caucus who felt that we should force the premier to continue with the debate and hearings. His argument, based purely on the political perception of events, was undoubtedly correct. It was clear I had opposed the agreement from day one, and the anger of the province would be directed, not towards me, but towards the premier. We would come across as the party representing the people. If I had only been interested in power surely this was the decision to make, but I could not allow this to colour my judgment. The important thing now was to consider our nation and our province. I told the caucus that, in the best interests of both, the amendment had to be withdrawn, and it was.

The House quickly adjourned, and after discussions with Gary Doer and me, the premier announced that a task force on the Accord would be convened in the spring and would travel the province to solicit the opinions of Manitobans. Jim Carr and I became the Liberal representatives on this six-member task force, seven with the addition of the chairperson, Wally Fox Decent, a professor in the political science department at the University of Manitoba. Gary Doer represented the NDP and James McCrae, Minister of Justice, Darren Praznik, legislative assistant to the premier, and Gerry Hammond, Minister of Labour, were the government members.

I knew that by participating in this task force I was literally giving the constitutional agenda to the premier. Had I been more driven by political ambition, perhaps I would have refused to participate, or would have allowed backbenchers to sit on the task force and refused my approval to the recommendations. But I was driven by the need to get a deal if such a deal was indeed possible, and I was prepared to let the political chips fall where they may. I have said often that this country is more important than Brian Mulroney, but as I said on the day of my resignation, it is more important than me, too.

The Meech Lake task force met several times in private before we began our travels across the province. We went to Thompson and The Pas in the north, Dauphin, Brandon and Winkler in Manitoba farm country, and to Island Lake to hear from the Aboriginal community. I was not on this last trip, and so I missed one of the more interesting sessions, in which the members were briefly held hostage (their plane would not be allowed to leave the community) until they signed a recognition of Aboriginal rights.

Everywhere we went the message was the same. Manitobans were opposed to the agreement. It became a bit of a joke among us to find the connection between the federal Progressive Conservative Party and those in Manitoba supporting the Accord. Who was doing what favours for whom? Of course we heard from PC MPs from the province—Dorothy Dobbie, Jake Epp and Lee Clarke among them—extolling the virtues of the Accord, but there was no challenge in identifying them. The fun came with identifying Holly Beard, now the recipient of a federal court appointment, Yvon Dumont, now the Tory-appointed lieutenant governor of Manitoba, and Brenda Leipsic, one of Dobbie's employees. Then there were the genuine supporters of the deal, people like Michael Decter, the former clerk of the Legislative Council in the NDP administration and presently the Deputy Minister of Health in Ontario, who honestly believed in the agreement and whose presentations came from the heart and were neither self-serving nor scripted. Then there were members of the PC Party like Vaughan Baird, who had represented Roger Bilodeau in his case to the Supreme Court of Canada, and who spoke so eloquently against the Accord.

For me, the highlight of the presentations was one given by an Aboriginal Manitoban, who, like so many others, had spent many years incarcerated in jails throughout this nation. Victor Payou said:

I have always looked upon every Canadian as being a Canadian and I don't distinguish between people or where they come from. As far as I am concerned, they are all Canadians, whether they are French, Germans, Czechs, or whatever. For me, Canada is a homeland and to most of the Canadians today it is a new home and will be a new home for many more new Canadians who arrive in this country looking for a better life, which this country can provide.

If this Accord goes through, it would be like building a country within a country. I think it would create some friction among other people. What's to prevent Quebec from using the Accord their own way, hold other provinces hostage with the Accord that they have?

There's a lot of things that can be changed. There's no such thing as you can't change. You can change anything you want to change, including this Accord, the Constitution. I think the best thing, in my own personal opinion, to do is that you sit down and talk about the things that need to be changed in this Accord. If you can't get it done right away, there's always time. Everybody's got time, whether you're a politician or not.[3]

Victor Payou is a simple man, neither well educated nor easily eloquent. Yet he was able to speak from his heart about what it meant to be a Canadian. He also identified with the majority of Canadians who in 1992 in the Referendum vote clearly told politicians that they would decide for themselves what was in their best interests and would not be rushed into decision-making.

I was pleased with the performance of my MLAs during this, their first session. But I knew there was still a great deal more work to be done. The learning curve was demanding. Some were up to the challenge; others, unfortunately, were not.

thirteen

It's Still Alive But Failing Fast

The task force began its private deliberations following the completion of public hearings on May 3, 1989. It was clear that the majority of Manitobans were opposed to the Meech Lake Accord. What was not so clear was the order in which they wanted changes made. In addition, there were different priorities among caucus members and among the caucuses themselves. There was, for the most part, a desire to come up with a Manitoba position to which we could all subscribe, and to that end all three parties put their political differences on the back burner.

This led to some strange bedfellows. Normally we faced one another across the floor and critiqued most of what each other said. Now we were forced to spend hours together hammering out an agreement. It led us to a better understanding of one another as human beings. But it also led me to be too trusting. Jim McCrae was in the most difficult position. As leaders, Doer and I could more or less speak for our caucus. McCrae always had to speak to the premier before he could agree to anything.

The meetings went on for months. The PC members were off-side with the Liberals and the NDP on the need to commit ourselves to a strong central government. The NDP was offside with the Liberals and the PCs on Senate reform. For me the protection of the Charter of Rights and Freedoms was the most fundamental issue, but it was clear that neither the NDP nor the PCs favoured the abolition of the notwithstanding clause.

The most innovative idea came from Jim Carr. As we tried to find ways to limit the power of the distinct society clause, Jim suggested that we needed a more inclusive clause, one that represented the whole country. This idea gave birth to the "Canada clause," which, in a much bastardized form, ultimately found its way into the Charlottetown Accord. The purpose of our Canada clause was to place in historic order those who settled this land and gave to it the dynamic known as Canada. We began our Canada clause with a recognition of our Aboriginal peoples, followed by the French, the English and the multicultural peoples, who came both before and after Confederation. Finally, the clause contained a commitment to the nation as a federal state. We deliberately used "unique" instead of "distinct society" for the francophone peoples because we knew that the latter phrase was interpreted negatively across the land.

We were ready to table our recommendations for reform to the Meech Lake Accord by the autumn of 1989. But Frank McKenna beat us to the punch.

In October of 1989, the New Brunswick Select Committee of the legislature tabled its report. New Brunswick was the only other province to go to a public hearing process. It essentially dealt a free hand to the premier, Frank McKenna, whose Liberal Party had control of all of the seats in the legislature. We were disappointed because, until this time, we had seen McKenna as an ally. It now appeared that he was capable of shifting with the wind. We presented our report the next day. While the Quebec media responded with some sympathy to the New Brunswick report, Manitoba's was vilified. Some interpreted it as a rejection of the Accord in its entirety. That is not at all the case.

Jim Carr had suggested to me and to the Liberal caucus that, out of courtesy to the other Liberal provincial premiers, particularly Ontario's David Peterson and Quebec's Robert Bourassa, we should deliver copies to them personally and explain why we made the recommendations we did. He and I made a quick trip to Toronto and Montreal, visiting the premiers and the editorial boards of *The Toronto Star*, *The Globe and Mail* and *Le Devoir*. This had been arranged some days before the report was officially tabled.

In Toronto we were asked to meet first with Ian Scott, the attorney general of Ontario, and then with the premier. In my experience there is no one more devoted to a cause than a new convert. In the case of the Meech Lake Accord, both Ian Scott and David Peterson had originally been opposed. However, they had now seen the light and, with the convert's zeal, intended to show those of us in opposition the error of our ways.

The opening meeting with Scott didn't go well. He was obviously part of a planned "bad cop/good cop" strategy of intimidation. He harangued us and, in my opinion, acted the role of a first-class bully. By this time Jim Carr knew this was the worst possible technique to use on me. As Scott became more and more aggressive in his arguments, I become more and more silent. Jim had to manage the discussion. I have a habit of retreating from conversations of this nature; my silence is my protection— otherwise I would blow my stack. By the end of the meeting I had completely tuned Scott out.

Then Jim and I were left waiting for almost an hour for the premier. While we were waiting I took a phone call from Clyde Wells, who told me we had not gone nearly far enough in our recommendations! It was clear that we were not going to lose him, at least, as an ally. When we finally had our meeting, David Peterson was warm and gracious, obviously enjoying his "good cop" role However, I was so incensed with Scott that Peterson might just as well have been blowing in the wind.

We moved on to Montreal. The next morning my staff alerted me to a cartoon in *Le Devoir*, whose offices we were to visit immediately after our meeting with Bourassa. The cartoon depicted the three leaders in the Manitoba legislature as members of the Ku Klux Klan. It is not widely known that during the Dirty Thirties, the KKK had an active presence in western Canada, particularly in Saskatchewan. In this country their hatred and bigotry has been directed towards Catholics, Jews and French Canadians. There I was, a Catholic by birth and training, born of a French mother accompanied on my trip by my Jewish deputy leader, being depicted in a cartoon along with the other leaders as a member of the KKK. To me it was clear that the purpose of the cartoon was to paint the three leaders in Manitoba as racists. The Quebec media is quick to take offence at any slight, perceived or otherwise, from English Canada. Nevertheless, they feel they can offend with impunity.

I was not prepared to tolerate this or any other accusation of racism directed towards me or the other leaders. I informed the publisher that there was no point in discussing the findings of the task force if a cartoon depicting its authors as racist reflected the editorial opinion of the paper. Presumably they had already made up their minds about Manitoba's position, so what was the point of further discussion? I asked for an apology, but it was not forthcoming, so I cancelled the meeting. Some of the media in Manitoba thought I should lighten up—freedom of the press and all that. I am the first to respect freedom of the press, and I have certainly come in for my fair share of nasty cartoons. But this one was inciting hatred, and I will not tolerate that.

The prime minister met with the other first ministers on the economy in November, at which time private discussions on the Constitution were held. David Peterson is reported to have told his caucus after this meeting that Filmon was prepared to move, but that I had a gun to his head. Filmon obviously thought he could sway the NDP if only he could get me to change my mind, but thought there was little chance of that. Senator Lowell Murray went on a cross-Canada trip to meet with the premiers individually. He made the mistake in Manitoba of also asking to speak with me, which resulted in the premier's nose being put out of joint. As a result, a meeting was held with members of the task force. We informed Senator Murray that, although ours was not an absolute bottom-line position, we had done most of our compromising during the task force meetings and there was not much further compromise possible.

The premier of Manitoba now began to make noises about a parallel accord, a proposal originally made by Frank McKenna. However, my position was that it didn't make much sense since it would have to come into force and effect at the same time as the Meech Lake Accord, so we might just as well amend that. The media made what it could of an apparent crack in the Manitoba alliance, but without much success. Of course McKenna's idea was that the parallel accord could take effect later, which meant literally passing Meech as it was, and that was unacceptable. Meanwhile, Bourassa, at the behest of the Parti Québécois, endorsed a resolution in the National Assembly rejecting any amendments or modifications to the Meech Lake Accord. Canada had arrived at a stalemate.

On March 22, 1990, the prime minister appointed Jean Charest to chair a parliamentary committee to examine the McKenna resolution regarding a parallel accord. Newfoundland, meanwhile, rescinded its approval of the Meech Lake Accord and made it clear that Manitoba and Newfoundland would be offside together.

Although the Meech Lake Accord dominated most of my activity, the federal Liberal Party was also in the midst of a leadership campaign. On Saturday, March 31, 1990, the leadership hopefuls gathered in Winnipeg for one of a series of campaign debates.

The day before the debate, Eric Maldof arrived in my office. I had known of Eric as the president of Alliance Quebec, an anglophone group in that province, but I had never met him personally. He was accompanied by Eddie Goldenberg, who was an active worker on the campaign committee to elect Jean Chrétien as national leader. They spoke with me about the possibility of breaking the deadlock on the Meech Lake Accord. They gave me a document that they wanted to have delivered to Clyde Wells, but according to them only I could get him to consider it seriously. They also said that he had not seen this proposal. I sent the document to Clyde and discovered two things: first, he had seen the document before and had discounted it; second, clearly Maldof was playing a double-agent game and was therefore not to be trusted. Eddie and I had been friends for some years and so I assumed that Eric had not given him the full story either. Eddie certainly denied knowing Wells had received the document previously. But I now suspect that Eddie was in full knowledge of what Eric was up to and was a willing participant in a strategy that would see me put pressure on Wells, without my knowing I was doing so.

It is impossible to separate the growing dissatisfaction of the people of Canada with the Meech Lake Accord from the Liberal leadership race. Sheila Copps and Paul Martin, two of the front-runners in the campaign, were in favour of the agreement. Jean Chrétien, who had a wide lead in delegate support over these two, was opposed. John Nunziata was also opposed, and Tom Wappel seemed to be sitting on the fence. By April of 1990 Lloyd Axworthy was no longer in the race and was now supporting Jean, although he had earlier been one of John Turner's strongest supporters, and Turner was a strong advocate of the Accord. In other words, the federal Liberal Party was in a mess over this issue.

During the leadership debate that weekend in Winnipeg the divisions became even clearer. But what struck me more was, once again, political sexism.

During the 1984 leadership race Monique Bégin, a Trudeau cabinet minister, had supported John Turner because she said Chrétien didn't have "class." The deeper implication was that he was somewhat sexist. She had been joined in this smear campaign by Judy Erola. But it was Turner who patted Iona Campagnola's bum during that election, an action for which he never believed he should apologize. Now both Paul Martin and Sheila Copps attacked my Meech position from the podium. I had not known I was a candidate, but their obvious ploy was to attack Chrétien through me. There they were, Sheila and Paul on a platform, telling Jean to get the Liberal leader in Manitoba onside. Since they were not making similar demands of Chrétien to get Wells and McKenna onside I could only interpret this as getting the little woman to fall into line! Talk about sexism. Under what delusions they were labouring I do not know, but Chrétien knew, as they should have, that I didn't take orders from him or anyone else.

I first met Paul Martin in Vancouver in 1986 when he was addressing a meeting of the British Columbia Liberal Women's Commission. He told his audience that when women enter politics they have to learn to think like a man. I challenged that view from the floor. I said that if women in politics had to think like men then there was absolutely no point in our participating. It is in bringing our own life experiences, experiences that are much different from a man's, experiences that represent 52 percent of the adult population of this country, that we make our true contribution! He obviously had learned nothing about me or the role of women in politics in the ensuing four years. As for Copps, I find it insensitive in a man to put down a woman, but unforgivable in another woman, particularly one who has experienced the same put-downs herself. In reality, Jean Chrétien was and is the greatest feminist of them all. At no time has he ever treated me as less than an equal, and that is all that I ask. I don't wish to be given special status, and my experience with Jean proved to me that he was gender-blind.

Manitoba Liberals were divided at this meeting. Some would have liked to have seen Axworthy on the candidates' podium, and I was blamed by many of them for his not being there. After six years of working around Lloyd but never with him, there was no way at all that I would support him. It was not my lack of support, though, that did him in. I am sure it would have helped if he had been able to show that his own provincial leader supported his candidacy, but this would have been a factor only if he also had wide public support among his federal caucus colleagues and Liberals across the nation. He did not. His inability to raise money was a smoke screen. Bill Loewen, now the president of the national party to which he has given $4 million of personal money but then the chief executive officer for Comcheq Services Limited, was prepared to raise the money. There simply was no support base.

The question of Lloyd's possibly throwing his support behind Jean Chrétien resulted in some interesting calls, and it shows, I think, the difference in style, not only between me and Lloyd, but between me and other politicians. I received a phone call from Eddie Goldenberg, who was negotiating with Tom Axworthy, executive director of the Charles R. Bronfman Foundation in Montreal, former principal secretary to Trudeau and

Lloyd's brother, about it. It was clear that because of my long-term support of Jean and also my problems with Lloyd they were not going to make a move without my approval. He told me that Lloyd wanted to support Chrétien, but there were certain conditions. The first condition was that Lloyd be recognized as the senior MP from Manitoba. My reply was that he *was* the senior MP from Manitoba. He then said Lloyd wanted to be made the critic for External Affairs. I replied that he would make an excellent critic. I went on to say that I had always admired Lloyd's ability and that, while I did not like him as a human being, I thought he was bright and articulate and had always done a good job in cabinet. The final condition was that he be made a member of the campaign committee. I replied that if this could help Jean swing even more support, then do it.

There was a long pause on the other end of the line. Obviously Eddie thought I would object to these conditions. However, I thought the name of the game was to elect Jean Chrétien leader, and it was no skin off my nose to do everything in my power to facilitate that victory. To say that Eddie was in a state of shock is to put it mildly, and he obviously didn't quite believe me because within two days I had exactly the same conversation with John Rae, current Ontario premier Bob Rae's brother and the chair of the Chrétien campaign. He, too, obviously did not believe me, or perhaps Chrétien wanted to hear it directly from me. Chrétien called and the conversation was repeated a third time. Jean finally asked me if I had any conditions at all. I told him that my only condition was that at some time in the future when decisions were being made about Manitoba I would like to be consulted. I did not ask for control over those decisions, I simply wanted the opportunity to have input. He agreed, but with my resignation that commitment is obviously no longer binding. It was clear that I did not play the power game as "the boys" did, perhaps to my peril.

Throughout the spring, as the leadership race dragged on, I participated in a number of national forums on the Constitution. In March I flew to Montreal to tape two segments of "The Journal." The participants were Claude Ryan, a Bourassa cabinet minister, Marc Lalonde, a former Trudeau cabinet minister, Brian Peckford, former premier of Newfoundland and signatory of the Meech Lake Accord, and me. It was clear that the CBC was taking a pro-Meech stand even then. It was also clear that Barbara Frum did not consider me to be in the same league as the other three, despite the fact that I frequently had background information she wanted that the other three did not have. I am devoted to the CBC, but it certainly aroused my ire in its treatment of Meech.

In April I attended a forum at Carleton University at which the panelists were Peter Russell, a political science professor at the University of Toronto, Al Johnson, a former federal deputy minister in the Pearson and Trudeau years and past president of the CBC, Monique Bégin, professor at Carleton and a former cabinet minister in the government of Pierre Trudeau, and me. I had not liked Monique since the days of the 1984 leadership campaign when I considered her comments about Jean's "lack of class" to be both false and in poor taste. During this debate she forever lost any respect I had left for her.

One of the issues that has bothered me so much during both the Meech and Charlottetown Accord periods was their attendant revisionist history. Quebec was most assuredly not left out of the Constitution in 1982. Quebec did not sign the constitutional agreement of 1982, but that did not make it any less a Canadian province than any other. Quebec did not sign because there was a separatist government in the province, and it was unlikely it would have signed any agreement short of a recognition of sovereignty association. It certainly continued to function as it had previously and made lavish use of the Charter's notwithstanding clause. I agreed with those who said some accommodation should be found with Quebec to make her feel more comfortable within the Canadian family. However, to say that it had not been considered part of that family in 1982 is simply false.

In this debate Bégin decided to rewrite Canadian history even further. She spoke of how shamed she had been in 1982 when Quebec, her province, had been left out. Here was a woman who

had been a member of Trudeau's cabinet, who had voted for the
constitutional package in the House of Commons, who was now
telling people how shamed she had been. I might have respected
her had she admitted, in hindsight, that she had made a mistake;
we all make those. But if she was shamed even then, as I wrote to
her later (a letter which has never generated a reply), she had the
God-given duty to resign from cabinet and to stand up for her
people. She did not, and indeed remained in cabinet until the
1984 election campaign. So much for principles!

The parliamentarians who worked on the Charest report,
examining the McKenna parallel accord resolution, were the first
to genuinely open the consultation process to those outside the
inner circle of first ministers. Not only did I hear from Lloyd
Axworthy throughout their deliberations, but also from David
Berger, a devoted anti-Meech crusader. My conversations were
not limited to Liberals. One day, to my astonishment, I heard
from Svend Robinson, the NDP member from British Columbia,
who wanted to assure himself that what was being said on my
behalf was indeed correct. As with the Manitoba task force
report, there was a genuine attempt on the part of the participants to find an agreement that we could all live with. The
Charest report was tabled on May 17, 1990.

The news reports of the day, after the report was read, clearly
showed an air of cautious optimism. The Manitoba leaders, plus
Clyde Wells and Frank McKenna who had, at this point, indicated they had problems with the original package (although
McKenna's position was far weaker in context than the others),
all expressed the opinion that it was a good starting point to
further the negotiations. Bourassa, as always, was cautious in his
comments. I had been led to believe, and so, I assumed had the
other Manitoba leaders and Clyde Wells, that Bourassa had been
consulted each step of the way, as we had been, and had given
tacit approval to the direction the Charest report had taken.

The optimism became irrelevant that weekend when Lucien
Bouchard, once a great friend of Mulroney's, stormed back to
Ottawa and resigned from cabinet. The prime minister literally
removed the Charest report from the bargaining table. It

appeared we were back to square one, and the deadline was June 23, 1990, for passage by all provinces. Manitoba and New Brunswick had never passed the Accord, and Newfoundland, because it had rescinded its original vote, also had to get it through its legislature. The days passed, and it was not until Sunday, June 3, 1990, that the first ministers were called to dinner in Ottawa. They had twenty days to come up with a deal, and I was to begin the worst week of my entire life.

fourteen

The Worst Week of My Life

During the week leading up to the first ministers' dinner at the Museum of Civilization in Hull, meetings took place on a fairly regular basis among the three Manitoba leaders. The paper flow between Ottawa and the provincial capitals was heavy, although different messages seemed to flow with the paper. Certainly I was of the opinion, one I believe shared by Filmon and Doer, that the documents we were receiving were proposals for a solution to the Meech Lake stalemate. Other premiers, including McKenna, appeared to have been under the impression that this solution was to be McKenna's parallel accord, with a commitment to negotiate these provisions after the deadline for the passage of the Meech Lake Accord. Had I known there was absolutely no intention on Mulroney's part to deal with changes at this time, I would never have gone to Ottawa. In retrospect I wish I never had. My dismay at this process was the reason I refused later to attend the meetings in Charlottetown. I was not going to get caught up again in a master game designed by the prime minister, to which only he knew the rules.

Filmon left for Ottawa on Sunday, June 3, and Doer and I were to join him the following day if the meetings were going to continue in the form of a first ministers' conference. Our plane was scheduled to leave at 5:00 a.m. Late Sunday evening I had a call from Filmon. He was discouraged, saying nothing had been resolved at the dinner meeting. He told me we should delay our flight since he would be in a meeting with the first ministers in the morning and we could not meet before 1:30 p.m., at which time he would brief us. If a formal first ministers' conference was to be held it would not begin until later in the day, he told me. As it turned out there never was a formal conference, and all the negotiations took place behind closed doors.

Doer and I, along with more of the premier's staff, arrived in Ottawa just before lunch on Monday. As the plane was taxiing to the arrival location, my cellular phone rang. (My cellular phone became part of my anatomy for the next week and led to several interesting problems. First, the premier told me at one point that my phone conversations were being repeated to him inside the meetings. It was clear that someone was listening in on my conversations, possibly the staff of the prime minister's office. Second, the phone led to a remark by pollster Angus Reid, who said that it made me look like Gary Filmon's secretary. It was an interesting comment, since Gary Doer was equally at the premier's beck and call, and yet he was not referred to as anyone's secretary.) On the other end of my cellular phone was Eddie Goldenberg, who asked me to come immediately to Jean Chrétien's law office. The enticement was a document that had been presented to the premiers that morning. According to him he wanted to make sure that I was fully briefed.

When I arrived for the meeting there were Eric Maldof, Eddie Goldenberg and a constitutional lawyer from Toronto. They made it clear to me that this document—a compromise proposal —was not acceptable, and they were fearful that Filmon would go along with it. As there was no real protection for the Charter in the document, it was unacceptable to me, too. I left, in order to meet with Filmon at the Chateau Laurier, but made arrangements to meet with Eric and Eddie later in the day at their suite, also in the Chateau Laurier.

Filmon was not upbeat about the two meetings held thus far —it was clear they were going nowhere. He seemed very reluctant to discuss the suggestions contained in the document Eddie had given me. I kept raising them, only to get blank stares in return. Finally he asked me what I was reading from, since I had the paper in front of me. I told him it was the document he had received that morning. He was livid. At first I thought he was angry simply because I had got hold of it and his nose was out of joint, but it quickly came to light that neither Filmon nor any of the other first ministers had seen this paper! I immediately committed to sharing with him every document I received. He was not as open in return. However, I believed the name of the game was to do the best we could for the country, and I was prepared to do everything I could to find a compromise, if one was possible.

When I met later with Eric and Eddie it was clear that Filmon had blown his stack at the meeting of first ministers that followed. Stanley Hartt called Maldof to complain that I had been given something which was strictly for Chrétien's eyes. Hartt knew better than that, but there were games within games being played. It was clear that the document had been prepared by the prime minister's staff for distribution, but for reasons known only to him he had withheld it. However, Hartt had given it to Maldof to use as he saw fit, and by giving it to me, Maldof had let the cat out of the bag. Maldof and Hartt were working closely together, but their strategy was to make me think that Maldof was my friend. One afternoon while in Maldof's suite at the Chateau I listened to one side of a phone conversation between Maldof and Hartt. The language was foul—at least on Maldof's part. I think I was supposed to be impressed by Maldof's defence of my position. In fact, because yelling and swearing have never impressed me, I left. To me it is just another example of male bullying.

My second stop that afternoon was at the Newfoundland government delegation offices on the second floor of the Conference Centre, located across the street from the Chateau Laurier. During this entire week the participants rarely moved outside of a two-block radius! They arranged a special pass for the meeting, as my pass entitled me to have access only to the first floor. (It was only later in the week that the colour of my pass was changed to allow me to move to the other floors.) I met with Deborah Coyne, Senator Eugene Forsey and other members of the Newfoundland delegation. I explained to them that I was at the meeting alone since I had been denied additional staff passes. It was essential, I told them, to keep in contact with me on a fairly regular basis. I told them I thought Filmon would capitulate if the pressure was great enough because he really wasn't, in his heart of hearts, totally opposed to the Accord. If Manitoba was to be kept as an ally I had to know what Wells was doing. After getting their assurances, I left.

I had only one other contact with the Newfoundland delegation, and that was a phone call that I made to them the next day, at Maldof's request, because he wanted to speak with them directly about some compromise proposals. Deborah Coyne was obviously unhappy with the source of the call; her tone was far less than cordial and we had no further conversation. This was unfortunate because it made a fundamental difference to my thinking on Friday, when the chips were down. It was clear they did not trust Maldof, but I had no choice but to maintain some relationship with him since he was the only source of information, other than Filmon, that I had.

I was totally alone that week. Members of Parliament with whom I was friendly were busy working on the various Liberal leadership campaigns and were not around. Indeed, while the lounge at the Conference Centre fairly overflowed with Tories and New Democrats, there were few, if any, Liberals. In addition to having no staff with me, my family was also out of circulation. This was the week of graduation ceremonies at Harvard University, and Cathi was graduating with an Honours B.A. (or A.B., as they call it). We were terribly proud of her achievements, and I desperately wanted to be with her. John had gone to Boston, along with his father, so she was not alone, but I still wanted to be there. As a result of the celebrations, John, my most important adviser, was also not available to me. He offered to come, but I felt that Cathi's needs were more important than my own.

I was forced to turn more and more to Maldof and Goldenberg, who I knew were more interested in protecting Chrétien than me, and with good reason. They both had their own narrow perspective. Both Eddie and Eric are anglophone Montrealers, and they see Canada from a Quebec point of view. While both are well

trained and educated, the dominant issue for them in any constitutional discussion is what happens to their home if Quebec
separates. That is obviously of concern to me, too, but it does not
dominate my thinking. I have dealt, in my own mind, with the
very real possibility that Quebec will leave Confederation. I have
also come to the reluctant conclusion that only the people of
Quebec can decide if they wish to remain a part of Canada, and I
am not prepared—have never been prepared—to have them stay
at the expense of the rest of the nation. Therefore, we brought
two very different perspectives to our discussions. They were the
only ones holding out the hand of friendship, though, and I
accepted it, with reservations. John Rae, chair of Chrétien's leadership campaign, was also frequently at the meetings we held, but
his usual contribution amounted to ordering me Earl Grey tea—
bless him. I think he alone understood the personal agony I was
going through each day.

The meeting on Tuesday, June 5, appeared to find Filmon in a
slightly better mood. I, however, could find nothing to take
comfort in when the meeting was reported to me. If anything, I
was losing more faith in the strength of Filmon's position. This
was the first night Filmon told me of polling going on in Manitoba. Apparently Manitobans were being polled nightly, and the
results indicated that they wanted a deal, and they would take
one if it was acceptable to all three leaders. Each night, I was told,
the results reflected this point of view at higher and higher
percentages. In the fall of 1991, after I had determined I wanted to
write a book about my experiences with the Meech Lake Accord,
I tried to get access to these poll results through Freedom of
Information in the province of Manitoba. I was informed that the
government had conducted no such polling. When I wrote and
asked the premier where these poll results were, he said that they
had been private party polls and he would not share the results
with me. If indeed these polls were conducted, something I now
seriously doubt, the Filmon government must be the only government in history to have paid for polls out of party funds when
they could have been considered a legitimate government
expense!

By Wednesday we had a collective bunker mentality. There we all were in our foxholes waiting for someone to fire a shot. For the most part the weather was lovely, and although that fact was totally irrelevant to the participants, it did encourage people to gather outside the Centre, hoping that a deal would be struck and they would be there at a moment of history in the making. The pervasive mood of those gathered was that the country would fall apart if the first ministers couldn't come up with a solution. Of course, this all played into the prime minister's game plan, which was to force a deal on the recalcitrant premiers. The media joined in the circus, uttering doom-and-gloom scenarios hourly. Occasionally there would be a report of a breakthrough, only to be followed by even more gloom when it was later announced that there had been no deal struck. Barbara Frum, during one of the interviews we were all constantly subjected to, actually asked me what it felt like to be responsible for the break-up of the country!

By Wednesday noon I was ready to leave and go to Boston. It was obvious we were getting nowhere. On Thursday morning, Gary Filmon actually told me he was sorry I was not able to be with Cathi. In all our years together it is about the only compassionate thing he ever said to me.

Thursday, June 7, was a crucial day for all of us. I was depressed because it was the actual day of Cathi's graduation. I spent part of the day wandering through shops looking for a special graduation gift and finally settled on several gold bracelets. I had not intended to buy her another gift, but was so disturbed that I wasn't with her I wanted her to know in a tangible way that she was always in my mind. At four o'clock, shortly after I returned to the Conference Centre, I was called to a meeting with Filmon. I thought I was told to go to the Chateau Laurier, but perhaps I just assumed that was where I was to go since all of our other meetings had taken place there. In fact I was supposed to go to the fourth floor of the Conference Centre, and everyone spent a half hour looking and waiting for me. When I arrived I found the meeting was not just with Filmon. Gathered on the fourth floor of the Centre were legal experts from across the country, as well as

Filmon, Wells and Doer. The meeting had been called to assure us that the wording of the distinct society clause had no meaning in law, but the "assurance" was farcical since no two of the lawyers had exactly the same opinion. I was far from reassured.

After the experts left we were joined by Bourassa, who again insisted, as he had done for months in private conversations, that he simply had no room to manoeuvre. It had always fascinated me that he said this with such a straight face, because he seemed sublimely confident that he was the only politician in Canada with his back to the wall. In his view, he was the only one whose electorate would accept nothing less than what they had been given. While I tried to understand his position and the strength of the nationalists in his province, I really never thought he had any notion that other premiers had similar problems. Perhaps that is what made him such a good negotiator. He simply blocked out the other points of view.

After Bourassa left, Wells, Filmon, Doer and I discussed the concept, not a new one, of a letter to be added to the Accord, signed by legal experts across the land stating to the courts that, in their opinion, the distinct society clause conferred no additional powers on the province of Quebec. We knew the letter would not be fully binding but would provide direction as to the intent at the time. Wells said we should get the letter signed by legal experts from all provinces, perhaps even the premiers. I told him I did not think he could get such a document because at about 2:30 that afternoon, while the first ministers met, I had been asked to have a private meeting with Gilles Remillard, Bourassa's constitutional minister. He had told me Quebec would not agree to the letter. Wells assured me he would get it, and with that he and Filmon went back to the meeting of first ministers.

I went into a state of shock when I was confronted by Joy Malbon, the CKY national reporter assigned to Winnipeg, shortly before midnight and told that Doer and I had said no to a deal the premiers had worked out that afternoon. I told her she didn't know what she was talking about. She explained that she'd got the story from Norman Spector and Stanley Hartt at the

PMO's news conference (held each night at the end of the day's events). CBC had bought the story hook, line and sinker and had featured it on their late-night broadcast. Joy knew me well enough to know that I didn't lie and that I was genuinely surprised. The CTV network did not repeat the CBC story, and they were correct not to. At no time during the afternoon session were Doer and I ever told that the first ministers had reached a deal. We thought we were being asked to provide Filmon and Wells with our opinions on the legal letter and any future positions they should take!

By the time I returned to my hotel room Thursday night I was exhausted, discouraged and angry. I phoned Eric Maldof and demanded he do what he could to arrange a meeting with Clyde Wells so I could learn first-hand exactly what had happened on the previous day at the first ministers' meeting. I did not contact Deborah Coyne. In her book about Meech, *The Rolling of the Dice*, she accuses me of "getting into bed" with Maldof and Goldenberg. To some degree she is correct. Unfortunately what she failed to realize was that I didn't "get into bed" with the Newfoundland delegation because I didn't think there was a bed for me there!

By 1:30 a.m. Friday, June 8, it was arranged that Wells and I would have breakfast in his suite at the Chateau Laurier about six hours later. It was rare during this week for any of the participants to have more than five or six hours of sleep. All of this led to frayed tempers and poor negotiating skills. The prime minister was using all of his skills as a labour negotiator, but we were not negotiating a labour-management contract. We were supposed to be coming up with a plan whereby Canadians could live in harmony together for generations to come. This was not the way to do it.

John Rae picked me up at my hotel at about 7:15 a.m. and we drove to the Chateau Laurier to be met by Goldenberg and Maldof. As we proceeded to the suite we were followed by television cameras. Obviously someone had notified the media of this "event." This was typical of the week. None of the participants could go anywhere without the media pack in hot pursuit. Clyde Wells looked as awful as I felt. He was tired and discouraged.

He told me that he did not believe the morning session would last very long, and he was prepared to tell them he was going back to Newfoundland if the stalemate continued. I told him that if he walked he could count on my support, as I would also return to Manitoba. I was convinced I would be back in Winnipeg that night. He also told me that the previous day had been one of the worst of his life. He said, "I will never let anyone do what they did to me last night." These words, and others uttered by Wells over the next few weeks, were the basis of the stories that he had broken down the previous night. Other stories circulated that he had been physically tackled by Don Getty when he tried to leave the room. My sense was that he had been browbeaten in a way he wished he had not, and he had lost his temper. Certainly I was told by many that he had cried. If he did it was irrelevant. The important factor in my mind was that on Friday morning he was more resolved to withstand the attacks of his fellow premiers than he had been the previous day, and I was prepared to support him in this.

I returned to the Conference Centre after the meeting and was besieged by the media, most of which had bought the CBC story that Doer and I had scuppered the deal. I told them one after another that no such deal had been presented to me. They did not, for the most part, believe me. After all, it was my credibility against that of the Prime Minister's Office and the mighty CBC. I remember one persistent reporter yelling, as I tried to end the scrum, "You simply cannot walk away when there is an obvious discrepancy of truth here." I told him that all I could tell him was the truth and walked away. Doer was being besieged in the same way, and gradually, as the morning passed, it was becoming clear we were telling the same stories, and there appeared to have been no contact between us. There was a grudging acceptance from some that perhaps we were telling the truth after all.

I waited and waited, hour after hour, for the meeting to end. When it didn't I gradually came to the conclusion that a deal was being made. Otherwise, I was convinced Wells would have walked.

Finally, at 5:00 p.m., Doer and I were called to a meeting with Wells and Filmon. The deal was placed before us. There was no written text, but the outline was clear. I was heartsick since it seemed to me that this deal was acceptable to both the Newfoundland and Manitoba premiers. It was at this moment that I specifically asked Wells, "Is this acceptable to you?" He said, "Yes." It was not a qualified yes. It was a one-word yes. Clyde Wells does not believe he said yes, or perhaps he doesn't even believe I asked the question. I know that I did, and I share the belief with Doer and Filmon that at that particular moment the deal was acceptable to Wells. This was the most significant moment of the week for me. I knew that Manitoba could not stand alone, I had known that from the beginning. Manitoba's history since 1890 regarding our francophone minority, which had originally been the majority of our province, was dismal. If we were the only province to reject this agreement we would be portrayed, once again, as a bigoted province. The Quebec media had portrayed us on many occasions, both during the Meech debate and the French-language confrontation of 1983, as prejudiced, and I knew that this unfair accusation would be levied again. That was not a legacy I could leave my children. As long as we were one of two, Manitoba could stand tall on this issue. Now it was impossible.

Wells left the meeting to negotiate further on the legal wording and to speak with his own delegation. Filmon, Doer and I agreed that we would support the deal. Filmon was required to return to the negotiations, and I was asked by the premier's press staff to alert the media that a deal was in the making. I was to warn them that no legal text was yet available, but the principles of an agreement had been worked out.

Of course I was not prepared for Wells to seemingly change his mind! I was so absolutely convinced in my mind that he had agreed to the deal that I either missed the nuances of what he said the next day or they simply took on new meaning as the days passed. When I left Ottawa on Saturday, actually early Sunday morning, I was convinced that Newfoundland was supporting this package.

Saturday had its own drama because of a clause missing from the legal text of the agreement. In fact it was not a significant part of the agreement, because it did not change the agreement to any great extent, but it seemed to give inspiration to Wells.

All that we had gained was a letter from legal experts stating that, in their opinion, the Charter had not been weakened. The letter had no real meaning in law. We also had the promise of Senate reform to take place some time in the future and a process by which the rights of our Aboriginal peoples could be recognized. It was better than what was on the table when negotiations had begun the previous week, but not by much. However, we had saved the country!

What a sham that was. It is hard for me today to relate to the feelings I had during that dreadful week in Ottawa, but at some point I, too, became convinced that the country would fall apart if we did not reach an agreement. All the media hype and the discussions I had with "ordinary Canadians" who stood at the barricades night after night in front of the Conference Centre made that appear to be the prevailing view among the people of this country. Now I know that it was all a misrepresentation, and more than anything else, it was this discovery that convinced me that this was no way to negotiate a constitution. We were all so out of touch with the feelings of the majority of Canadians.

Filmon wanted to leave Ottawa as soon as he could, and he asked Doer and me to be on standby to leave on the government jet as soon as possible after the signing of the agreement on Saturday night. Both of us wanted out of Ottawa as much as he did, and we agreed.

The signing ceremony began at about 10:30 p.m. As the premiers entered the room I reacted only to the arrival of Filmon and Wells and gave both a standing ovation. Despite my personal feelings about Filmon, I thought he had done the best he could during a difficult week. For Wells my applause was the loudest. They all sat down and the prime minister began to speak. He began with, "This is a great day for Canada." I immediately felt sick to my stomach and knew I had to leave the room or I would be physically sick at my seat. I left and went back to the hotel. I turned on the television set and muted the other premiers but listened to the speeches by Wells and Filmon. Despite his words—that he was going to let Newfoundlanders decide for themselves—I was still convinced Wells was onside. It was only in watching his press conference on his arrival in St. John's the next day that I began to have a feeling in the pit of my stomach that something was wrong.

Filmon, Doer and I boarded the plane to return to Winnipeg as soon as we could. On the plane we discussed strategy for the next few days. We agreed the House should sit as soon as possible; it appeared that Monday would not be realistic, so we would begin at 1:30 p.m. on Tuesday, June 12. Filmon's staff informed us that they had booked television time for each of us to speak to the people of Manitoba. I offered to take the first taping slot because Doer wanted more time to speak to his staff about his presentation. I would be writing my own on Sunday. I told the premier I thought I would have the majority of caucus onside, although I could not demand that all of them support the agreement. Gilles Roch had joined my caucus because of my stand on Meech, and if he saw our acceptance of the deal as a reversal, I refused to impose caucus discipline. Indeed, all members had been given a free vote and they would continue to have it, but I felt most could be persuaded to vote yes. The premier indicated that he had some members who would be difficult to convince, but since all three leaders were in agreement he would probably be able to persuade the others to also vote yes. Ironically, Doer was the only real optimist on board. He expressed the opinion that all of his members would be onside. As it turned out he was the one with the greatest numbers willing to jump ship almost immediately.

Drinks were passed around and, as usual, I refrained. Doer and Filmon finally fell asleep. I stayed awake the entire flight. My mind was not easy, and the exhaustion I suffered simply became more acute.

We arrived in Winnipeg in time for the sunrise. Obviously the premier's staff had done their homework and several hundred cheering Tories were on hand to welcome us home with, of course, the ever-present media. After I had completed a scrum, Al Munroe, who had, of course, come to the airport to meet me, drove me home.

Exhausted, sick at heart, but with a resolve to see this thing through to the end, I told my husband the highlights of the events of the week past. He made me some tea, my comfort food, and I tried to sleep. Finally, I got out of bed and proceeded to call each member of my caucus, asking them to meet me in our caucus room the following morning. There were several I couldn't reach, but the vast majority of them knew the contents of the agreement before we met Monday morning.

I spent the next hours drafting my words to the people of Manitoba, to be taped the following morning and broadcast Monday evening.

I arrived at the office early Monday morning so that Marguerite could type my speech on monitor paper in preparation for the broadcast. It would have been much easier if we had agreed to go to one of the television studios. The legislative staff did not have a proper monitor and their improvisation was not effective. I pride myself on my ability to tape a speech in one take. This one, which was so highly charged emotionally, we had to do over and over again. I was a walking zombie.

At the caucus meeting at 11:00 that morning when I began to tell everyone about the worst week of my life, I broke down. I struggled to gain control but it was difficult. I realized that most of my colleagues were confused. Some, like John Angus, were totally unsympathetic. However, my greatest disappointment was with Jim Carr. Jim and I had been in contact every day while I was in Ottawa. He alone should have known what I had gone through, but he stood in stony silence. It was only much later that I learned he had not been providing regular briefings to other members of caucus. I had assumed that our conversations had not been for his ears alone, but his to share with the others. For some reason, known only to him, he treated them as private confidences.

Several days later when I was somewhat restored, owing to a mild tranquillizer prescribed by Dr. Gulzar Cheema, I was in the CBC studio having my make-up done prior to an interview when

Mike McCourt dropped by to see me. McCourt was at this time the co-host of "24 Hours," the local 6:00 p.m. news show. Mike is a friend of both Otto Lang and Adrian Macdonald. He and his wife Lorraine had been at our home, and John and I at theirs. When he asked me how I was doing I took it as a friendly question and not the question of a news reporter. I replied I was doing okay, nothing that a few tranquillizers and some sleep wouldn't cure.

A week later, long after I had stopped taking the pills, Mike conducted a series of interviews with the three leaders about the impact of Meech week on us. One of my questions was, in paraphrase, "I understand, Mrs. Carstairs, you took some tranquillizers." I suppose I could have lied, but that is not my style. Besides, I thought it important that the people of Manitoba understand in full the impact of that week on all of us. I suspect if I had said I had had a few stiff drinks no one would have looked askance. But somehow or other my use of tranquillizers, coupled with the fact that I was a woman, had a negative impact the likes of which I could not possibly have imagined. To be fair to Mike McCourt, I do not think he thought his remark would raise the question of my suitability for public life. It was clear, however, that there was a double standard at play here. When Pamela Wallin had asked John Turner, several years before, if he had a drinking problem, within days the story had turned from Turner's response to the acceptability of Wallin asking the question. No one in the media questioned the acceptability of Mike McCourt asking his question. During this same interview I also expressed the feeling that I was not sure I wanted to remain in public life. Again this was seen as a weakness on my part, and the phrase "If you can't stand the heat get out of the kitchen" surfaced. I was dismayed by this reaction, and sick at heart.

It was not that I could not stand the heat; my diary for the week shows me at work every day and attending three or four events as well. I simply was not sure I wanted to remain in a profession where the ethics, in my opinion, had reached an all-time low. The NDP, in the election campaign to follow, actually broadcast a television ad with a woman answering, in response to a question, that she did not think she could vote for a woman who couldn't make up her mind whether to remain in public life or not. The public say they want their politicians to be honest with them. Surely part of that honesty is to portray our feelings, our doubts and our concerns. The lesson I learned was that this was not what the public wanted at all. They did not want a leader who expressed self-doubt, at least not if that leader was a woman.

Filmon, Doer and I met on Monday afternoon and it appeared as if the process of ratification would begin in the legislature on Tuesday, as planned. But shortly before the session was to open it became clear that the Aboriginal community—who had been opposed to Meech because it did nothing to further their goal of self-government—had found a way to delay the procedure, at least for one or two days. Proper notice for tabling the resolution had not been followed, and therefore the tabling would require unanimous consent. The Aboriginal community had persuaded Elijah Harper to refuse permission. In essence, this was a delaying tactic while they examined other legal options. I was approached by Jack London, legal counsel for the Assembly of Manitoba Chiefs, and asked if I would give permission to have the House rules regarding unanimity changed, and, if not, would Elijah at least be given the opportunity to make his statement without intimidation. I said I would agree to no change in House rules, and if Harper could use the rules to his advantage so be it.

When the three leaders met on Tuesday, June 12, Doer was convinced that the delay would only be for two days. He also explained that Elijah was a most reluctant participant in all of this, but the chiefs were putting enormous pressure on him and he was caught between loyalty to his party and loyalty to his people. All of us were annoyed at the clerk of the Assembly who, along with the Speaker, Denis Rocan, and his assistant Rick Mantey, had given us incorrect information on procedure and had thereby allowed Elijah to do what he did. Some of the Tories went so far as to accuse Harper of legislative terrorism.

My caucus was very divided. Kevin Lamoureux had come to see me on Monday evening to express his personal concern for me as well as his desire to work to ensure the caucus was united behind me. I told him they could have my resignation if they wanted it, but I considered it a slap in the face that they had insisted I go to Ottawa when that offer had been made by Filmon, and I had taken it to caucus for their approval, and now they would not accept my judgment. When I read the papers the next morning I found that two of my MLAs had told the media they would vote no and four others were said to be uncomfortable with my decision. Because events were to unfold that took the decision-making right out of the hands of the MLAs, we never held a formal vote in caucus, and to this day I do not know how many would have voted no on the final day. I do know that Gulzar Cheema, one of the confessed doubters, came to tell me he would do whatever I asked of him. To my delight and surprise, Gilles Roch, who had joined my caucus on the issue of Meech Lake, came to see me to say he trusted my judgment and I could count on his support, even though he had earlier said he would vote no.

On Wednesday, June 13, what should have been the second day of debate in the Manitoba legislature, once again denied by Harper, Jim McCrae, Gary Doer and I were invited to speak with the Manitoba chiefs at a conference at Fort Garry Place in Winnipeg. When McCrae tried to leave the meeting because he had another engagement, he was physically barred from doing so. We were told in no uncertain terms that the chiefs would do everything in their power to block the passage of the Accord in the Manitoba legislature. It was already clear that hundreds of Aboriginal people had registered to attend public hearings. Jim Carr, on my behalf, announced to the media at the legislature that no vote would take place until everyone had been heard.

This meeting was also the first time I observed the support network the Aboriginal community was now providing Elijah. He was always accompanied by members of Aboriginal police forces. There were always members of his community in the gallery of the legislature supporting him when he would answer

"No" to the question, "Is there unanimous support to proceed with the debate on the Accord?" He was never without his eagle feather, even though, technically, this was a violation of House rules since we were not allowed to use props of any kind. But no one was about to suggest the removal of the eagle feather. Elijah Harper was the first Aboriginal elected to the legislature of Manitoba and the first to be appointed to cabinet. While to this point he had been relatively ineffective, during this week he became a different person. With the support of his people he gained in stature and maturity. He no longer spoke for himself but for them, and he became quite eloquent. It was like watching the transformation of a person before your eyes.

It was now clear to most knowledgeable observers that it was unlikely we could pass the Meech Lake Accord before the deadline.

Once again I had to assure Jack London, clearly to his astonishment since he came back again to ask the same question, that I would do nothing to thwart any legitimate attempt to delay the process. Even though the agenda was changing I wasn't changing my mind. No longer was this a French or Quebec issue, it was an Aboriginal issue. No longer did I feel Manitoba would be portrayed as bigoted. The Aboriginal people were taking hold of the agenda, and my fears about accusations directed towards Manitoba had disappeared.

I was concerned for Robert Bourassa. It appeared to me that the federal government was totally discounting the effect the Manitoba chiefs were having on the process in Manitoba and I believed Bourassa should hear first-hand what was happening. I placed a call and, to my astonishment, he immediately came on the line. I told him exactly what I thought was happening, and that I did not believe the Accord would pass the Manitoba Legislature by June 23. He told me, "Sharon, this conversation has not taken place." I presume he did not want the prime minister to know he was getting information from me. I said I would respect that and have, until now. Whether or not this conversation had anything to do with the arrival of Senator Lowell Murray in Manitoba, resulting in a promise of a royal commission on Aboriginal issues, ultimately rejected by the chiefs, I do not know.

By Thursday Jack London had found another way to delay the procedure in the Manitoba legislature. It appeared we had not given the required time for translation of the notice of the resolution, and the House could not begin deliberations until Wednesday, June 20, 1990, three days before the required deadline of passage.

By Saturday, June 16, I had said to the media that I supported the Aboriginals in killing the Accord.

The morning I made that statement I woke as usual to see my husband placing the *Winnipeg Free Press*, *Winnipeg Sun* and *The Globe and Mail* on my bed prior to making breakfast. It is a family tradition for me to be served breakfast in bed, and it's one of the many ways my husband has spoiled me over the twenty-seven years of our marriage. He is a morning person, one of that disgusting breed who wakes up bright-eyed and bushy-tailed with enthusiasm to get on with the day. I am much slower to rouse, and breakfast in bed was one of his ways to get me to talk to him. I usually start with the *Sun*, move to the *Free Press* and spend the majority of time with the *Globe*. At any rate, that morning began normally.

I am not a screamer, but after beginning to read an article by Susan Delacourt in *The Globe and Mail* I let out a blood-curdling yell that brought my husband running from the kitchen. I had read, as thousands did that day, of the prime minister's master plan, his "rolling of the dice." It was clear that the choice of timing of the meetings by the prime minister was to guarantee a pressure cooker atmosphere. Arguments were made that changes couldn't be made to the document because there simply wasn't enough time. Those who opposed would have to accept the document as it was. Any belief on behalf of those opposed that genuine negotiations were to take place was clearly an error and they would have to eat their principles. All of the agony I and so many others had gone through the previous week had all been by design. He had deliberately allowed the negotiations to go to the bitter end. I no longer felt I had any responsibility to any of the players in

Ottawa. If the Aboriginal community could defeat the Accord they not only had my full support, but my help if I had any to offer.

The following day I had a bodyguard assigned to me as a result of a death threat. Someone had phoned my office and threatened to kill me because I had capitulated on Meech. I suppose this should have been more of a worry, but it was simply an inconvenience.

Throughout the week I had contact with Newfoundland, primarily with Clyde Wells himself. He wanted to believe what I was telling him, which in essence was that the Accord would fail, but he was getting contrary information from Ottawa.

On Thursday, June 21, the premier came to my desk in the legislature to tell me that the prime minister wished to speak with the three leaders at approximately 5:30 p.m., and would I please meet him in his office. I told him I didn't really want to speak with the prime minister and he grimaced in agreement. But I went anyway. When the call was put through it was not the prime minister, it was Senator Lowell Murray. Once again we were told we must suspend the public hearing process and pass the Accord the next day. Doer and Filmon politely informed him that that was not possible. I gave up all pretence of politeness, and when it was my turn, I, who rarely swear, said, "There is no God damn way, Lowell." We were told the prime minister was at that moment meeting with Clyde Wells and that Newfoundland would be passing the Accord the following morning. When I arrived home my husband was holding the phone. Clyde Wells was on the line calling from St. John's, where he and the prime minister had just had dinner. Clyde told me that Mulroney had told him that Manitoba would be holding its vote tomorrow, and if Newfoundland voted no it would be the odd province out. Obviously Mulroney was playing both sides off against one another. I once again assured Wells that no vote would be taken in the Manitoba legislative chamber. He, in turn, told me that in his opinion the free vote in the Newfoundland legislature would result in rejection of the Accord. His concern was how he would know what was happening in Manitoba the following morning. I told him we would keep a phone line open between my office and his from the moment the Manitoba House opened until it closed, and that either I or Jim Carr would phone him personally when we adjourned.

On Friday, June 22, 1990, at 12:30 p.m., the normal time for adjournment, Elijah Harper refused permission to extend the session. We adjourned and, according to House rules, would not sit again until Monday, June 25, at 1:30 p.m. The Meech Lake Accord had failed to be ratified by the deadline in the legislature of Manitoba.

The media were jammed into the foyer outside of the legislature, as they had been all week. The premier stepped to the microphones to explain, from his perspective, what had just occurred. I was in line waiting my turn. My secretary, Marguerite Martin, came to drag me out of the line; Clyde Wells wanted to speak with me.

He was furious at the most recent ploy of the federal government, which was the announcement by Lowell Murray that they could delay the process further for Manitoba because our House rules had made passage impossible, but, of course, it could not be delayed in Newfoundland. I told him that the premier of Manitoba was already on record as saying this was not a valid option and that I would be commenting in the same way. The federal government was prepared to try every trick in the book. The Meech Lake Accord had been passed in the Quebec legislature on June 23, 1987. This is what had started the three-year process. According to provisions in the Canada Act, it became invalid if it was not passed by the House of Commons and all ten legislatures by June 23, 1990. Indeed there was some question that it had to be passed by June 22, 1990, since June 23, 1987 had counted as a day so June 23, 1990, could not.

Wells told me that he did not believe Newfoundland should even hold its vote, and I agreed. If Newfoundland said no then it would definitely be seen as a rejection of Quebec, and all their anger would be directed towards that province, since it would be argued that Manitoba would have voted yes if it had been given sufficient time. If, on the other hand, Newfoundland voted yes, then all the anger and bitterness would be directed against Manitoba. It was my opinion, and also that of Wells, that we should hang together in this and have the anger directed against both provinces, particularly as it was no longer clear to me that there would have been a yes vote in Manitoba if one had been taken. Wells announced his decision in the Newfoundland Assembly that no vote would be taken because Manitoba had been unable to vote. The Furies were loosed.

John Crosbie, the Newfoundland federal minister, accused Wells of breaking faith, as did Mulroney at every opportunity he could find over the next few days. Gary Filmon, who could have protected Wells and accepted some of the blame for Manitoba, did nothing. At a press conference the next day he stated that each premier had to make his own decision. I was disgusted. The leaders in Manitoba had worked so closely with Wells, and it was unthinkable, in my view, to hang him out to dry like this. However, it obviously suited Filmon's and the prime minister's agendas to do precisely that.

After the phone call with Wells I told Jim Carr about what was going to happen in Newfoundland, and then took questions from the media. I was incensed at the pressure tactics of the PMO over the previous twenty-four hours, and I pulled no punches. I spoke of my absolute lack of respect for all who worked there, from the prime minister down. Jason Moscovitz, in an interview for CBC radio news during Meech week in Ottawa, had asked me if I should not show Brian Mulroney more respect because of the office he held. I responded that you only get the respect you deserve, and he deserved none. I was even more convinced of this on June 22, 1990.

Meanwhile, there was the federal Liberal leadership convention to be dealt with. It was being held in Calgary from June 21 to 25. On Friday, the second day of the convention, Jim Carr, Neil Gaudry and I left the legislature and flew by private plane to Calgary. As we were all Jean Chrétien delegates, we wanted to be there in time for the candidates' speeches, which were to take place that night. We arrived in Calgary tired and in no mood to attend a convention.

Upon our arrival, I was again mobbed by the media, who were asking me to explain what had happened in Manitoba and what the future held with respect to the Constitution. Al Munroe and John whisked us away from the airport—they had arrived earlier in the week—and took us to the Stampede Grounds to register. As I entered the convention floor more media swooped down and followed me to the Chrétien box. In retrospect I realize I should not have sat with Chrétien and his family, as I was now a political liability for him. He must have known that, but he put friendship above the politics of the hour and greeted me warmly.

I had hoped to be of use to Chrétien that day but I was too exhausted to do anything but give the occasional cheer. It was clear he had the delegate support. His speech was received with thunderous applause, although, in my opinion, it was not as good as the speech he had given in 1984. (That speech had been panned by Senator Keith Davey, the Liberal guru, who was supporting Turner. Why anyone took his opinion on the speech seriously, considering he had already taken a personal stand in support of Turner, I never understood, but they did.) This 1990 speech was safe, and if it didn't swing any votes, it didn't lose him any either.

The day was over: Meech was dead; Chrétien looked like a sure bet. These two things would have thrilled me once, but not now. Since I had fought so hard against the Meech Lake Accord I suppose I should have felt some satisfaction. Instead my overwhelming feeling was one of disgust with the process of constitutional reform and a dislike, so deep and abiding, of the prime minister that it coloured my view of him forever. My respect for Wells, who had confused me in those last few days at Meech, was not diminished. I simply was not capable of judging what had been going on in his mind. I knew he had done the best he could. All of us are human and all of us, on occasion, make mistakes.

The following day Jean Chrétien was elected leader of the Liberal Party of Canada. I had worked for this since 1984 and should have been elated. I was pleased for him and the party, but I was now in a state of unease, a state that would last for the rest of 1990. The Meech Lake Accord had claimed me as a victim, and I had lost confidence in myself and my decision-making abilities.

John and I returned to the Calgary Delta Inn to celebrate the result but didn't go to any of the parties. We had a quiet dinner together and went to bed. It was such a contrast to the 1984 convention. Both of us had worked so hard on the convention floor during that race. We had been caught up in the hoopla and were devastated for Jean when he lost. We were delighted he had won in 1990, but elation was simply not there.

fifteen

A Question of Influence

The next day we came home. If I had been thinking clearly I would have taken some time off. I was concerned with the prospect of a fall election, though, and rushed ahead, working to ensure that all was in place to achieve victory for the Liberal Party in Manitoba. My plan was to work through July and begin holidays on August 5, for two weeks, in the hope that I would be rested for a campaign to begin after Labour Day.

During the weeks following Meech week in Ottawa, the premier made a commitment to both Doer and me that he would not call an election until the fall. I still have the handwritten memo, which I copied to all of my MLAs following my meeting with Filmon, in which I told them of his promise and declared that I thought he could be trusted. He obviously was of the belief that "all is fair in love and politics," because he announced the election on August 7, 1990, which by no one's calendar could have been considered the fall.

The campaign was a disaster from start to finish. On Wednesday, July 18, I met with Ernie Gilroy, my campaign chairman, Jean Paul Boily, who as my executive assistant was to be the day-to-day manager of the campaign, and the representatives from McLaren Advertising in Toronto, who were putting the final details together for our media strategy. Among the things we approved that afternoon was the poster of me to be used in the campaign. But I hated it and I still do. Unlike the one we used in 1988—a black-and-white picture taken by Eric Hope, an amateur photographer, that showed me smiling from ear to ear, this one was in colour, and I had a severe, set look about me. In my opinion I look almost grim. The rest of those in the room loved it, and I was clearly outnumbered. I was even more dismayed when they told me they had mechanically fused the body from one picture and the head from another, and wasn't it a wonderful job! To me this epitomized the whole campaign, which can best be described as disjointed.

Shortly after the 1988 election we had spent a great deal of money having Arthur Gillman conduct a rather avant-garde poll to measure the moods and impressions of the electorate rather than actual voter support. The information that he put together, all valid for the fall of 1988, was the basis for the strategy of our 1990 campaign.

But of course everything had changed. Filmon was no longer considered a wimp and I, on the other hand, had sacrificed my principles, according to the Manitoba electorate. Manitobans from across the province would stop me for the next year and tell me how much I had let them down in Ottawa. I would say to them, "You mean all the leaders." Their reply was always, "No, you." They would go on to say, "We never trusted the other two, we trusted you, and you let us down."

The television ads were all to portray me as strong and Filmon as weak, particularly in his relationship with Mulroney. Again, this no longer rang true with the voters.

The final blow came when Ernie Gilroy announced he would be stepping down as campaign chairman to run in the Wellington constituency. David Walker took his place. Walker was the member of Parliament for Winnipeg North Centre. Like all the other Manitoba MPs (with the exception of Axworthy), had been able to piggyback on our electoral strength in April of 1988 to win his seat in the November 1988 federal election. David had a great deal of experience in campaigns, having chaired several of Axworthy's, and he did the best he could. It was simply not ours to be won.

Perhaps the greatest deficit to the campaign was me. I had been the strength of the 1986 and 1988 campaigns, but this time I was the weakness. I had lost confidence in my own ability. I knew the strategy was wrong at that July meeting, and I told them so. In other campaigns I simply would have insisted it be changed, but this time I went with the flow, and I was wrong.

I was in Ontario the morning of August 7. John and I had gone to Minaki Lodge to celebrate our twenty-fourth wedding anniversary on August 6. There had been rumours about the call, but the more favoured date seemed to be August 21, so I thought it was safe to leave. Darrell Neufeld, my press officer, called early in the morning to say the election call was almost certain, so John and I left immediately on the three-hour drive back to Winnipeg. We heard the actual announcement in the car. Everything had been arranged, so our kick-off, which took place early that afternoon at the Holiday Inn, went off without a hitch. Hundreds of Liberals gathered. We had the cheering crowd, I wore my newest acquisition (yet another red suit), and the press releases were issued. It was the last thing that would go well for us until the dying days of the campaign.

David Walker decided that the thrust of our campaign should be the economy. Announcement after announcement called for new strategies on the economy—more money for skills training, smarter spending and curtailment of government waste. The major problem with this thrust was that economic issues are considered Tory issues, and also male issues. The media couldn't figure out why the female Liberal leader kept talking about economic issues, appearing to be to the right of the Tories. The public couldn't figure it out either—and worse, neither could I. However, I dutifully gave the speeches, but without my usual spark or enthusiasm. Donald Benham wrote an article in which he depicted me as being aloof not only from the issues but also from the people. He said that after a press conference I had turned away from a group of people who had wanted to speak with me as if I had not even seen them. He was right, I had not! But his article made me rethink what I was doing. I once again took possession of the campaign agenda, but by that time it was too late. Although, if our internal polls were correct, it did prevent the campaign from sliding still further.

I refused to make another economic announcement and demanded the remaining media events be related to social issues. It was at this point that we announced a centre for midwifery in the province. We also announced that we would establish a Literacy Corps. Though patterned on the federal Company of Young Canadians program of the 1960s, it would be provincial and would focus on literacy training for those in the public school system experiencing difficulty in learning to read. Those who were accepted as tutors would be given an honorarium of $100 a month for a year of service, plus free tuition for the following year at the post-secondary institution of their choice in the province of Manitoba. This was the old Sharon. The media responded, and once again I saw smiles on the faces of voters.

Nominating candidates in 1990 was a relatively easy procedure throughout the province. We had a base of twenty sitting MLAs who were seeking re-election. The only exception was our twenty-first MLA, Gilles Roch, who had crossed over to us from the PCs in 1988. Gilles decided it was unlikely he could win his riding because the boundaries had changed for all fifty-seven constituencies, including his. This should have been to the Liberal Party's advantage since two fewer seats would be located outside of Winnipeg and two more would now be located in the city, and we were primarily an urban party. However, Gilles's rural riding had literally been cut in two. One of the potential seats in which he might choose to run had become even more Tory in its demographics, and local Liberals decided they did not want him to be the candidate in the riding with the stronger Liberal demographics.

As in past campaigns, I tried to go to as many rural constituencies as possible during the campaign. The urban media criticized that because they felt I should have targeted ridings in Winnipeg, where we had electoral strength and where we had to obtain more if we were to form the government. However, they failed to realize that I had a motherly attitude towards all of my candidates. The Liberal Party, the candidates and the members were all part of my extended family. If anything, I felt a greater obligation to those running in rural Manitoba than I did to those in Winnipeg. After all, the Winnipeggers had a chance of winning! Like a good mother, I had to be with those who needed me more.

I insisted on a tour that would take me, at least once, to every riding. It was gruelling, and I was still suffering from deep-seated exhaustion as a result of my Meech experience. At one point the organizers decided that, rather than use the campaign bus, it would be quicker if I travelled in a mobile home. What a disaster! Not only did I become car-sick in the back of the mobile home while trying to conduct an interview with Dan Lett, a reporter with the *Free Press*, who had been assigned to the Liberal campaign, but our driver lost his way on the back country roads! Fortunately Al, who was always to be trusted, was watching out for me. He was supposed to have gone cross country to meet me several stops down the road. However, he didn't have complete confidence in my young driver and had followed us. When he realized the Young Liberals on board the mobile home had us completely lost, he shot ahead and directed them to our next whistle-stop. At that point I left the mobile home and travelled with Al for the duration of the trip.

Once again Jean Chrétien came to lend his support. He too had been battered by the Meech Lake Accord. Following his election as leader of the Liberal Party of Canada, the Quebec press had been vicious, one paper going so far as to call him a Judas for his opposition to the Accord. His participation in the Manitoba campaign, by my side, was not going to help him in Quebec, but once again he put friendship before politics.

Neither he nor I had the enthusiasm of other campaigns and, as he told me the night of the election, he knew that the support that I'd had in 1988 was simply not there. The spirit, he said, was gone.

It was during Jean's trip to Manitoba that Ontario's election was held. To everyone's shock and surprise, Liberal David Peterson went down to utter defeat, even in his own riding, and the NDP were elected with a majority government despite having only 38 percent of the popular vote. This had an instant impact in Manitoba. New Democrats who had voted Liberal in 1988 because they felt that casting an NDP vote was wasted, or because they were furious with their government over Autopac, decided they could return to the NDP fold.

But the worst moment of this campaign for me came after the televised debate. I was the first leader to leave the studios, and I was met outside by a group of Young Progressive Conservatives, all in their teens. They began to chant "Filmon, Filmon" as I was leaving. But that wasn't all. They crowded around me, making it almost impossible for me to get into the car, and even after I was inside, they banged on the car with their hands and their signs, shaking it and damaging it. It was absolute hooliganism and a sign, in my opinion, of the Americanization of our political and social system. This kind of violence is becoming more and more acceptable in Canada.

On election night, September 11, 1990, I went as usual to my headquarters in River Heights to watch the returns. My personal victory was announced, but I was filled with despair as Liberal after Liberal was defeated. The election results in Manitoba were interesting, if devastating to me. The Tories formed a majority government with 41.86 percent of the popular vote, an increase of only 3.59 percent from the previous election. Indeed, only 158 more votes were cast for the Conservatives in 1990 than in 1988! Their majority was caused by a low voter turnout. Many of those who voted in 1988 because they saw an exciting phenomenon occurring simply did not vote in 1990. There were 46,587 fewer ballots cast in 1990 in a province with relatively stable population figures.

The NDP increased its popular vote by 5.15 percent, obtaining 141,328 votes or 28.72 percent of the popular vote. The Liberal vote had declined by 7.37 percent, almost all of it lost to the NDP. However, we still had 28.07 percent of the popular vote, only .65 percent behind the NDP. The NDP had received 3,182 more votes than the Liberals, but with these votes were able to elect twenty members to our seven! It made me believe even more strongly in a proportional representation system for Manitoba and Canada.

We were grossly underrepresented in the Legislature, and the Tories and the NDP were overrepresented. However, the name of the game was seats, and the media has never made reference to the popular vote, only to the number of seats, since that time. Some of our losses were particularly tough. Five ridings were lost by less than 300 votes, four of those by less than 118 votes, and all were a direct result of the upsurge of NDP votes, shown by our polling to be the result of the NDP victory in Ontario.

I felt very sorry for the MLAs who lost, and I took personal responsibility for some, if not most, of the defeat. Had I taken more time to rest, had I not lost my confidence in my own ability, the campaign would have been structured differently. Hindsight is a wonderful thing. I am not sure, in the end, if I could have done it any differently at that time.

The media stories all depicted us as having suffered a great defeat. This for a party who six short years before had a popular vote of 5.54 percent. The party was not as strong as it had been in 1988 but, other than the 1988 election, it was much stronger than at any time in its history since 1966.

The one media story about election night which infuriated me was written in *Maclean's* by Bruce Wallace. He wrote, "Later, she burst into tears during an encounter with reporters and had to be led away."[4] I am dismayed that when men cry it is seen as a sign of tenderness (remember Wayne Gretzky in tears when he was traded to the Los Angeles Kings; and Jake Epp had a tear in his eye when he recently retired). However, when a woman cries it is always considered a sign of weakness. Yes, I was in tears, but I certainly did not "burst into tears." Practically everyone I spoke with that night was in tears, and I followed suit. To say that I was led away as if I were a child was unfair, insulting and untrue. It is all, unfortunately, rather typical of the way women are portrayed in the media.

The following morning our much-reduced caucus met in the caucus room, which would soon be transferred, because of the numbers, to the NDP. It is fair to categorize all of us as downhearted, but my colleagues were all very supportive of me, for which I was grateful.

John and I decided immediately to take a trip to Bermuda. We had planned to return to our honeymoon island the following summer to celebrate our twenty-fifth wedding anniversary, but we both thought the trip was needed now. I had some thinking to do as to my own future and that of the Liberal Party in Manitoba.

Leadership of a political party requires of the leader a constant re-evaluation of the ability to lead. The questions are clear-cut. Do you have the loyalty of the caucus and the party, and will the public look to you in the future to form a government? These were the questions I was to put to myself during our ten days in Bermuda.

My primary concern was for the members of caucus. These were the men—unfortunately they were all men after the 1990 election—with whom I would work on a daily basis until the next election campaign. Was one of them ready and able to take over the leadership? Not really. Reluctantly I had come to the conclusion that, although Carr was the one I would feel most comfortable with in terms of policy direction, I did not believe he was prepared to devote the hours necessary to rebuild the party as I had done. The party was, and still is, fragile. It needed constant stroking in terms of personal visits by the leader to constituencies all over the province in order to add to its growth and strength, and this was not where Jim Carr's priorities lay.

I also looked to Paul Edwards as a potential successor. Paul, too, had been elected in 1988 and, in addition to being an MLA, practised law on an almost full-time basis. He is a prodigious worker, often dedicating late-night hours and weekends to the job. He, too, is a family man with three young children. The problem with Paul was that he was only twenty-nine years old in the fall of 1990, so if I was to retire and he was to succeed, the question of the electorate would invariably be, "Is he old enough to hold the office of premier?"

I decided that I would remain, continue to rebuild the party and examine my leadership in each of the following two years to measure our popularity and myself as an asset or a liability to the Liberal Party in Manitoba. Meanwhile I would try to give the remaining members of the legislature a higher profile.

This was easier said than done. Politics in the western world has become more and more leader-fixated. The media wants its sound-bite every day, and in their minds the best story of the day is generally the one that comes from the leader. The only stories credited to backbenchers are those related to scandal, usually their own! Cabinet ministers can still get coverage of a new announcement, but, in my experience, the media would prefer to get the response from the leaders rather than the opposition critic. The game becomes even more tricky if one of the leaders responds. They are considered the more "senior," so the critic for the other party is often ignored. This attitude on the part of the media is particularly pervasive during Question Period. Time after time, while I was leader of the opposition, I tried to give the lead questions to members of my caucus. The reaction of the media was invariably that if I had not asked the question it could not have been very important! As a result the caucus insisted I take the lead questions since they wanted us to generate as much publicity as we could. But then I was vulnerable to accusations of not grooming a successor. It is a dilemma that I, for one, have not yet resolved.

It was during this period, as well, that many people approached me to seriously consider entering the federal arena. Most observers thought that there was a strong possibility that the Liberals would form the next federal government. Some assumed that, on the basis of my close friendship with Jean Chrétien, I would probably be asked to join the cabinet. Jean Chrétien and I have had only one conversation about my running federally, and at no time was it ever suggested I could participate in any cabinet he formed. I made it clear during our conversation that I had no desire to enter federal politics. He respected my reasons for making the choice I did.

In Canadian politics and in the minds of Canadian voters, there is a hierarchy of political service. For some reason understood only by the voter, you are considered most important if you are a federal politician, least important if you are a municipal politician and somewhere in the middle if you have chosen provincial politics. This is a true tragedy since it means the "lower" levels are frequently used as a training ground for the others, and service to these so-called lesser levels of government is coloured by a politician's future political ambition.

I personally chose provincial politics because of the issues involved. Education, family services, health care—these are all delivered by a provincial government, and these are the issues of most fundamental concern to me. It is not that I am uninterested in Canada's foreign, trade or defence policies. It is simply that, on a scale of priorities, they fall far short of where my primary interests lie. I was also not interested in living apart from my husband. Our life together is number one on any scale I have for the important things in my life, and I was not prepared to sacrifice that closeness for any ambition.

However, the media speculation continued. Each time Jean Chrétien and I met, one or more of the media would ask if we had discussed my entry into federal politics. I told them honestly and straightforwardly that no, we had not. The media speculation even continued after it became very clear that one of the Liberal MLAs, Reg Alcock, would be seeking the federal nomination in Winnipeg South, the riding touted as being the one selected for me. The media now went so far as to say he was a smoke screen for me.

This media game is simply that, a game. In their speculation pieces they write as they please, giving credence to rumours they hear, from goodness knows where, and the public buys into it. I cannot remember how many times I have been asked when I was going to announce I would be running for a federal seat. In addition to my reservations based on the fundamental issues of family and policy, I would never have put Jean Chrétien in the very difficult position of having to explain my presence to the media of Quebec. I want Jean Chrétien to be the next prime minister, and I, for one, will do nothing to hurt his achieving that goal. This county needs him. His friendship, clearly shown, is enough for me.

When the legislature reconvened in October of 1990, the NDP were now the official opposition and Gary Doer the leader of the opposition. They now experienced many of the same problems we had faced in 1988. A number of their previous cabinet ministers—Jay Cowan, Bill Uruski, Maureen Hemphill and Harry Harapiak—had chosen not to run in 1990. Many of the new members elected had no experience and, like many of ours in

1988, had no expectation of winning; neither, might I add, had their party! They were now the amateurs, and we the experienced members of the House. They were not, however, examined with the same close scrutiny as we had been, which I considered unfair. Perhaps it was because everyone knew they had a full four years or more to grow. Our growth was expected to be instant because of the minority government and the possibility that the government could fall at any time. They have been given the opportunity to grow by both circumstance and the media.

In January 1992, Jim Carr announced that he was resigning from the House to accept an appointment to the editorial board of the *Winnipeg Free Press*. I was not surprised that he left, but his method of leaving disturbed all of us in caucus. There had been some warning of his movement to civic politics, but he dropped this bombshell on me forty-five minutes before he held a press conference! Some of the caucus members learned only minutes before the public did. It was clear that Jim was going through a mid-life crisis, having reached his fortieth birthday. He was questioning, on an almost daily basis, what he was going to do with the rest of his life. This was a wonderful opportunity to return to his first love, journalism, to receive better remuneration than he received as an MLA and to have the kind of family life he and his wife desired. It is hard to fault someone for these reasonable ambitions. But from my perspective, as one who was still trying to rebuild a party, it was disastrous. How was I to attract new candidates when one of those perceived as being the closest to me was quitting? In the media's minds this had to mean that Jim felt that the party was going nowhere.

Media speculation heightened with the rumours of Alcock's running for a federal nomination. This is in stark contrast with the media treatment of the NDP, however. They, too, have recently lost two members: Elijah Harper resigned in the fall of 1992 to pursue other ambitions, and their deputy leader, Judy Wasylycia-Leis, has just announced she is resigning to seek the NDP nomination in the federal riding of Winnipeg North. There has not been a single speculative piece on what this means for the NDP! Apparently they are still not subject to the same scrutiny as the Liberal Party. There was not even any comment when it became clear that Elijah's new move was to accept the Liberal nomination in the federal constituency of Churchill.

In spite of all the adversity, I was far happier in my role as leader of the third party in the House than I had been as leader of the opposition. No longer did I feel bound by the rules imposed on the official opposition, those which required us to be critical of everything the government did. I again had the opportunity to be the positive opposition I had tried to be from 1986 to 1988. In the minds of the voter, those in opposition oppose every single thing the government does. The reality is far from it. Most of the bills passed in the Manitoba legislature and in Houses throughout this country are passed with unanimous consent. Much of the legislation is housekeeping—the upgrading of legislation so that it meets the standards required by the day. Even policy issues of the government, if they are perceived to be reasonable, are supported by all parties. However, these events are not newsworthy. The events reported to the public are those in which we are shown as opposed. As a third party you have the unique opportunity not to "just say no" to everything noteworthy but to side with the government on some issues and with the official opposition on others. This is a particularly advantageous position for the Liberal Party since we are, by policy affiliation, between the other two.

I was much more comfortable and confident in this role. I only wish I had had the courage to play this role more often when I was the leader of the official opposition.

sixteen

The Charlottetown Accord

I was elected to the Manitoba legislature in March of 1986. From April of 1987, with the Meech Lake Accord approved by all eleven first ministers, the Constitution dominated the lives of provincial and federal politicians until October 26, 1992. Five and one-half years of this country's creative energies were directed towards a goal that created nothing. While Canadians were, throughout most of this time, going through the greatest recession in sixty years, and while those same Canadians were faced with changing global trading patterns and the need for retraining and evolving social patterns, the politicians—me included—could not get their heads out of the sand of constitutional wrangling. What a waste! Why did we do it?

For me it was primarily the impact of the ego of Brian Mulroney. Canadians have debated the Constitution throughout most of their history, and yet there were no real fundamental changes to it between 1867 and 1931. The Statute of Westminster in 1931 did create a fundamental new direction when Canada, for the first time under the Constitution (or the BNA Act), took control of her external affairs. However, the substantive change was gradual, and in 1931 Canada simply had constitutional control of something she had been taking practical control of, gradually, since 1867. That is, in my opinion, constitution-making at its finest, a gradual and very careful evolution.

Several times in our history, serious and almost successful attempts to patriate our constitution—to bring it home from

Britain so it could be amended in Canada—were made. The Fulton-Favreau Agreement in 1965 almost made this final step towards our total sovereignty possible. It failed because Quebec rejected it. There was no gnashing of teeth or threats to leave the country; it simply did not work out, and the players decided to try again sometime in the future. In 1970 the first ministers tried again at a meeting in Victoria; once again it was thought success had been achieved, and once again it was rejected by the province of Quebec. We heard so much in the Meech Lake Accord about how the rest of Canada was rejecting Quebec, but the media spoke little of the historic fact that the Fulton-Favreau and Victoria formulas had been accepted by the rest of Canada but rejected by Quebec! That is constitution-making: sometimes you win and sometimes you lose.

Finally in 1982 the pieces were put together. A constitutional deal was struck, albeit without the approval of the government of Quebec. It was really quite a simple agreement. Canada would bring the British North America Act, our constitutional document, home to Canada and rename it The Canada Act. At the same time we would place within this Canada Act a Charter of Rights and Freedoms, one almost identical in tone and content to the Quebec Charter of Rights and Freedoms, and we would have an amending formula.

Our history tells us that, while the Quebec members of the National Assembly did not give approval to this document, which was hardly likely since the majority of the day were separatist, seventy-four of the seventy-five Quebec members of Parliament voted for this constitutional agreement. In addition, polls in the province of Quebec supported both the inclusion of the Charter and the patriation of the Constitution. A little-known part of this history was that, in the first instance, it was not only Quebec that said no. Manitoba also rejected the agreement, and, ironically, if they had continued to maintain that position, the case could never have been made that Quebec had been left out of the Constitution. History would simply have shown that eight provinces said yes and two provinces said no. However, since the new amending formula now required that, in order to pass an amendment, approval must be reached by seven out of ten provinces representing at least 50 percent of the Canadian population, the agreement had met the test for ratification. The Supreme Court of Canada had ruled that under the British North America Act the federal government could act unilaterally and without the approval of any of the provincial governments, although they had tempered their judgment with the recommendation that it would be better if the federal government had the approval of at least the majority of provinces. Manitoba changed governments in November of 1981, and Howard Pawley and his new government approved the amendments that would constitute the new sections of the Canada Act.

After the 1982 amendments went through, there was general agreement that the Constitution could be put on the back burner for some time. Pierre Trudeau, the prime minister of the day, spoke of a hiatus of at least ten years.

Within two years Trudeau had resigned and been replaced by John Turner, who was, in turn, defeated by Brian Mulroney. For reasons fully clear only to Mulroney himself, the prime minister decided to open the constitutional can of worms once again. I am personally convinced that his ego was so great that he convinced himself he could do what Trudeau had been unable to do—make a constitution with the full support of every province, an almost impossible task. Donald Johnston, a Liberal member of Parliament from Montreal, a Trudeau and Turner cabinet member until 1984 and an opposition member until 1988, has said often that in the period between the patriation of the Constitution in 1982 and the striking of the Meech Lake Accord on April 30, 1987, he did not receive a single letter from a constituent demanding changes be made to the Constitution! The idea of changes to the Constitution seemed to be primarily the brainchild of Brian Mulroney, prompted by his desire to upstage Trudeau.

It must be remembered that Mulroney had forged a very strange alliance in his bid to become prime minister. There was virtually no Progressive Conservative Party in the province of Quebec. He, therefore, joined forces with the Quebec nationalists and, as a result, had an agreement with them to obtain a new deal for the province. This alliance was not understood in other parts of the country. Had it been, I venture to suggest he would never have been given the support he received in western Canada in 1984 or 1988. Westerners, rightly or wrongly, have little patience with the desire of Quebec for more power or special status.

Having failed with the Meech Lake Accord and having torn the country emotionally apart over it, one would have thought the prime minister and the media would let sleeping dogs lie. However, circumstances had taken on a life of their own, and it was this dilemma that led to the revival of the discussions, and eventually the Referendum, following the agreement known as the Charlottetown Accord.

In February 1990, the Quebec Liberal Party, under Bourassa's leadership and with his approval, created a task force to be known as the Allaire Commission, to study the Constitution. This was a deliberate move to put pressure on the first ministers to forge an agreement on the Meech Lake Accord. All politicians knew that any recommendations made by this group would call for more power to be given to the province of Quebec than that proposed in the Meech Lake Accord. The red flag waving was a threat: "Give us Meech or we will ask for more."

There was, however, another way to look at this commission, and it concerned me. This was the interpretation that Meech was simply the Liberal Party of Quebec's first step towards greater and greater power and independence. There was a naiveté among first ministers. They seemed to believe that if Quebec obtained what it wanted through the Meech Lake Accord it would then go away satisfied, and Canada could go happily into the twenty-first century without further constitutional wrangling. My opinion was that if Quebec obtained all they wanted in the Meech Lake Accord this would simply whet their appetite, and demands for more power would quickly follow. Allaire substantiated my thinking in spades.

Jean Allaire went out and listened to the people of Quebec, particularly those in the Liberal Party. When he made his report in late January of 1991, recommending broad new powers to the province of Quebec, it was accepted by the provincial party, including its leader. Allaire and those who had worked with him had every right to expect their views would be reflected by the leadership of the party. Robert Bourassa was playing with fire when he gave Allaire the powers that he did, and further, he in no way repudiated Allaire's report, despite its recommendations for powers that no one, including, I suspect, Bourassa, ever thought Quebec would achieve. For example, the report recommended giving Quebec exclusive authority over agriculture, unemployment insurance, the environment and health and language. In fact, the only areas in which the federal government would have exclusive control would be defence, customs, currency and common debt, and equalization. Indeed if they had achieved those powers Quebec would have been virtually a sovereign nation. Claude Ryan, a Bourassa cabinet minister and the former leader of the Quebec Liberal Party, understood the fire they were playing with and did his best to block approval of the Allaire report during the meeting of the Quebec Liberal Party in the spring of 1991. However, Bourassa supported it. Why, therefore, was he surprised, or indeed disappointed, that Allaire rejected the Charlottetown Accord and fought against the Referendum? In Allaire's mind it didn't go far enough! This is what happens when leaders fail to influence the course of events at the right time.

Giving the people of a country or province the right to participate is fraught with problems. If politicians tell the the public they can make presentations, and they will not only be listened to but their majority views carefully considered, then politicians must honour their promise. If Canadians are offered a referendum and told their vote will count, then their expectation will be that the politicians will respect the process. But apparently politicians will do whatever they like, regardless of their promises. The population of Canada is cynical about politicians, and politicians, in my opinion, are primarily responsible for this!

Leading Canadians to believe their expectations would be met was also going on at the federal level. In November 1990, the prime minister commissioned Keith Spicer to find out what Canadians wanted from their Constitution. The mandate of Spicer's Citizens' Forum on Canada's Future was to seek out the opinions of ordinary Canadians on what this country's problems were and how to solve them. Of course, the politicians had no real intention of listening to these opinions unless they coincided with their own ideas! Canadians know that at least $25 million was spent on this giant think tank. The jobless were scornful of this massive expenditure when they needed employment, and their opinion of elected officials sank even lower than usual. Still, many Canadians chose to participate in this project—16,000 in Manitoba alone. They set up discussion groups; they contributed their ideas and their concerns; and they were devastated when they learned that no one was really listening.

Spicer's report indicated that the overwhelming concern of Canadians was their dislike of the prime minister! His words were, "There is fury in the land against the prime minister." It is quite mind-boggling that, given that sentiment, the prime minister still thought his government had the mandate to negotiate the Constitution.

It was clear from the presentations to the Citizens' Forum that the majority of Canadians felt that no province should have special status. The presentations documented over and over that Canadians wanted equality of all Canadians, and yet the commissioners recommended that the Constitution give special status to the province of Quebec. Is it any wonder the voters are turned off by the political process?

The commissioners also recommended settlement of land claims for Canada's Aboriginal peoples, a review of bilingualism, a new focus on multicultural grants to ensure immigrants are provided with the skills necessary to adapt to Canadian life, programs to reduce racism, reform of the Senate and House of Commons and the elimination of waste in government. Some of these found their way into the Charlottetown Accord, but in far different forms than those recommended by the citizens of Canada.

Since nothing concrete in the way of an "offer to Quebec" had resulted from the Citizens' Forum, Mulroney established yet another committee. To my mind he was once again practising the strategy we had seen during Meech—pretend that something is going on when it really isn't, meanwhile move closer and closer towards the deadline. The deadline for this round was a more artificial one, May or October of 1992, the dates Bourassa had set for a referendum in Quebec on either a new offer from Canada or sovereignty!

In the fall of 1991, one year before the deadline set by Quebec, the prime minister announced that Senator Claude Castonguay and Dorothy Dobbie, member of Parliament for Winnipeg South, would head a Special Joint Parliamentary Committee for a Renewed Canada. It was a fiasco from day one, but it was a wonderful delaying tactic on the part of the prime minister. Once again Canadians would be asked to participate. Once again the final results would not be what the people of this nation said they wanted.

In reality, because of our constitutional amendment process, the only real negotiating committee of importance is the one made up of the first ministers. They are the ones who must take an agreement back to their provinces for passage. Since they were unwilling to give up their authority to a constituent assembly or the Citizens' Forum, the question was, why were they not meeting now, rather than awaiting yet another committee report? The answer was strategy. They were to be brought to the brink yet once again.

Members of the Castonguay-Dobbie committee quickly decided they were educators and gave themselves the mandate to explain the position of the government to the people, rather than to listen. When the media reported the concerns expressed by P.E.I. citizens to the Castonguay-Dobbie committee regarding the distinct society clause, they were chastised by Dorothy Dobbie! In a presentation in Toronto, Sheldon Godfrey, appearing on behalf of the Ontario region of the Canadian Council of Christians and Jews, normally considered a highly tolerant organization, found himself subjected to attack when he made the statement, "We must not allow cultural groups in any part of the country to be more equal or less than equal. To create a distinct society in any part of the country could have that effect." This modest statement from the council resulted in committee members wanting to bar him from speaking further! Two of the Tory members of the committee wouldn't even stay to hear the presentation. It was clear that members of the committee were only willing to hear what they believed, not what Canadians wanted to say.

The committee's arrival in Manitoba was not well planned. Notices of meetings went out barely days before their arrival, and, for the most part, there was no time for preparation. I asked to appear before the committee but was denied. The reason given was that the Manitoba Constitutional Task Force, on which the Liberal caucus had a member, was going to appear. But since the task force had not yet developed its stance, it would essentially have nothing to report, and the committee knew this. I wanted to speak on behalf of the Liberal Party. Neither Gary Filmon nor Gary Doer had asked to appear and, therefore, I was to be denied! The committee finally agreed to pay my way to Ottawa, along with that of the other two leaders, in order to hear my presentation there. It was an example of how badly organized they were that Manitoba political leaders would not be heard in Manitoba but would have their way paid to be heard in Ottawa. I accepted some months later. The committee did have the time, in Manitoba, to hear from Patrick Riley, who, along with D'Arcy McCaffrey, had established in 1990 a two-member group called Friends of Meech Lake!

When the committee moved to rural Manitoba, the lack of careful planning became evident. When they arrived in St. Pierre they were greeted by a completely empty hall. The Right Honourable Joe Clark immediately ordered the committee back to Ottawa for reorganization.

It was clear the committee was in chaos. What I found fascinating was that all the blame was directed towards the anglophone co-chair, Dorothy Dobbie. Why was Senator Claude Castonguay not criticized for his part in this fiasco? Was everyone so afraid of Quebec that criticism of a Québécois francophone was now off limits? The calls for Dobbie's head were loud and clear, but there was nary a word against Claude Castonguay, who eventually resigned, citing ill health, and was replaced by Senator Gerald Beaudoin. Finally, on March 2, 1992, they tabled their report. In my view and that of most Canadians, it did not reflect the perspectives of the thousands of Canadians who had participated.

The Dobbie-Beaudoin report recommended the inclusion of the distinct society clause in the Charter. In other words, not only would a designated "distinct society" not be subject to the Charter (my major concern during the Meech Lake debate), but now the Charter would be interpreted in a way consistent with the distinct society clause. Whereas there may have been some question as to whether the distinct society clause in the Meech Lake Accord would weaken the Charter, now it was perfectly clear that this was its intent. I knew at this moment that if this became acceptable to the first ministers, then I would fight any such agreement with every breath in my body. I had sacrificed my principles on the Charter once, in the dying days of Meech week in Ottawa, and I vowed I would never do it again. If it cost me my political career, so be it.

The report also called for a massive shift in powers from the federal to the provincial governments under the guise of efficiency. I do not believe there is a single Canadian who would oppose efficiency, particularly if it meant reduced taxes. However, there is a difference between efficiency and the dismantling of the federal government's ability to be involved in decision-making. Programs should be directed by those closest to the people, often municipal and provincial governments. However, the funding of those programs, and most importantly the policy thrust of those programs, often requires de facto intervention from the federal government. It is only the federal government that can assure a level of service somewhat equal across the country. It is only the federal government that can guarantee that citizens from Newfoundland to British Columbia to the Territories are given the same opportunities to maximize their talents and abilities. Air and water flows, for example, do not recognize artificial lines drawn on a map reflecting provincial boundaries. So the federal government indeed has a legitimate role in setting national standards on the environment.

Education, often seen as a wholly provincial responsibility, must have a federal thrust. The need for nation-wide testing, skills standards and equivalency standards is becoming more and more evident in this country. We must stop looking to the Canada of 1867 and to narrow provincial agendas and recognize that Canada is part of a global village. The parochialism of the last century in areas like education must disappear. The Dobbie-Beaudoin report called for further responsibilities in education to be given to the provinces, a backward step. The administration of all education programs should be provided at the provincial level, but to entirely eliminate the federal presence is inane.

The report did recommend the recognition of the inherent right of our Aboriginal peoples to self-government, and this was its most positive aspect. On Senate reform the report was very weak. While it recommended that the Senate be elected by a system of proportional representation, it said nothing about the powers of the Senate or the equality of its representation.

Obviously as a sop to the Tories on the committee, the report recognized the entrenchment of property rights in the Canadian Charter. This led to an interesting exchange between myself and Jake Epp.

Jake Epp was, at this time, the senior federal cabinet minister from Manitoba. He asked to meet with me and members of my caucus the day the Dobbie-Beaudoin report was tabled in Parliament in order to explain to us personally, as he would to the other two caucuses in Manitoba, the provisions contained therein. I agreed, and we met in my office. When I questioned him on the practicality of the inclusion of property rights in the Charter, Epp admitted that there had to be something in the report for Tory supporters.

Just as the meeting was breaking up, Jim Carr and Jake Epp entered into a dialogue about the extension of the river walkway from The Forks, a wonderful Winnipeg development project at the junction of the Assiniboine and Red Rivers undertaken by the three levels of government. The walkway was to be continued from The Forks to the legislature, but five landowners were refusing to donate their land without certain conditions being met. Most had insurance and liability concerns, not payment concerns. Epp and Carr were in full agreement that these businesses were not acting in a responsible manner. When I pointed out to Epp that this was exactly what property rights were all about, he seemed shocked! It has always fascinated me that people, including politicians, can always "understand" an issue as long as they are not personally affected.

Finally, the report called for a so-called economic union and a social charter, both so nebulous in their definitions as to be mostly meaningless.

Meanwhile, yet another committee on the Constitution was at work in Manitoba. Shortly after the election in 1990, Gary Filmon had announced the formation of a Manitoba Task Force on the Constitution. The purpose of this group was to put forward Manitoba's concerns on changes to the Canada Act. Manitoba wanted to have its desires clearly stated prior to the presentation of a federal deal. In this way it would not find itself reacting to some other report or deal as it had been forced to do with the Meech Lake Accord. This committee would have only one representative from the Liberal Party, and I asked Jim Carr to do it since he had been part of the 1989 Meech Lake task force. The NDP were represented by Oscar Lathlin, an Aboriginal member of the legislature, and Jean Friesen, both new members to the process of constitutional reform. The government members were Jim McCrae and Darren Praznik, both members of the Meech Lake task force, and Shirley Render. The chair was once again to be Wally Fox Decent. Significantly fewer Manitobans made presentations to this task force than the previous one, but their comments about the future direction of this country were almost identical. It was clear Manitobans had not changed their opinion about what kind of country they wanted since Meech Lake.

The real battles took place behind closed doors when the participants on the committee hammered out the report. The final recommendations called for either the abolition of the Senate (a sop to the NDP) or its replacement with a new chamber that would be more equal, elected and effective. It also stated that the Aboriginals' inherent right to self-government would be recognized within the Canadian legal structure, a difficult agreement to obtain from the Tory members. The Canada clause would recognize the distinct society of Quebec but, as with all other aspects of the Canada clause, it would be subject to the Charter. Finally, the report contained the recognition of the need for a strong central government while at the same time recognizing the need for efficiencies.

I insisted that a Liberal minority opinion be expressed in the report to the effect that the notwithstanding clause should be removed from the Charter of Rights and Freedoms. Neither the NDP nor the Tories supported this position. However, it was my signal that I would tolerate no further weakening of the Charter. To the contrary, I wanted the Charter to receive additional protection. Why anyone was later surprised by my position on the Referendum I do not know. I suppose they were simply revealing their lack of awareness of what was happening in Manitoba.

The Manitoba report was tabled on October 28, 1991. It was in many ways antithetical to the Dobbie-Beaudoin report.

In the spring of 1992 it was finally decided that the first ministers, or their representatives, should meet to discuss the report. Robert Bourassa had refused all along to meet with the first ministers or their designates as a result of the Meech Lake Accord's failure, and he maintained that position. I urged Gary Filmon not to allow our government to attend any meeting on the Constitution without the presence of Quebec. However, my opinion was discounted. The way I saw it, we were once again playing the game by Quebec's rules. Everyone was prepared to admit that the failure of the Meech Lake Accord was, for the most part, attributable to the fact that it had been perceived by Canadians to be a deal for Quebec only. With great fanfare the Charlottetown Accord was now being touted as "the Canada Round," and yet one of the major players in Canada, Quebec, was not to be at the table.

What a fool's game they were all prepared to play. The very fact that Quebec was not at the table made that province the most important participant. Quebec, and Quebec alone, was in the advantageous position of rejecting everything that was decided. Anyone close to the negotiations knew that, while the province was not an active participant in the sense that it did not take its seat, its spirit was pervasive. No discussion took place without someone at the table saying, "Would this be acceptable to Quebec?" So Quebec dominated the debate in ways it could not have if it had been at the table. Once again it was calling the tune.

Back and forth to various meeting sites across the country went Jim McCrae, Manitoba's Justice minister and the Minister Responsible for Constitutional Affairs, as did the representatives of other provinces. Week after week he made reports to the Manitoba legislature that were effusive in their expressions of good will but totally lacking in concrete proposals. Always we were assured that Manitoba's delegation was not deviating in its commitment to the task force recommendations. Finally, in July, the first ministers themselves gathered in Toronto. Upon his return from this meeting Gary Filmon provided the opposition leaders with the first bits of actual documentation.

Incredibly, this document, entitled *Status Report, The Multilateral Meetings on the Constitution* and stamped "Personal and Confidential," was shortly thereafter released in full, and indeed in more detail, in *The Globe and Mail*. In other words, opposition politicians were again being provided with less information than the media, either deliberately or by design.

In the meeting my caucus had with Jonathan Scarth, principal secretary to the premier, and other members of Premier Gary Filmon's team, a number of questions were raised. My overall concern was that the Charter did not appear to be appropriately protected. I was assured by Scarth and Greg Yost, the legal adviser, that, despite what the Status Report said, the distinct society clause was not going to be in the Charter. Out of concern and the desire for clarity, I asked Brian Bohunicky, a member of my research staff responsible for the Constitution, to write to Jonathan Scarth to obtain further clarification. This letter was sent on July 14. In addition to concerns with respect to the Charter, the Liberal Party also asked for clarification concerning the following provisions: gender protection for all Aboriginal peoples; the powers of the Senate, particularly with respect to the initiation of bills but also concerning the double-majority rules; the legal impact of equalization payments; a broader definition of the Canada clause; and a further explanation of the provisions concerning the devolution of powers from the federal to provincial governments.

The lack of adequate explanations for these provisions would become my fundamental arguments during the Referendum campaign. However, they should not have come as a surprise to the Filmon government. I was still prepared to support the government if they brought home a document that fully met the aspirations expressed by the people of this province. However, I also wanted the government to clearly understand where the Liberal Party thought this document fell short. I did not want the premier getting any-last minute surprises from me or my party.

On July 22nd I received a letter from Jim McCrae, Manitoba's constitutional minister. It read in part, "I should point out that Manitoba did not endorse the release of the 'final' Status Report in its current form. We felt that, in at least two areas—the references to the Canada Clause and Charter, and the references to Established Programs Financing—the summaries did not reflect our understanding of the consensus on those subjects." This suggested to me a repeat of the paper shuffle we had been subjected to during the week leading up to the meetings in Ottawa in June of 1990. It was clear then that the federal government was not giving provinces the same information nor relaying information correctly from one province to another. This letter prompted my concern to the extent that I released it to Don Campbell, a *Winnipeg Free Press* reporter. Since it was not marked "Confidential," I felt at liberty to release it. I knew this would damage my relationship with McCrae, and it did. He refused to release other documentation. However, I believed it essential to warn the people of Manitoba and Canada that the Meech Lake games were being played all over again. Documents were being released, and were portrayed as official and as having the approval of governments, when this was simply not the case. Regrettably, no one seemed to think there was anything seriously amiss.

Bourassa finally agreed to rejoin the negotiations, and a deal was struck during first ministers' negotiations held in Ottawa between August 18 and 22. Many stories have been told of Filmon using his calculator to work out numbers of seats in the House of Commons and Premier Bob Rae borrowing a lap top computer from the Native Council of Canada to work out the wording on the Aboriginal clauses. But what has not been given the time I think it deserves is this question: By what authority did the first ministers come to agreement on issues never before discussed with the Canadian people, and further, why did they expect the Canadian people to buy into them? In none of the committees or discussion groups among Canadians that I know of was the guarantee of 25 percent of the seats in the House of Commons being granted to Quebec in perpetuity ever discussed. Why, then, were the first ministers so shocked when the people of British Columbia rejected this outright? Canadians had consistently demanded a strong federal government, and even the prime minister was somewhat surprised at the giveaway to the provinces during the meeting of premiers in July! Why did they think Canadians would be any less so? The people of this country demanded the equality of all Canadians, and although both the Spicer report and the Dobbie-Beaudoin report called for special status for Quebec, it was against the expressed views of Canadian citizens. The first ministers were not speaking for the Canadian people. They were speaking for themselves. This was not "the Canada Round," this was "the Premiers' Round"!

I was at our cottage on Saturday, August 22, when I received a call from the media reporting that a deal had been struck in Ottawa. My first question was, "What has happened to the Charter?" When they reported to me that it appeared that the Charter would be subject to and interpreted in accordance with not only the distinct society clause for Quebec but also with the inherent right of our Aboriginal peoples to govern themselves, I knew that I would have to oppose the deal. This document would do what was abhorrent to me: establish classes of Canadians citizens, the antithesis of what I believed the Charter of Rights and Freedoms was all about. As soon as I finished my media call, essentially saying I had concerns but would reserve full comment until I had received a copy of the document, I phoned all of my MLAs. Some I did not reach until the following morning but most heard from me on Saturday night. I told them I would not be supporting the Charlottetown Accord. They could vote as they pleased since they had a free vote, as they had had on the Meech Lake Accord.

I was particularly concerned for Neil Gaudry. Neil represents the constituency of St. Boniface, where the majority of Manitoba francophones live. The Société Franco-Manitobain would, I was confident, come out in favour of the agreement. Their primary concern is the protection of the French language in Manitoba, and they understand that if Quebec is no longer a part of this nation then the chances of Canada remaining a bilingual country are minimal. This colours their thinking, and I wanted to assure Neil that if he felt required to represent this point of view he should cast his vote accordingly.

It was not yet clear that there would be a referendum, although I had come out fully in support of this concept soon after the failure of the Meech Lake Accord. I personally felt I had misjudged the feelings of the Canadian people in June of 1990, and I was not willing to ever put myself in that position again. Since the people of this nation would have to live by this document for generations to come, they, and they alone, should have the final say on its ratification. The Referendum was announced by the prime minister on September 3, 1992. It would be held on October 26.

During this period there were two by-elections being fought in Manitoba. Ed Connery, a former Tory backbencher fired from his cabinet position by Filmon, had resigned his Portage la Prairie seat in the spring, and the constituency of Crescentwood had been without a member since Jim Carr's resignation to join the editorial board of *The Winnipeg Free Press*. Both by-elections were called for September 15, 1992. This was in the early days of the debate on the Charlottetown Accord, so it did not play a major role. However, the by-elections gave me a number of media opportunities to make my position on the Charlottetown Accord clear. With Avis Gray being elected in the constituency of Crescentwood, the Liberals won back the seat we had previously held. The Tories held on to the riding of Portage la Prairie.

On September 11, I announced that I would be leading the "No" forces in Manitoba while, at the same time, my MLAs would be free to vote as they pleased. Even if the Referendum had passed, it would still require passage in the House of Commons and legislatures because that is what the amendment formula requires. I felt that all citizens should vote as their consciences dictated, including those who were elected to office. I also stated that Izzy Asper was prepared to bankroll the "No" campaign. I pre-empted Izzy on this, although he had not asked me to refrain from using his name when he told me earlier in the week that this was what he was prepared to do. However, I did not suspect that he would receive phone calls, one in particular from John Turner, warning him about the negative impact such a stand would have on his corporate affairs. I, too, was subjected to this kind of pressure.

In early October I received a letter from George Richardson, President of James Richardson and Sons, Limited, informing me that he would not donate to the Liberal Party in Manitoba in 1992 because of the position I was taking in the Referendum campaign. He wrote: "The proposed agreement is not perfect and there are many areas I wish were different but I feel very, very strongly that a 'No' vote will jeopardize the future of Canada and cannot even be considered by loyal thinking Canadians. I feel so strongly on this matter that as long as you are proposing to lead a 'No' campaign, we are unable to provide financial support." I replied that he could give his money to anyone he pleased, that was his right. However, under no circumstances did he have the right to call me a disloyal Canadian, and I pointed out that my family history in this country was not only longer than his, but was one filled with public service. He later apologized for his "inappropriate" use of the word loyal, and, although there was no donation in 1992, the party has received a donation for 1993.

I took a week off following the by-elections, in which I had campaigned almost every day either in Portage or Winnipeg, and began the Referendum campaign in earnest on September 28 with an appearance on Peter Gzowski's "Morningside," on CBC Radio. From this day until October 26, I had at least two appearances each day of the Referendum campaign, and sometimes as many as five. On Wednesday, October 21, for example, I began my day at 7:40 a.m. with an interview in the local CBC studio. I was at Kildonan East Collegiate for a debate at 10:30, followed by a local phone-in program at 12:30 p.m. At 3:30 I flew to Saskatoon for a speech at 7:30 and flew back to Winnipeg, arriving at 12:45 a.m. The following morning I left at 6:45 for Toronto, where I taped two debates for "The Journal," flew back to Winnipeg in the afternoon and gave a speech on literacy that evening to the Reading Council of Winnipeg. This energy level was reminiscent of that which I had experienced during my 1986 and 1988 election campaigns, though it was absent from my 1990 campaign. I considered this the campaign of my life, and I fully understood that there was a downside.

When I announced my support of the "No" side on September 11, I was asked by Donald Campbell, the *Winnipeg Free Press* legislature reporter, if I understood that there might be a political price to pay for my position. I replied, "Yes, and I am prepared to pay it." I am not sure any of them understood as fully as I did that I was putting my political life on the line. At the time of that announcement the polls were showing that 67 percent of people residing in English Canada supported the Charlottetown Accord.

This was similar to the early poll results on the Meech Lake Accord. The fundamental difference was twofold. First, we had had three years to debate the fallacies of the Meech Lake Accord with the Canadian people, and to gradually convince them that it was not in their best interests. We had only a month and a half on the Charlottetown Accord. Second, other than myself, there was not another public figure in opposition to the Charlottetown Accord. Fortunately, I was soon joined by Gordon Wilson, then the leader of the opposition in British Columbia, and Pierre Trudeau. But still, the pickings were slim.

Within days, Paul Walsh, the former president of the River Heights Liberal constituency and the co-chair of the constituency's 1986 campaign, demanded my resignation as leader of the Liberal Party in Manitoba. Others joined him, both publicly and in letters to me. I had no intention of resigning at this time, although I did inform Al Munroe that if we lost the vote in Manitoba—a clear possibility at this juncture—then my resignation might be essential. Out of interest, since Paul Walsh was being portrayed as a significant member of the Liberal Party, I asked party offices if Walsh was indeed a card-carrying member. As it turned out, he had not renewed his membership since the spring of 1990, when he had failed in his bid to be a Paul Martin delegate to the national leadership convention.

There were benefits to being the underdog. Canadians had a deep and abiding dislike of the prime minister. Every time he opened his mouth, support for the Charlottetown Accord dropped. The public also had a dislike for politicians in general, and when they tried the slick, hard-sell campaign, with glitzy ads and lots of money spent, the campaign was rejected in favour of the amateur productions of the "No" forces. Finally, the "Yes" campaigners, particularly the prime minister and Joe Clark, aided and abetted by the corporate giants, tried the threats of economic doom and gloom and of the country falling apart that had been so much a part of the dying days of the Meech Lake Accord. They had forgotten Abraham Lincoln's observation that you can fool all of the people some of the time, and some of the people all of the time, but you can't fool all of the people all of the time. Canadians were simply not buying the rhetoric this time around. Indeed, every time it was used, not only did the people not buy into it, they became more and more resolved to vote "No."

The media, particularly CBC TV, also decided to play a different role in this campaign. No longer did they portray themselves as saviours of Canada. This time they decided to provide, in as unbiased a format as possible, the facts, and allow Canadians to make up their own minds without heavy editorializing.

This was a significant factor in their two hour-long programs aired Sunday, October 11, which asked the question, "What Will Happen to Canada if Canadians Vote Yes?" and Sunday, October 18, which asked the question, "What Will Happen to Canada if Canadians Vote No?" Following the first program, which had more "Yes" than "No" supporters on the panel, I asked them to measure the time given each side. When they learned more time had been given to the "Yes" side, they increased the number of "No" panellists the following week.

The two debates taped for "The Journal" were scrupulously fair to both sides. However, there was some irony at play here. Robert Jackson, a professor at Carleton University, and I were the participants on the "No" side. Kim Campbell and Sheila Copps debated the "Yes" side. In the days leading up to the debate we were told that the rules would provide for a two-minute opening on each of six questions, three each night, and a one-minute rebuttal, followed by a free-for-all. Each side would introduce three questions, and rebut on three. Jackson and I quickly decided which of the three we could best handle and prepared ourselves accordingly, not worrying whether he or I would get the greater amount of time on either of the two nights. After all, the object was to win the debates, not to score political points.

Copps and Campbell, however, couldn't come to this arrangement. I can only assume that for political reasons they were afraid one might get more coverage, so instead of building their argument for the two minutes, they each took a portion, thereby weakening the argument and making it disjointed! Jackson and I loved it. In addition, just before going into the taping room, I told Jackson that at some time over the course of the two debates Copps would speak about her daughter. Jackson asked, "Why would she do that?" I replied that it was standard. She had done it throughout the leadership debates in order to soften her image. He asked me how we should counteract it. I said it was quite simple, I would speak of mine! Sure enough, in the middle of the debate Sheila told the audience she was supporting the Charlottetown Accord for her daughter, who was too young to vote for herself. I immediately replied that I didn't have to speak for my daughters, they were both old enough to speak for themselves and they could not support a document that eroded their rights in this country.

Throughout the Referendum campaign I made four principal arguments. I told audiences about the undermining of the powers of the federal government, a particular concern for the small "have-not" provinces, of which Manitoba was one; the reduction of the real power of the small provinces in the institutions of this nation; the muddling of the Charter; and the failure of the Charlottetown Accord to live up to the Manitoba Task Force on the Constitution.

The premier of Manitoba kept telling Manitobans that this province had received everything it wanted. But that was simply not true because, in clause after clause, the deal fell short of what had been requested by Manitobans. In the Canada clause, developed in the first instance in Manitoba, one of the most important provisions was the affirmation that the rights and freedoms contained in the Charter of Rights and Freedoms apply to all Canadians. Judy Rebick, who on behalf of the National Action Committee on the Status of Women announced on September 13, two days after my announcement, that they would oppose the agreement on the basis of the weakening of the Charter, was not alone in taking this position. On October 22, thirteen constitutional lawyers from across this country released a detailed legal analysis, the only one to be done, which showed clearly the debasement of the Charter in this Accord. Gary Filmon is not a strong believer in the Charter; he was part of the Sterling Lyon government that opposed the inclusion of the Charter in the Constitution in 1981. However, Manitobans do believe in the Charter, and they said so clearly in two separate task forces in this province.

The Manitoba Task Force recommended certain principles for the new Senate. It was to be elected, seats were to be distributed equally or equitably, and it was to be given the role of reviewing significant appointments as well as the power to review federal programs with a direct impact on the provinces. In other words, the new chamber was to be effective. Gary Filmon became so hung up on equal, which was not required by the task force—more equitable would have done—that he dismissed as unimportant the assurance that this new chamber be effective, particularly with respect to those programs that had their heaviest impact on smaller, less advantaged provinces.

This reform was not achieved. The loading of the House of Commons with additional members, particularly with the guarantee of 25 percent for the province of Quebec, ensured that the only authority this Senate would have would be the so-called moral authority spoken of by Clyde Wells. This was simply not good enough, and I would rather maintain our present Senate, with all of its problems, than bring in a new Senate with no power in perpetuity. At least we can hope for changes to the present Senate. With the Charlottetown Accord no changes would have been possible in the future because of the unanimity provision in the amended Canada Act. The Manitoba Task Force report also called for a strong central government and constitutional entrenchment of funding for the Established Program Financing initiatives, which is the means by which the federal government provides funding for health and post-secondary education. Nothing was gained other than a further weakening of the federal government.

The people of Manitoba had been betrayed by the Accord and they knew it. It was not my popularity that resulted in 61.7 percent of Manitobans saying "No" to the Referendum, it was the deal itself, combined with the people's lack of respect for those selling the package. I was careful throughout my presentations to tell Manitobans not to reject this deal because they disliked Brian Mulroney. Indeed, Jeffrey Simpson, a columnist for *The Globe and Mail*, after hearing one of my speeches at Murdock Mackay Collegiate on October 5, wrote that I was purring like a kitten. Referring to a woman politician as a kitten or a cat smacks of a certain amount of sexism; however, he seemed to recognize that my tone was different from others engaged in the Referendum debate. I found that telling my audience, first, to hear from the "Yes" side and, second, to remove Brian Mulroney from their decision-making were among the strongest arguments I could make. It set the stage for the audience to truly listen to the other arguments I would develop.

Perhaps the most interesting group position throughout the Referendum campaign was that of the First Nations. Ovide Mercredi had been elected grand chief of the Assembly of First Nations on June 12, 1991. He was opposed by a number of other Aboriginal leaders, but his major opponent was Phil Fontaine, the grand chief of the Manitoba Assembly of First Nations. Both men were from Manitoba. Phil Fontaine was born and raised on the Fort Alexander reserve, now known as Sagkeeng First Nation, in the eastern part of Manitoba. Mercredi came from Grand Rapids, a northern Manitoba reserve. Fontaine had stayed close to his community throughout most of his life, serving as chief for a time. He was replaced by his cousin, Jerry Fontaine, who had run for the Liberal Party in 1986 as a provincial candidate. Mercredi was a lawyer and, according to many Manitoba Aboriginal people, had become more remote from their concerns.

I personally gave small donations to both election campaigns because I wanted a Manitoban to be elected to this position, and because I liked and respected both men, although my favourite was Fontaine. I knew Fontaine would have a tough time, partly because he was not as well known among the national chiefs as Mercredi, and also because Fontaine had achieved so high a profile during the Meech Lake Accord, providing the support network for Elijah Harper. There was a sense that he would not consider himself to be one among equals. Women politicians understand this since we often have the support of women until we are considered to have achieved too much, at which point that support is removed. In a tough, four-ballot battle, with Fontaine ahead on the first two ballots, Mercredi prevailed.[5]

For the most part Manitoba chiefs were furious that Mecredi had defeated their grand chief, and to some degree that was a factor in their decision not to support the Referendum; they were reluctant to accept a deal he had negotiated. However, they also had a more serious concern. They questioned whether their treaties had been adequately protected. A fundamental concern had to do with the redirection of powers to provincial governments from the federal government. Aboriginal people know the federal government has a fiduciary responsibility to them. That has been well documented by the courts. They were concerned that the courts would not see that same level of fiduciary responsibility on the part of the provinces. Elijah Harper called for more time for his people to study the agreement, but they were not to be given that time. Finally the chiefs in Manitoba called for a boycott, suggesting that Aboriginal peoples simply not vote. However, they further recommended that if their people wanted to vote then they should vote "No." As Referendum results were announced, poll by poll, it became clear that the majority of status Indians had voted "No," not only in Manitoba but across the country.

Aboriginal women had their own concerns, and in this they had my full support. In the weakening of the Charter by both the inclusion of the distinct society clause and the clause on Aboriginal peoples, they were concerned that their rights were in jeopardy. There were other clauses causing them concern as well, particularly those that referred to Aboriginal traditions. Studies clearly show that Aboriginal women and children are among the most disadvantaged people in this nation, and Aboriginal traditions have not protected them. This Accord would only make things worse in their minds, and in mine also. Only the Charter, unencumbered, could protect them.

It was clear from his body language and his unwillingness to speak with me when we met during the Referendum campaign that Ovide Mercredi was angry with me. When we appeared in Montreal together on "Sunday Night Report," he did not even acknowledge my presence. Because he would not speak it was impossible to discern the issues on which we disagreed. On the other hand, I had a number of conversations throughout the Referendum month with representatives of the Indigenous Women's Collective and chiefs in Manitoba, and I knew that I had their support.

As the Referendum debate continued, it became more and more clear that the "No" side was gaining support. Polls released by Angus Reid, which had earlier shown support for the "Yes" side at 67 percent in English Canada, showed the support at 50 percent by September 26. By October 17 the Angus Reid poll was showing that six provinces would be voting "No," including Manitoba and Quebec.

By Referendum Day I considered my role to be finished. I had done what I could to convince Canadians to vote "No." The final choice was theirs alone. At no time had I any doubts about my role. Throughout the last six months of the Meech Lake Accord I had felt heavily burdened with the responsibility of having to decide on behalf of Canadians. Now they were to decide for themselves, and my role had been to present the arguments against to the best of my ability. This I had done, and I was satisfied.

As I sat in the CBC studio in Toronto watching the results, I might have been expected to feel some elation, particularly with the "No" vote in Nova Scotia, the narrowness of the "Yes" decision in Ontario and the substantial "No" vote in Manitoba. I did not. I had already decided to resign and had told my husband of that decision on the weekend. I had informed Adrian and Donald Macdonald of my decision just before I left for the studio. I was content that I had done what I believed was right for Canada, and it was now time to step aside and let others lead Canada into the future.

I returned to Manitoba and was hailed as the hero, but I did not feel that way. I had another agenda to deal with. However, while the media was making a fuss about "my victory," Axworthy and others were making noises about splitting the federal and provincial wings of the party. It was clear that my opposition to the Referendum was to be no more acceptable than my support for Chrétien had been some nine years earlier. It simply reaffirmed my decision to leave the leadership. If I had required any other impetus to resign I received it that night when watching the CBC six o'clock news. They had sent a team out on the street to interview Winnipeggers about what they thought of my role in the Referendum. Most interviewed portrayed me as a hero, but one woman, expressing the cynicism so deeply felt by so many in Canada, said, in paraphrase, well she was just playing politics, she knew how we would vote and that's the reason she took the stand she did. This was simply false, since the polls had clearly shown when I took my stand that Manitobans would vote "Yes."

It was essential for me to resign if for no other reason than that this woman, whom I do not know, and others, can have some faith in politicians again. Politicians do not make decisions for political reasons only. I am convinced that many politicians voted "Yes" because they honestly believed the Charlottetown Accord would be good for the country. I voted "No" because I believed it would not. It was as simple as that.

seventeen

Leaving on a High Note

Making the decision to retire, which was obviously the difficult part, was now done. What remained was to let those close to me know what I'd decided. In order not to offend anyone, since there were many people I wanted to tell personally the reasons for my decision rather than having them hear it through the media, I spent most of the next week on the phone. I think it is a tribute to all of them that there was little or no media speculation about my decision until just hours before the announcement, and that was prompted by a release from my office stating that I would be holding a press conference to make an important announcement. I phoned my brother, Dennis, and sisters, Catherine and Patricia in Halifax and Maureen in Calgary. None of them was surprised. I think they believed I had made my contribution and it was time for me to move on to other endeavours.

My daughters had a little more warning. When they were home in the summer I had discussed with them the possibility of my stepping down before the next election. I told them I would do so if the party fortunes would benefit from a new leader. Both had encouraged me to step down after Meech week in Ottawa. I suspect the reason was because, for the first time in their lives, they saw their mother truly vulnerable. They had to deal with a mother who was not as strong as they always had assumed her to be. They fully understood and supported my participation in the

Referendum campaign but knew that it, too, had taken its toll. They both encouraged me to do what I wanted to do.

The caucus had planned a retreat in Hecla, a provincial park on Lake Winnipeg, about one and a half hours from Winnipeg, for November 4 and 5, and I decided that would be the appropriate time to tell my colleagues. I wanted Al Munroe and Marguerite Martin to know before I went out of the city, because if one of the caucus leaked the news to the media, either purposely or by accident, then they would be hurt. So I told them both before I left. Marguerite, I think, expected it. She had been through so much with me that I suspect she recognized the signs.

Marguerite always had an intuitive sense about me. It was she who pointed out, months after the provincial election in 1990, that I was still punishing myself, and she knew it had nothing to do with the election. It was she who clarified for me that I had never forgiven myself for the decision I had made in Ottawa. She asked one day in late fall 1990, "You have never been one to cry over spilt milk. What is wrong?" I knew what was wrong. I had betrayed both my principles and the people, and I was wallowing in it. It was with her help that I put it behind me, while at the same time I made the decision that if I had the opportunity to stand by my belief in the Charter's protection of individual rights a second time, I would not waver.

I asked Al to meet me at my home. He turned ashen when I gave him the news. For over eight years he had been my side-kick. He had supported me in every decision I had made. It was tougher telling him than members of my family. He didn't really understand, and to some degree still does not, but his faith in me is convincing him that it must be the right decision.

I asked both Al and my husband to come with me to the caucus retreat. For some reason we were late leaving Winnipeg, and a blizzard was setting in. The roads became impassable so we decided to drive into Gimli, about halfway there, in order to get a road report update. The RCMP advised us to get off the road. I promptly checked us into a hotel in order to pre-empt any arguments from Al about proceeding. In typical motherly fashion I kept phoning Winnipeg and Hecla trying to track down the other members. Finally they had all arrived in Hecla, with the exception of Neil Gaudry, who had remained in Winnipeg because his mother was seriously ill. Only the leader was stuck in Gimli, some believed by design. In fact I was truly stranded, but they thought Al went through any weather. (What they didn't know was that I don't. Over the years, after several white-knuckle driving experiences, Al and I established a protocol. We would carry on after the first and second vehicle we saw in the ditch. The third vehicle always meant a change in plan. This was a three-vehicle day.)

The caucus continued with the retreat and I arrived the next morning. They informed me of plans they had made with respect to strategy for the next session, which was to open later in the month. Finally the agenda turned to party matters. I took that opportunity to inform them I was going to resign the next day.

Sherry Wiebe, the caucus research director and a close friend, was the only non-caucus member there. She was not surprised, and that was obvious from the expression on her face. She and I had had lengthy discussions about our futures over the previous year and this seemed to her a well-reasoned decision. All of the caucus members respected my decision, although both Kevin Lamoureux and Gulzar Cheema were deeply disturbed. I immediately drove back to Winnipeg, since there were a number of others who needed to be told and I wanted to do it in person, if possible. Marguerite tracked down Neil Gaudry and asked him to come to a meeting in my office, where I told him.

I phoned Scott Gray and Lore Mirewaldt in The Pas, Peter and Liz Rampton in Dauphin and Laurie Evans in Ste. Anne. I then made personal trips to offices and homes of very special people: Doreen Froese, my first secretary and a constant supporter; Lynne Axworthy, who had chaired all of my campaigns in River Heights and whose efforts had made those victories possible; Brian Head, my constituency president who had guided the constituency so carefully for the last two years; and Berenice Sisler, who had many roles over the years but above all was my mentor because I had such faith in her judgment. Ernie Gilroy, who had chaired the provincial campaigns of 1986 and 1988 and had been a candidate in 1990, was not home, so I reached him later that evening by phone. I also called Rae Scott, who had volunteered in all of my campaigns, even though in the last one her health was failing and she was in her mid-eighties! After nine years it seemed like such a small list, and yet these were the people who had always been there for me in very special ways. This group had done more than any leader had a right to expect.

I went to sleep that night completely at peace with myself. I knew I was doing the right thing for me and for the party for which I had worked for forty-four years. The following morning at 9:00 a.m. I announced my decision to the staff, and at 11:00 a.m. to the media.

The next two days were filled with media interviews, some accepting what I had said as the gospel truth, others trying to ferret out different reasons for my decision. No one had forced me out. If the people of Manitoba had voted overwhelmingly "Yes," perhaps there would have been a push, and maybe it would have been successful. However, I had the people on my side, and to have tried to replace me at this time would only have resulted in a backlash against those federally leaning Liberals who might have tried. It is safe to say there was some rejoicing in the federal caucus, although not from the leader. Jean Chrétien was in Florida and we had spoken the day before my resignation, not as leaders but as friends. He was genuinely shocked by my decision and his obvious concern for me was expressed in the warmest of terms. But a friend reported overhearing a conversation between David Dingwall, Sergio Marchi and Lloyd Axworthy in the halls of the West Block in which they were discussing the "great news" from Manitoba. I suppose from their perspective it was good news. I had been a thorn in their sides, and now I would be gone. It is always a relief when the sting goes away.

Why did I retire? It's really very simple. I was tired of working sixty- to eighty-hour weeks, but I didn't know how to do my job properly without that time commitment. I was tired from carrying so much of the burden of the party on my back, from fundraising to policy development to caucus. I was tired from having worked seven election campaigns in nine years. I wanted time for

John and for Cathi and Jennie, and I wanted time for friends, and reading and teaching. Above all I was tired of the public spotlight. As I said in my closing press conference, I certainly wouldn't miss the comments on my hair, my clothes, my figure, my make-up and my voice.

I really wonder why women in the public eye, be it media or politics, are subject to such invasion about personal choices like clothes and hair. Why did people, particularly women, think they had the right to comment on the length of my hair, its colour and its style? Every time I received a letter on issues like this I felt it was such a putdown. If someone was prepared to take the time to write a letter about my hair, but not an issue affecting the province, did it mean that all that person saw when I spoke was my hair? Do they subject male politicians to the same kind of scrutiny? I think not. Certainly those with whom I have spoken don't receive letters on such personal topics.

Shortly after I was elected leader of the opposition, a card arrived at my office. Marguerite assumed that it contained a congratulatory message, so she put it on my desk unopened. I took the card out of the envelope and read the outside message which said, "WHAT IS AN EIGHT LETTER WORD FOR WHAT YOU NEED?" Inside it read, "AGOODLAY." These kinds of missives were infrequent and could not match the hundreds of good, positive letters I received over the years, but they had a tendency to wear me down at a much faster rate than the others built me up. I am not sorry to be moving on to another stage of my life.

When I evaluate the years I have given to the Liberal Party and the people of Manitoba, several things come immediately to mind. Without a doubt I have received an education second to none over the past nine years. I have learned more facts, figures and policy issues than in all the years I spent in academic institutions. Since I have a natural curiosity to know more and more, I thoroughly enjoyed the constant challenge to learn. I also saw, perhaps more than I wanted to, human nature—most on the positive side, but much of the darker side of life too. For the first time I had to deal with far too many takers and not enough givers, and it was a struggle to constantly ensure that the takers, because they demand so much time and attention, didn't always win the battle for that valuable time and energy.

Above all, my enthusiasm for and love of this country and its people grew throughout my leadership. Canada is not the country of my youth. Canada is now a vibrant, multicultural society where people live together and contribute in ways not experienced in my childhood. I am thrilled when parents tell me that their children are "colour blind," for many of them indeed are. They do not see their friend as Chinese or Filipino, African-American or Aboriginal. They see their friend who, like them, is a Canadian! When I watch television and I see a group of high school students prepared to take on racism and all its ugliness, I am filled with confidence in the future of my country. If I have been able to make any of these young people feel more comfortable with one another because of statements I have made—and some have told me this is the case— then my political career was a success.

One of the great thrills of my life is to have a woman, particularly a young woman, say to me that I opened new doors for her. Often I have done nothing other than be a woman politician, but women were able to take strength from that, and surely that must be considered on the scale of success.

Do I regret never having been premier? I can honestly say I don't know. I certainly feel no dissatisfaction in what I have achieved, so perhaps the answer is no. When I was elected leader of the Liberal Party in Manitoba in 1984 no one would have realistically given me a chance of being the premier, so it certainly was not one of my long-term goals. It did become a short-term goal between 1988 and 1990, but I was so disturbed by what I had done in Ottawa that it was almost as if my "big chance" disappeared without my even noticing.

The only regret I have in not being the premier concerns the policy I was unable to implement. However, knowing how slow the pace of change is in government, there is no guarantee I would have achieved any of it even if I had been premier! Had I been given the chance, there were three major initiatives I would have pursued.

First, I wanted to change the face of the civil service in Manitoba so that it was more reflective of the population at large. I wanted to ensure that more women and members of visible minority communities held senior positions. There is still far too much tokenism in affirmative action and it must change. The Old Boys' network must not be allowed to continue into the twenty-first century. After all, the majority of people in Canada today are most certainly not "one of the boys"!

My second thrust would have been in the area of education, my first love. The young people of this country are simply not getting the education they need or deserve, and, for the most part, this is not a funding issue. Teachers are under siege, being asked to perform tasks they are not qualified to do, while, at the same time, they are forced to ignore many of the tasks for which they are receiving their paycheques. If the schools are to be expected to be child-care centres, nursing stations and deliverers of social services, then let us give them the dollars and facilities to be multidimensional institutions; but let us stop asking them to do all these things with education dollars. Education dollars must be focused on teaching children to read and to communicate, to compute and calculate, to think and to reason and to problem-solve.

No longer can we live with curricula designed primarily for socialization. Curricula must be designed for learning, and right now our children are underchallenged and undermotivated. By all means, let us use modern technologies to teach skills in new ways, but testing is as valid today as in my day, and children need to know there are expectations placed upon them. We live in a society that values competition on the hockey rink and on the football field but tells us we should not ask our children to compete in school. Life is a competition, and children have to be prepared to participate in it.

Let us not use testing to try to evaluate teachers, because it rarely does this. Let us use it to identify where additional resources are needed, and let us be flexible enough to be able to move those resources quickly. There is no excuse for the poor performance of Canadian children on international tests. We have the ability to be the best and should accept nothing less.

My final thrust would have been the empowerment of Aboriginal women and children through the upgrading of their living conditions and economic opportunities. Nationally and provincially we have to eliminate the authority of the Department of Indian Affairs and help Aboriginal communities to help themselves. To me this is the essence of self-government. Yes, they will make mistakes and there will be abuses. So what? That is what they are experiencing right now with the predominantly white culture in charge. The only way for them to have a future is for their own people to demand and obtain change, and this will only happen when they have education and employment opportunities that empower them.

Now I can only sit back and hope others will take these ideas and move them forward. I am frequently asked if, after I have had a rest, I will return to public life. The answer is no. I have given my best years to public life, and it is now time for others who are younger and brighter and who have enthusiasm for the battles.

I will return to teaching young people, perhaps to inspire a few of them to take up the challenge. Our country needs all of us to take some time from our limited span of years and devote that time to the enhancement of this nation. It is such a very special place, but it will remain so only as long as Canadians believe in themselves and are able to turn that belief into action on behalf of others.

Notes

1. Wade Kojo Williams, Letter to the Editor, *Winnipeg Free Press*, January 2, 1993.
2. Oscar Lathlin, Member of the Legislative Assembly of Manitoba, quotation from *Hansard*, December 7, 1992, 329.
3. From an oral presentation by Victor Payou to the Manitoba Task Force on the Meech Lake Accord, Friday, April 28, 1989.
4. Bruce Wallace, "Taking the Prize," *Maclean's*, September 24, 1990, 14.
5. Jordan Wheeler, "Mercredi wins the battle," *Windspeaker* vol 9, no. 7 (June 21, 1993): 3.

Index